D1325837

Experimental Statistical Designs and Analysis in Simulation Modeling

Experimental Statistical Designs and Analysis in Simulation Modeling

Christian N. Madu and Chu-hua Kuei

Quorum Books
Westport, Connecticut • London

HF
1017
·M28
1993

Library of Congress Cataloging-in-Publication Data

Madu, Christian N. (Christian Ndubisi)
    Experimental statistical designs and analysis in simulation
modeling / Christian N. Madu and Chu-hua Kuei.
      p. cm.
    Includes bibliographical references and index.
    ISBN 0–89930–695–0 (alk. paper)
    1. Commercial statistics. 2. Mathematical statistics.
3. Simulation methods. I. Kuei, Chu-hua. II. Title.
HF1017.M28   1993
650'.01'5195—dc20   92–37467

British Library Cataloguing in Publication Data is available.

Library of Congress Catalog Card Number: 92–37467
ISBN: 0–89930–695–0

First published in 1993

Quorum Books, 88 Post Road West, Westport, CT 06881
An imprint of Greenwood Publishing Group, Inc.

Printed in the United States of America

The paper used in this book complies with the
Permanent Paper Standard issued by the National
Information Standards Organization (Z39.48–1984).

10 9 8 7 6 5 4 3 2 1

Copyright Acknowledgment

Excerpts reprinted with permission from *Long Range Planning*, 24(5), C. N. Madu, C-H. Kuei, and
A. N. Madu, "Setting Priorities for the IT Industry in Taiwan—A Delphi Study," copyright 1991,
Pergamon Press Ltd.

To
Assumpta and Jan-Hwei Chen

CONTENTS

TABLES AND FIGURES

TABLES

FIGURES

PREFACE

This book illustrates the art of simulation modeling with emphasis on discrete-event simulation. Throughout the book, examples are used to illustrate in a clear and concise form how simulation models can be constructed, validated, and applied in decision making. The orientation is toward business applications of simulation with emphasis on the use of personal computers (PCs). Since simulation modeling and output analysis will often be useless without the application of statistical designs and analyses, we illustrate in a concise and simple manner how such difficult techniques can be applied.

This book is intended primarily for practitioners and students majoring in business and computer information systems who need to be able to build sound simulation models without getting into the rigor of statistical simulation modeling. A basic background in probability and statistics is enough to fully comprehend the methods discussed in this book. Simulation is often impossible without the use of computers. Fortunately, there is an increasing number of simulation languages that are being developed for PC application. This provides convenience to many people who dislike the arduous task of using mainframe computers. All the applications presented in this book are PC-based and can easily be applied to IBM PCs or IBM compatibles.

The prerequisite required for this book is familiarity with PCs. Knowledge of computer programming, though helpful, is not required in order to effectively use this book.

The book is unique in several ways: (1) It is written primarily for the less technical simulation modelers who also need to use the existing knowledge in the area of statistical designs and analyses to build sound simulation models. (2) It discusses how simulation models can be generalized within well-defined boundaries of the problem domain by emphasizing the construction of regression "metamodels." (3) It shows how Taguchi designs can be easily applied in determining the appropriate input levels in an experiment. Many more features of this book are rarely available in basic simulation texts.

Finally, although the target audience includes primarily practitioners and business majors, those in industrial engineering, computer science, and other technical majors may find this book a useful reference.

This book originated from our class outline in teaching simulation courses. It can be used in a semester simulation course in both undergraduate and graduate courses. The arrangement of the chapters may be a useful sequence in which to offer the course. This book may be used with any discrete-event simulation package.

ACKNOWLEDGMENTS

We wish to thank Koula C. Kilaras, an excellent, professional secretary, whose impeccable work is always distinguishable. We thank our wives, Assumpta and Jan-Hwei Chen, and sons, Chinedu, Chike, Chidi, and Steve, for their passions and continuing support of our joint ventures.

Experimental Statistical Designs and Analysis in Simulation Modeling

Chapter 1

THE ART OF MODELING

INTRODUCTION

Most problems in the real world are difficult to analyze. Several factors, both controllable and uncontrollable, act on any particular problem and all of these increase the complexity of the problem. Even when information is available to solve the problem, it is often difficult for the decision maker to isolate all of the relevant information from the pile of information that may influence the decisions made. For example, a company's decision to relocate its manufacturing plant to a new site will consider factors such as demand shifts, taxes, availability of support services, cost of labor, rental fees, reaction of the neighborhood, competitors' reactions and responses, and relocation costs. It would be unwise to carry out the decision and then access the impact of the decision afterward. Rather, the decision maker would prefer to experiment with a model of this system of operation. Through the use of this model several options and strategies (i.e., alternative sites) can be evaluated and the response of the system to these options and strategies evaluated. Also, impending flaws of any of these decisions can be tolerated when models are used. Clearly, if these decisions are implemented on the real system, it becomes more risky and very difficult to change when unsatisfactory results are observed. In fact, it may be too late and impossible to restore the system when incorrect or bad decisions are made.

In some problems, there may be no real system with which to experiment. For example, if a company's strategic plan calls for the introduction of a new product, models may be used to analyze this plan before it is actually implemented. Models are, therefore, less expensive to experiment with and are often effective in understanding and interpreting real world systems.

DEFINITION OF A SYSTEM

Figure 1.1 provides a schematic description of a system. This figure illustrates the common components that should be present in any *purposeful system*. These are inputs, process(es), outputs, and control. A purposeful system must have an objective or a mission. A common objective as evident from Figure 1.1 is the transformation of inputs into outputs. It is also apparent that without a form of control or set of standards to measure the performance of the system, both desirable and undesirable outputs may be generated from the system. In a manufacturing system for example, outputs may include both items that meet the quality standards of the company as well as those that deviate significantly from such standards. Thus, rejects and scraps may also be produced. The institution of a control mechanism in this framework ensures that the established standards are being satisfied by the outputs that are generated from the system. Inputs into a system may include materials, objects, people, and so on, while processes may include machineries, objects, people, and information that are needed in order to transform the inputs into outputs. The primary flows into any system are, therefore, materials and information.

If we consider a hospital system as an example, we notice that the material flow into the hospital consists of patients of all kinds seeking medical services or treatment. At the same time, information about these patients flows along with them as they move through the various processing centers of the hospital. At the different stages in their processing, information on their medical records and history as well as their billing is collected and channeled to the appropriate processing centers. The patients receive treatment and are discharged. There are medical guidelines, however, to ensure that the right services are appropriately

Figure 1.1
Schematic Description of a System

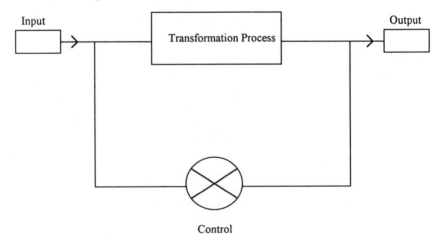

administered. For example, the right dosage of drugs as prescribed by the doctor must be filled by the pharmacist and administered by the nurse. Also, the doctor monitors the progress of the patients and signs discharge forms. The hospital itself is frequently evaluated by several agencies (internal auditors, state and federal governments) and people (patients, interest groups). Different performance measures used in the hospital may include the length of hospital stay for the different categories of ailment, mortality rate, average waiting time in the emergency room, number of occupied beds in the hospital, number of complaints, and of course, the number of malpractice suits. The monitoring and evaluation of the services provided by the hospital are helpful in improving the quality of future services rendered. Thus, the hospital is said to incorporate feedback.

Also, notice that some factors that affect the system performance may not be controllable. For example, the high cost of providing medical services may relate to inflation in the price of medical equipment and supplies and the high cost of interest rates on borrowed money used to finance some of the hospital's operations, and even on the high cost of malpractice insurance that hospitals often pay for their physicians. All of these factors, which are outside the hospital's control, may influence how the quality of health care provided by the hospital is perceived by its customers. Also, mortality and severity of ailments may be reduced if routine medical checkups are carried out. The hospital has no control over the patients in ensuring that this undertaking is carried out. Yet, this may affect the mortality rate at any given hospital. For example, hospitals in poor neighborhoods may experience relatively higher mortality rates. Factors that are external to the system of interest as discussed here are referred to as *exogenous*, while those internal to the system, such as the average time a patient stays in the emergency room before seeing a doctor, are referred to as *endogenous*.

TYPE OF MODELS

We shall adopt two definitions of a model as presented in Webster's *New Universal Unabridged Dictionary*.[1] These are:

(a) an imitation or copy in miniature of something already made or existing on a large scale; and

(b) a generalized, hypothetical description, often based on an analogy, used in analyzing or explaining something.

From definition (a), we can add that a model is really an abstraction of the relevant parts of a real system. For example, some realtors build new homes only on demand. Prospective buyers are often shown a model of what their home would look like when it is actually built. This model contains all the relevant

---

[1]Webster's *New Universal Unabridged Dictionary*, Deluxe second edition, Dorset & Baber.

aspects of the real house as well as interaction with the real home's environment. For example, buyers are shown the location of their lots as well as the potential location of other facilities such as parks, schools, churches, or synagogues. Buyers make decisions based on this model. Clearly, there are advantages in using the model. The realtor is, for example, lowering risks by not tying up limited capital on the construction of new homes until there are firm guarantees that such homes will be sold. Models, therefore, serve several purposes. Dervitsiotis [3] identified four of these purposes. We shall briefly describe each of these.

(a) Models are descriptive in nature. They are used to describe real systems.
(b) The functions and structure of a system can be understood by examining its model.
(c) Models are used to predict the behavior of the real system. Models can also be studied under different conditions to understand how the real system will react to such conditions.
(d) Models are useful in controlling the behavior of the real systems and in ensuring that the objectives of such systems are effectively achieved.

Models are very useful in decision making. First, as an abstraction of the real system, they are less expensive and are much easier to experiment with. Second, with models, we have the ability to study the system under different conditions, including adverse conditions. Valuable information on both the system's reaction and interaction with its environment are obtained. Third, from the second definition of a model (b), we can use the information obtained through a model to generalize about a particular system.

In the context of simulation, we try to use a model to understand a problem situation. There are often difficulties on how to abstract a real system. If a model is, for example, too simple and does not consider many of the relevant characteristics and interactions of the real system, that model will be ineffective in understanding the real system. On the other hand, if a model is too complex, it becomes expensive and difficult to debug and run. These problems make it difficult to fully comprehend and understand the system being modeled. Again, the ability to make inference to the real system based on this model is significantly hampered. Models must be developed to give true representations of the real system. They must consider all the important attributes of the system as well as its interaction with its environment. In some cases, it may be easier to decompose a system into different components that are easier to model and understand. However, it should be clear that all these components may interact and such interactions must be adequately considered.

Next, we shall describe the different types of models.

Iconic Models

Iconic models are models that have similar physical characteristics to the real system. Simple examples of iconic models are pictures, figures, diagrams, images, and statues. These models may be scaled down or up. For example, the model of the home we discussed above is a scaled-down version of a real home but it contains all the physical characteristics of a real home. Other examples include models for an automobile, a person's picture, an airplane wind-tunnel, and others.

Analog Models

With analog models, we explain a real system by comparing it point by point with a model. A commonly cited example of analog models is the inventory levels of a product. If a container is filled with water and the water is periodically discharged at a given rate, the inventory level for each rate of discharge can be assessed by measuring the water level after each discharge. Thus, this is an analogous model that is used to analyze the behavior of an inventory system.

Mathematical Models

Mathematical models allow for the use of symbols, variables, functions, and equations to represent the important characteristics of the real system under study. These models offer the most flexibility because they have wider applicability and can, therefore, be generalized to a wider range of problems. In fact, simulation itself is a mathematical model. A simple example, however, is in the basic $M/M/1$ queuing system where an equation is used to determine the average waiting time of customers in this queuing system. Rather than observing this real system as it unfolds, we are stating that if the assumptions of the $M/M/1$ are satisfied, then the average waiting time in the system can be derived using models that have already been established. Notice the flexibility of this model. The waiting line can be in a bank, in a supermarket, in a doctor's office, and so on. Once the same assumptions are satisfied and the input values supplied, the average waiting time can be computed with the same formula.

Although mathematical models have been very useful, especially in the pure sciences, there are considerable difficulties in several other areas of application. For example, in most socio-economic and behavioral problems, mathematical models have not been quite successful, with part of the reason being that such systems are relatively more complex to understand. However, greater attempts are being made to understand such systems especially with the use of computers. We shall discuss the different types of mathematical models in the following sections.

Static Models. Static models convey the notion of lack of progression. Models of this form are normally used in single period planning. An example of a single period planning model is the one period inventory planning model. An economic order quantity (EOQ) model or the Wilson lot size model that computes the order quantity, which is time invariant, can be considered as a static model.

Dynamic Models. When successive periods in a planning horizon are considered, and the new information obtained for each period included in the modeling, then, we are dealing with a dynamic model. Dynamic programming is an example of such a model where each of the successive planning horizons can be viewed as the different stages or states in a network. Some inventory models are also dynamic as the decision rules are different for the different periods in a planning horizon.

Deterministic Models. Deterministic models imply that there are no uncertainties in the behavior of the variables and the functional relationships between these variables. Thus, the models behavior can be completely determined. The EOQ model discussed earlier is a deterministic model because the assumptions made about the key parameters of that model, such as the demand rate, holding costs, and ordering costs, do not incorporate any uncertainties. Linear programming applications are mostly deterministic since uncertainties are also not considered and the functional relationship between the variables is known to be linear. Clearly, most real life models must consider some uncertainties. This brings us to the next model.

Stochastic (Probabilistic) Models. When it is necessary to consider the uncertainties in at least one of the system's parameters or variables, we are dealing with a probabilistic or stochastic modeling. Although the distinctions between probabilistic and stochastic models are often blurred, probabilistic models are often used to refer to models that consider uncertainties in the decision variables only for a single period. On the other hand, stochastic models consider such uncertainties for successive periods. The newsboy problem in inventory control is a probabilistic model. Here, an order is placed only to cover a single period. Since the attempt is to minimize both the costs of understocking and overstocking the item, the uncertainties in the demand of that item have to be considered. Queuing models are also examples of stochastic processes. If we consider the number of customers in a queuing system as a performance measure for the queuing system, we observe that the number of customers in the system will change in probabilistic manner at fixed or random intervals in time. For example, when a customer is served, the customer leaves the queuing system. At the same time, the arrival of a new customer will increment the number of customers that have gone through this system. We also know that these two events—the service and the arrival patterns of the customers—are probabilistic.

Irrespective of the model type, models are used to understand the behavior of the real system. All models can be categorized as either *descriptive* or *normative*. Descriptive models are useful only in describing a particular system. For example, information such as the average waiting time in a queue, the average equipment utilization, the proportion of time a server is busy, and so on, is descriptive of the performance of the system. Simulation is a powerful model for obtaining descriptive information about a particular system.

In most decision analysis, information is often needed in order to evaluate alternative decisions and, perhaps, choose the best one. Normative or prescriptive models are useful in making such decisions. For example, if we are interested in the optimum order size in an inventory problem or the optimum number of bank tellers in a multiple channel banking system, analytical models are useful to address such issues. As demonstrated later in this book, simulation results can also be applied with other models with some limits as a normative or prescriptive model.

MODEL BUILDING

As we discussed previously, models are used as representations of real systems. Imperatively, they must have something to offer that we may not be able to deduce directly from the real system. We have mentioned some of the reasons why models are used. Notable among these are the facts that the real system may not exist and when it does, it is difficult and more expensive to experiment with. In other words, models offer us information that may not be easily derived from the real system. For models to be effectively used, they must not be as complex as the real system they tend to emulate. On that note, the modeler must be able to identify the key variables and attributes that influence the system's performance. That is, the endogenous and exogenous variables that impact on this system must be isolated and studied. The good judgment of the model builder is necessary in order to identify these critical variables. The number of variables considered should be narrowed down in order to obtain a model that will serve as a satisfactory predictor of the system. Accuracy of the model is very important. Good models often use few critical variables to develop easier models of systems. Another attribute required of all good models is the ease of implementation. If the model is easily applied, model acceptance and adaptability is enhanced. In addition, the cost of implementing such models will be reasonable provided that the model's results are reasonable. Due to the narrowing down of the number of variables considered by a model, complexity of the system is reduced. Also, results derived from the model are often satisfactory solutions to the real problem.

Once models are developed, they must be tested for accuracy of prediction. Analogous systems may be used to compare the model's results to an actual system's performance. Validity is necessary to ensure that the model that has been developed actually represents the real system. Morris [13] identified five major attributes that must be present in any good model. These attributes are:

Relatedness: The model must be comparable to other well-developed models that have been adequately tested.

Transparency: The model must be clear and easily understood. This also relates to the interpretations derived from the model as well as the model's validity.

Robustness: This refers to the generalizability of the model. How useful is this model when certain model's assumptions are changed?

Fertility: The model must be productive. In other words, a variety of results should be deduced from the model. Also, these results must be valuable to the decision maker.

Ease of Enrichment: This discusses the issue of adaptability. How easily can this model be applied to other multifarious problems?

DEFINITION OF SIMULATION

Simulation is a process that uses computers to build a model to imitate a system. The system may represent a real-life operation, such as an assembly line operation, construction of a building, ship building, emergency services of a hospital, banking facility, ambulatory services, and so on. In many of these real-life systems, it may not be possible to use a set of variables to explicitly define functional relationships between the systems performance measures and all the variables (controllable and uncontrollable) that impinge on the system. Due to the complexity of most real-life systems, simulation is often used to analyze and interpret such systems. However, in some cases, mathematical relationships as obtained with functions or formulae may be adequate to model a problem. In fact, simulation is another form of mathematical modeling.

If, for example, we are interested in modeling the waiting line problem in a bank and the waiting line system has been described as having a single line where all the arriving customers must queue in order to receive service from the single teller, and also that at the completion of service the customer departs the line, it has been determined that the interarrival times as well as the service times follow the negative exponential probability distribution. The order of service is first in, first out. With some assumptions made about the stability of this operation within the time frame considered, this problem can easily be solved to determine information such as the average waiting time of a customer in the system, the average time spent on queue, the teller's idle time, and so on. Since this particular problem is not really difficult, existing queuing models, such as the popular birth and death process or specifically the $M/M/1$, can be applied to solve this problem. On the other hand, if some of these assumptions are changed, it may be difficult to solve the problem, for example, if multiple channels of service are allowed, and a limitation on the number of customers that can enter the system is imposed. In other words, there is *balking*. When an arriving customer observes that the system is full or that the waiting time may be high, the customer decides to leave. We may also have cases where customers may switch to the shorter lines assuming that each teller has a separate line. This particular case is often referred to as *jockeying* in the queuing literature. The more complex the problem becomes, the more difficult it is to use analytical models to analyze it.

Simulation is very effective when the problem is not easily modeled, and there is a need to consider some of the assumptions that may have been assumed away in order to obtain a tractable mathematical model. It is also easier and more cost effective to experiment with simulation than with the real system. If, for example, a major urban center is interested in expanding its emergency medical services (EMS), it would want to determine the added coverage, increased response time, and life savings in order to justify the cost of setting up new offices, buying or leasing vehicles, and hiring both skilled and unskilled workers. It would be ineffective to carry out this expansion and then see how it is helping to achieve these stated objectives. However, a simulation of this system may provide further insights into the nature of the EMS operation if expansion is carried out. Such insights may help in making the right decision on the extent of the expansion. In addition, because the method of simulation is much easier to understand, management is more likely to have higher confidence in the results obtained through it. This enhances the acceptance of such results and perhaps, the commitment of the decision maker to ensure that these results are seriously considered and implemented.

There is a misnomer that simulation is simply a computer programming of complex systems. In fact, model coding is just one aspect of simulation modeling. The art of simulation modeling is a "sophisticated systems analysis [10]." Law and McComas [10] noted that a typical simulation study must pay attention to activities such as problem formulation, data and information collection, probabilistic modeling, model building, statistical design, and analysis of simulation experiments, as well as model coding.

Simulation model coding can be accomplished by the use of computer programming languages such as FORTRAN, BASIC, PL1, PASCAL, and so on. However, these languages are not efficient for simulation purposes. Lengthy coding of even a simple system will be required, thus making it difficult to debug. Special purpose languages developed specifically for simulation modeling make this task much easier. More and more of these simulation languages and programs are continually being developed as the interest in the use of simulation continues to grow. Some of the most popular discrete-event simulation languages are General-Purpose Systems Simulation (GPSS), SIMAN, and SIMSCRIPT. GPSS is, by far, one of the easiest simulation languages. Although it is not as flexible as SIMSCRIPT in terms of allowing for integration of statistical analysis in the model coding, the extensions of GPSS to GPSS/H make it possible to incorporate FORTRAN-like codes in GPSS [1]. This improves the flexibility and the power of GPSS as a simulation language.

The use of simulation has also been enhanced by the increasing number of PC-based simulation languages including GPSS. A few years back it was almost impossible to conduct simulation on personal computers (PCs). Mainframe applications were then emphasized. Even then, the processing time and costs were quite high. With the advent of new PCs that use faster microprocessing chips (i.e., Intel 80286, 80386, 80486) and support math co-processors, the processing time and costs have been significantly reduced. With advances in both computer hardware and software, simulation is increasingly one of the most widely used operations research and management science techniques.

SIMULATION AND ANALYTIC MODELS

Wagner [15] in his classical operations research text noted that simulation should be used as a model of last resort. He emphatically stated that simulation should be used "when all else fails." This pessimistic view is often shared by operations research analysts because of the difficulties in building simulation models. However, since Wagner's book was published, a lot of technological advances have taken place in the computer industry. Also, the growing number of research studies in simulation have helped to address some of the issues that concern model builders, thereby improving the value of simulation models.

A major concern with simulation experiments is that simulation outputs are subject to random fluctuations. As a result, it is useless to use a single outcome to represent the output of an experiment. Several replications of the same experiment would be required in order to improve the confidence and the precision of estimates for system parameters obtained through simulation.

On the other hand, most analytic models such as optimization techniques will yield unique solutions when the solutions do exist. Replications here are not important since the same outcomes will always be observed. Such models lead to optimization decisions. It is, for example, easy to determine the optimum number of servers in a multiple channel waiting line system if adequate information about this operational system is provided and the assumptions of queuing models such as the $M/M/c$ are satisfied. However, such observations are not possible through simulation. Simulation will yield good solutions that are near optimum. Thus, simulation results can be said to be *satisficing* rather than optimal.

Outputs obtained through simulation may not be a true replica or representation of the real system that is being modeled. If this error is not identified and corrected, then the estimates generated from simulation will be a gross misrepresentation of the real system and will seriously and dangerously hamper the effectiveness of decision making.

In using simulation in modeling, there is a need to establish control points throughout the different phases of model building. These control points will help the modeler identify when the model is deviating from what is expected of the real-life system performance. Some of the GPSS PC programs are interactive, and this makes it possible for the modeler to follow each step of the model execution in debugging the model codes. However, this is just one aspect of the control points discussed here. Others include the validation and verification of the simulation model, and tests to see that the behavior of the model reflects that of the real system being modeled. Verification is used to measure the internal consistency of the simulation model while validation is used to compare the model to the real system that is being modeled.

Both simulation and analytic models show different degrees of flexibility. For example, it is much easier to model complex systems through simulation without limiting the usefulness of the model through a series of unrealistic assumptions.

With analytic models, however, such assumptions are often necessary to make the model more tractable.

On the other hand, analytic models are more flexible in that they apply to a wider range of problems that fit into the assumptions made in building the model. Simulation is often situation-specific. That is to say that once any of the input values is changed, the simulation model has to be rerun. Thus, it becomes difficult to use simulation in conducting sensitivity or "what if" analysis. There is, however, an increasing number of articles supporting the use of statistical experimental design techniques and the development of regression models from simulation outputs [2, 4–8, 11, 12]. Although this relatively new application has increased the flexibility of simulation models, they are often applied within a much narrower range than the analytic models. They become very useful, however, when analytic models do not exist or are not efficient for solving a particular problem.

ADVANTAGES AND DISADVANTAGES OF SIMULATION

Simulation experiments are often more costly and more time consuming. Data collection is not always easy and data/output interpretation and analysis are often difficult. For many complex systems, it is often difficult to obtain simple and realistic mathematical formulations. Even when a mathematical model exists for such problems, it may be very difficult to solve. Simulation becomes the only option to solve such problems.

Simulation is very useful when experimenting with a system that does not exist. Previously, we discussed the introduction of a new product line, the expansion of an existing facility, and the ramifications of such decisions if a model is not used to try to understand such systems. Thus, when systems are very complex and poorly understood, analytic models become inefficient in modeling them.

Simulation has also been very effective for training purposes. Areas where simulation has been applied in training include flight simulation and business and war games. Such training procedures cannot be done with analytic models.

Users of simulation are often concerned about when to use either of these modeling techniques. Although we do not have a direct answer to this problem, we shall suggest the following:

1. Simulation should be used to model complex problems when efficient analytic models do not exist or are difficult to apply. Also, if the existing models make assumptions that appear to be unrealistic and, therefore, an underrepresentation of the system of interest, simulation should be used.

2. Simulation should be used in training exercises where the costs and risks of experimenting with the actual situation are too high. Examples include pilot training, military training, and so on. The use of simulation in these cases will help to limit the

consequences of experimenting with the real system. It also shortens the learning period.

3. Simulation should be used in complex decisions where an actual system does not yet exist, and there may be need to conduct sensitivity analysis on various aspects of that system before implementation decisions are made.

There are also cases where simulation and analytic models may be jointly applied [8, 11, 14]. The resulting models benefit by combining the good attributes of both simulation and analytic models. One such example includes the building of regression models from simulation outputs. First, a statistical design technique is used to determine the combination of the input values for simulation. Simulation is then conducted using this set of input values. The simulation outputs are then analyzed through regression analysis to obtain a regression predictor model for a system's performance measures. If the model is not a good predictor of that system's performance measure, one of the strategies to improve the model will be to choose additional input values through the use of statistical design techniques and then run simulation for this new set of data points. These latter results are combined with the former. Regression analysis is conducted again to find a best-fit regression model. This approach has also been integrated with optimization techniques in order to apply simulation results in economic analysis and decision making [8, 11].

With this procedure, satisficing decisions are made while using the flexibility of simulation in modeling real-life systems. Moreover, a general model that applies within some defined ranges for the input variables is developed for the system performance measures. Thus, "what if" analysis can be conducted without rerunning the simulation.

TYPES OF SIMULATION MODELING

There are basically three types of simulation models. These are discrete-event, hybrid, and continuous simulation models. In order to understand these models, we shall first define the concept of a random variable. A *random variable* may be defined as a variable that assumes different numerical values as a result of the outcomes of an experiment. These numerical values are, therefore, due to chance occurrence. If we consider a parking lot as an example, we observe that the arrival and departure of cars in and out of this parking lot is a chance occurrence. However, we may be able to keep track of the number of arrivals or departures at a given point in time. Thus, the objects of interest here, which are the cars, are countably finite or infinite. Since they are countable, they are referred to as discrete. We can, therefore, view the parking lot as a discrete system where the number of cars in the parking lot changes over time as a result of either arrival or departure. On the other hand, continuous systems are not countable. Consider, for example, the flow of crude oil in a pipeline. We notice that the rate of flow changes continuously over time. In such systems, we may use difference and differential equations to measure the changes in the system variable over time. Thus, the flow of crude oil in a pipeline represents a continuum that cannot be separated into discrete units. A system does not have to be absolutely continuous or discrete. In fact, many systems may consist of both discrete and continuous elements. If we consider, for example, the traffic flow problem, we observe that it is comprised of both a discrete segment (e.g., the number of cars that pass through an intersection), and a continuous segment (e.g., the rate of flow of vehicles from one intersection to the other). The choice of model depends on the type of random variables that are involved. If we are interested in modeling the rate of flow of traffic, then *continuous simulation* will be required. However, if the interest is in modeling the number of vehicles that move through an intersection, a *discrete-event simulation* is required. There are, however, cases where it may be possible to combine the attributes of both discrete-event simulation and continuous simulation. Such a case is referred to as a *hybrid simulation*. This book emphasizes only discrete-event simulation. Discrete-event simulations incorporate the elements of mathematical models already discussed. They are "discrete, dynamic, and stochastic [9]." This implies that the state variables change over time, are countable, and again, that the values assumed by the state variables are stochastic or due to chance. As Law and Kelton [9] pointed out, deterministic models are, in fact, a special case of stochastic models. If you consider a stochastic problem where the probabilities are reversed to known, then the model becomes deterministic. Thus, discrete-event simulation is applicable in modeling both deterministic and stochastic systems. Digital computers are useful in conducting discrete-event simulation due to the large amount of data that has to be analyzed in order to understand a real system. As a result, discrete-event simulation is often referred to as discrete digital simulation.

REFERENCES

1. Banks, J., J. S. Carson II, and J. Ngo Sy. *Getting Started with GPSS/H*. Annandale, VA: Wolverine Software Corporation, 1989.
2. Cochran, J. K., and J. Chang. "Optimization of Multivariate Simulation Output Models Using a Group Screening Method." *Computers and Industrial Engineering* 18 (1) (1990): 95–103.
3. Dervitsiotis, K. N. *Operations Management*. New York: McGraw-Hill Book Company, 1981.
4. Friedman, L. W. "The Multivariate Metamodel in Queuing System Simulation." *Computers and Industrial Engineering* 16 (2) (1989): 329–337.
5. Kleijnen, J.P.C. *Statistical Techniques in Simulation*, Parts I and II. New York: Marcel Dekker, 1975.
6. Kleijnen, J.P.C. *Statistical Tools for Simulation Practitioners*. New York: Marcel Dekker, 1987.
7. Kleijnen, J.P.C., and C. R. Strandridge. "Experimental Design and Regression Analysis in Simulation: An FMS Case Study." *European Journal of Operational Research* 33 (1988): 257–261.

8. Kuei, C-H., and C. N. Madu. "Polynomial Decomposition and Taguchi Design for a Maintenance Float System." *European Journal of Operational Research* (forthcoming).

9. Law, A. M., and W. D. Kelton. *Simulation Modeling and Analysis.* New York: McGraw-Hill Book Company, 1982.

10. Law, A. M., and M. G. McComas. "Pitfalls to Avoid in the Simulation of Manufacturing Systems." *Industrial Engineering* 31 (5) (1989): 28–31, 69.

11. Madu, C. N. "Simulation in Manufacturing: A Regression Metamodel Approach." *Computers and Industrial Engineering* 18 (3) (1990): 381–389.

12. Madu, C. N., M. N. Chanin, N. C. Georgantzas, and C-H. Kuei. "Coefficient of Variation: A Critical Factor in Maintenance Float Policy." *Computers and Operations Research* 17 (2) (1990): 177–185.

13. Morris, W. T. *Management Science: A Bayesian Introduction.* Englewood Cliffs, NJ: Prentice-Hall, 1968.

14. Nolan, R. "A Recurcive Optimization and Simulation Approach to Analysis with an Application to Transportation Systems." *Management Science* 18 (12) (1972): B-676.

15. Wagner, H. M. *Principles of Operations Research,* 2nd ed. Englewood Cliffs, NJ: Prentice-Hall, 1975.

Chapter 2

CONSTRUCTION OF SIMULATION MODELS

INTRODUCTION

Figure 2.1 is the tenet behind the discussions presented in this chapter. This figure shows a step-by-step procedure to construct simulation models. Although each of these steps is sufficiently discussed with an example here, they are explained further in future discussions. The discussions on how to construct simulation models presented here are in some ways similar to those presented in many sources [6,9,11,13,14], however, we have added to this discussion the issue of experimental statistical designs since this is one of the major objectives of this book.

The major elements presented in Figure 2.1 for constructing simulation models are

1. Problem definition and formulation
2. Schematic development of the system
3. Data collection and analysis
4. Simulation model building
5. Validation and verification
6. Design of experiment
7. Simulation runs with the design points
8. Development of metamodels
9. Evaluation of alternatives, sensitivity analysis, and optimization
10. Decision making and implementation

Figure 2.1
Construction of Simulation Models

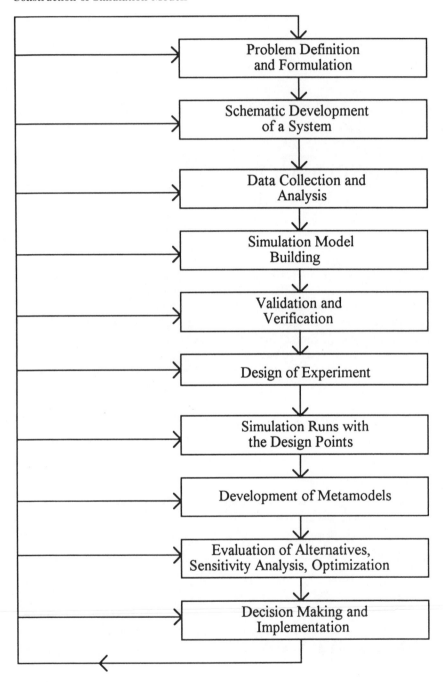

Although a sequential procedure is presented in Figure 2.1, the existence of feedback loops, as shown in this figure, indicates that some of the steps may be repeated as need be. The procedure is, therefore, iterative. We shall discuss each of the elements listed in this figure in the following sections.

PROBLEM DEFINITION AND FORMULATION

A critical phase of any model building is problem identification. If the wrong problems are identified, ultimately the solutions presented will solve ill-conceived problems. There are various problems that afflict an organization. Each of these problems competes for the organization's limited resources and is also influenced by the organization's environment. For example, an organization's decision to relocate its chemical plant to a new neighborhood is not only affected by factors of production but also by social and political factors that may be outside the control of an organization. Thus, in defining problems to be solved several criteria that influence the choice of the problems to be solved must be considered. A hierarchical structure of problems should be established so that the organization starts by solving its most critical problems and, if resources and time permit, descends to its less critical problems. Problems should, therefore, be assigned different priorities. One of the methods to achieve this goal is to use multicriteria decision-making models to rank problems on an importance scale [7,12]. Problem identification is important since the entire system's objectives may be derailed if inappropriate problems are solved.

To effectively define a problem its impact on the system and the need to make a change to redirect the system toward some form of order must be felt. Evidently, a problem exists when it is perceived that change is inevitable in order to control the system. If a problem is identified and clearly defined, the problem must also be diagnosed to identify its boundaries, constraints, and all the important variables both internal and external that influence the problem. Consider the machine repair shop problem which follows.

Example: Machine Repair Shop

Suppose that identical machines are used in a work station of an assembly line operation to produce a certain product. These machines are known to fail according to the exponential distribution and when a failure occurs, the failed unit is taken to the repair station where it queues for repair. There are a total of N repair stations that service these machines. Since the machines are all identical, they have the same priority levels, and service or repair is conducted on a first-come-first-served basis. After repair, the machine leaves the repair station. It has also been determined that the repair times are exponentially distributed. In order to minimize the waiting time of machines, the operations manager is interested in optimizing the number of repair stations. Of course, their are trade-offs involved. Minimizing the waiting time of the machines implies increasing the number of repair stations. Thus, while the cost of waiting may significantly decline, the cost of maintaining the repair stations will significantly increase. In addition, due to budget limitations the operation's manager may specify a tolerable average waiting time within which the optimization of the number of work stations can be conducted.

Evident from this problem definition is the fact that the machine repair shop is just a segment of the assembly line operation that is here viewed as an independent system. It is easier to analyze this system on its own. The problem of particular interest here is to minimize the time machines wait for repair. There are also alternatives to achieve this goal. One alternative is to increase without bound the number of repair stations. Now, how feasible is this option? It is apparent that space limitation, the cost of maintaining an infinite number of stations, the high proportion of idle time in the repair stations, and so on, may make this option infeasible. Another option is to establish trade-offs between the costs of machine waiting time and the number of work stations. This trade-off sounds feasible since increased cost of lost production may be attributed to the inability to repair failed machines in a timely fashion. A minimum cost approach can, therefore, be followed to determine the optimum combinations of waiting time costs and repair station costs. Based on this, appropriate decisions on the optimum number of repair stations can be made.

SCHEMATIC DEVELOPMENT OF THE SYSTEM

A schematic development of the system is necessary to really understand how the real system operates. In fact, this is also a form of model building. A blueprint of the model is established to show the processes that take place in the system, its environment, and constraints and variables that influence the system's performance. Figure 2.2 shows a schematic development of the machine repair shop problem already discussed. Evident from this figure is that there is only one line where all the machines wait. Notice that we have already described this line as first come first served. Also, observe that we have shown the N repair stations and that a machine awaiting repair is not selective on which repair station to choose. Once a repair station is idle, the machine next in line must proceed to that station for repair. We can deduce from this diagram that if more repair stations are open the average time a machine spends in the queue will decline if the machine's arrival rate and the repair station's repair rate are fixed. We can also try to identify some of the factors that influence this system's performance measures. These factors are classified as either exogenous or endogenous variables and are stated, with the objectives identified for this system, in the following list.

Objectives:

Minimize machine waiting time for repair

Minimize repair station's idle time

Minimize the cost of operating the repair shop

Figure 2.2
Machine Repair Problem

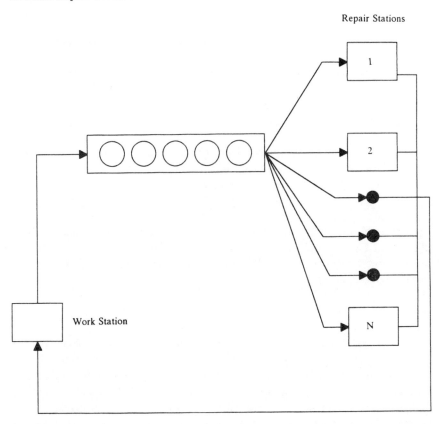

Exogenous Variables:

Number of repair stations

Arrival pattern of failed machines

Wages of repair personnel

Skills of the repair personnel

Diagnostic and repair technology

Decision to separate machines based on the severity of failure (i.e., machines with major failures may be treated differently from those with minor failures)

Endogenous Variables:

Waiting time for repair

Idle time of the repair station

Number of machines waiting for repair

Machine repair time

In Chapter 1, we defined exogenous variables as those variables that are external to the system of interest. Exogenous variables can be either controllable or uncontrollable. We observe from this problem that variables, such as the arrival patterns of failed machines, may be classified as uncontrollable. Failures follow a random process and are, therefore, probabilistic. The operation's manager has no control over this factor. Also, if the assembly line operation is unionized, the wages paid to the repair personnel may be influenced by the union and it is, therefore, not totally predictable. There are, however, exogenous variables that are controllable. For example, if the design of the repair shop has a fixed number of repair stations, the operation's manager may adjust the number of repair stations that are opened on a given time unit based on the demand for repair services. The manager may be able to control whether or not to open up a separate line for machines with major repairs. This may be a strategy to combat the long waiting times of those with minor repairs.

Exogenous variables mainly represent the input variables into a system. On the other hand, endogenous variables are used to represent the system's outputs. These variables are influenced directly by the exogenous variables and the model's design. For example, one of the major endogenous variables identified is the waiting time for repair. It is obvious that if the number of repair stations (exogenous) is increased and all other factors such as the arrival and repair rates are constant, then the average waiting time for repair will decrease. Subsequently, such increase may also lead to an increase in the proportion of idle time of the stations.

We have noted three objectives of this particular system. These objectives are not independent of each other. As noted earlier, there are trade-offs in trying to optimize any of these objectives. For example, in order to minimize the cost of operating this repair shop, we consider basically the cost of machine waiting time and the cost of operating the repair stations. We note an inverse relationship between the cost of machine waiting time and the number of repair stations that are opened to serve these machines. Also, as more stations are opened the cost of operating these stations goes up. A balance has to be achieved between these two costs. It is, therefore, not possible to achieve these objectives without some sacrifice.

Since the significant variables that influence this system have been identified and the interaction between these variables established, the next step is data collection and analysis.

DATA COLLECTION AND ANALYSIS

Data collection is an ongoing process. In fact, in defining and formulating a problem, reasonable data must be collected to explicate the problem. There are several ways of collecting empirical data. If we consider the example already presented, the type of data that may be of interest will be the interarrival times of the machines to the repair shop and the service times of the machines. Such data may be collected by manually recording the time that a machine enters into the repair shop and queues for repair. Service time may also be recorded at the point the machine advances to the repair station and at the time it departs. Manual recording is, however, tedious and it is not devoid of human errors. Incorrect recording of observations may be prevalent. Digital electronic devices may also be used to accurately record both the times of arrivals into the queue, the commencement of services, and the departure from the service system. Although automated devices are more accurate in recording data, they may be very expensive and need to be economically justifiable. Automated devices, such as pressure sensitive equipment often used in parking lots if equipped with timers, may provide more accurate information.

Once the data has been collected, it has to be analyzed. Data analysis is necessary in order to simplify model application. For example, it is obvious that the example presented can be solved as a queuing problem. However, suppose that the probability of interarrival and service times are unknown and it becomes necessary to analyze the observed data. Data analysis employs statistical techniques. If it is determined as stated previously that both the probability distributions of interarrival and service times follow the exponential distribution, then it is imperative to apply the well-established M/M/c queuing model in determining the proportion of idle time of the repair stations, the average waiting time of machines, and the minimum cost. Also, even when the assumption of these probability distributions is shown to be any of the other known probability functions, it becomes easier to make reference to such probability distributions when the simulation model is developed. Otherwise, the empirical data will be used.

SIMULATION MODEL BUILDING

At this stage, model building involves simulation model coding. This involves selecting the appropriate simulation language. As we are concerned only with discrete-event simulation, this choice is easily made. In order to effectively develop the simulation codes for a problem, we must understand how the system operates. The diagram presented as Figure 2.2 offers some insight on the operation of the physical system described in our example. In addition, construction of flow charts would help to demonstrate the sequence of events and how the variables change over time as well as how the system's performance measures are computed. The flow chart of Figure 2.3 is used to illustrate the machine repair shop example.

Of critical importance in model coding is the identification of the transactions of physical entities that are in the system. The transactions flow through the system and are processed at different points in the system. Using our example, we observe that the transactions in the machine repair shop problem are the machines that are in queue to be repaired. These transactions are temporary entities that are randomly generated. They are subsequently destroyed after ser-

Figure 2.3
System Flow Chart for the Machine Repair Shop Problem

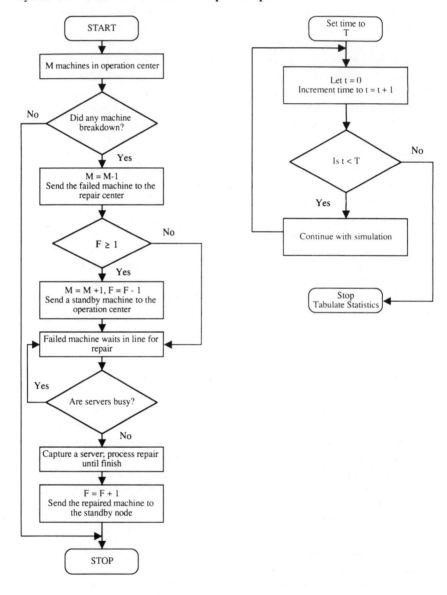

vice has been rendered. Thus, temporary entities are used to represent the transactions that enter and leave the system during the course of the simulation [5]. There are also cases where a transaction may be involved in series of activities within the system and may be represented as a permanent entity, however, permanent entities often refer to those objects that remain throughout the simulation. With the machine repair shop problem, the number of repair stations, the diagnostic devices, and the repair persons in those stations are permanent and are not destroyed during the course of simulation.

The simulation model should be helpful in determining the sequence of events, tracking the flow of the transactions, tracking the state of the permanent entities, and controlling the simulation program. For example, if the state of the repair station is classified as busy, that should trigger the next transaction to wait until the busy signal is removed. Also, there must be a termination point for the simulation program to avoid a loop. The program may be terminated, say, after a certain number of transactions have gone through the system or after some prespecified time has elapsed. The simulation should also have the capability of sequencing the next event based on specified rules.

Random Number Generation

The transactions in simulation are generated using a random process. For example, a random number is generated to represent a particular failed machine that is seeking repair. This random number is sampled from the probability distribution defined for the interarrival times. These random numbers are often referred to as *pseudorandom numbers* since they are not really random and are in fact deterministic. The algorithms for generating random numbers are already incorporated in most simulation programs, however, the process for generating such numbers will be presented in a later chapter. Pseudorandom numbers are generated using mathematical formulas. These formulas generate pseudorandom numbers that are between 0 and 1. This process is similar to the use of random number tables presented in most statistical texts and also in this book without the affixation of the decimal points. However, the usage is precisely the same. The formulas rather than the random number tables are used in most computer simulation programs because storing the random number tables will require excessive storage space.

Program Debugging

Debugging is a process of tracing the errors in a computer program. Debugging is a necessary component of programming to ensure that the logic and flow of transactions represent that of the system being modelled. The process of detecting errors in the program, especially when the program has been submitted for execution, may be time consuming. Many of the General-Purpose System Simulator (GPSS) programs use batch debuggers that take an exceedingly long time. Interactive debugging facilities that use a windowed environment are presently available with GPSS/H [1]. This allows the modeler to control the execution of the model. Information about the status and attributes of the transactions are readily displayed if a test video option is invoked.

VALIDATION AND VERIFICATION

In validating the program, we establish a correspondence between the model and the real system. The process of validation is, therefore, to ensure that the behavior of the real system is adequately represented by the simulation model. There are various ways to validate a model. One approach is to compare the model's result to the performance of an existing system and measure the deviations. If there are statistically significant differences between the performance of the model and the real system, this provides evidence that the model is inadequate. A second approach is to have the model reviewed by those familiar with the system. Although this approach is not objective, further insights about the operation of the system and potential problems with the model may be gained if the right people are used. Alternatively, the simulation program may be reevaluated and cross-checked for errors especially with the logic. Finally, the probability distributions used in the model may be tested to see that they are actually a representation of the random process observed in the real system.

Validation is an ongoing process. In fact, every phase of model construction as presented in Figure 2.1 needs to be continually validated. It is apparent that if errors occur in any of the prior stages, the simulation program will end up misrepresenting the system. Thus, validation of simulation models should not be constrained only to the simulation program. It also should be extended to the problem definition and formulation and to data collection and analysis.

While validation is used to compare the performance of the simulation model to the real system, verification is concerned with the internal consistency of the simulation model [3]. Emphasis is placed on the behavior of the model itself without linking it to the real system. For example, the output measures may be observed to see if they are reasonable. Some of the consistency checks may be to see if the queues are building up when fewer numbers of repair persons are maintained. We may also want to verify that the transactions are terminating at the right points in the system. Also, if the model is designed so that all the transactions that enter the system must depart before the close of business, for example in a bank, it must be verified that the model's performance is consistent with this assumption. This we can check easily by keeping track of the transactions that enter and leave the system. Validation and verification are, therefore, important aspects of simulation model building.

DESIGN OF EXPERIMENT

The design of experiment is critical in conducting simulation experiments. Here, the model builder decides what values of the independent variables identified in the section on schematic development should be used in the experiment. The values of these independent variables are chosen so that their respective effects on the system's performance measures (dependent variables) are understood. The exogenous and endogenous variables identified in the schematic development section represent the independent and dependent variables, respectively. It is not always easy to determine the typical values that should be assigned to the independent variables, because this often depends on what type of outcome is expected. Data collection and some preliminary experiments may be conducted at this stage to establish the appropriate input values. Also, existing information, such as historical data on similar systems and the subjective judgments of decision makers, may be useful to accomplish this goal.

Again if we consider the example presented earlier about the machine repair shop problem, it becomes apparent that there are the following independent variables: failure (arrival) rate, rate of service (repair rate), and the number of repair stations. We also have some other input variables that are very uncontrollable. These are the arrival and service times probability distributions. Assuming that the conditions for applying the analytic model are not satisfied, this problem can then be modeled via simulation. With the first three input variables specified, we may want this system to experiment under different levels of these input variables. Suppose we denote the lowest level at which we want to study any of the input variables, which we now call y_i, as a_i and the highest level as b_i, then any of these independent variables can be expressed in a range of $a_i \leq y_i \leq b_i$. In this particular example, $i = 1,2,3$ while the functions of the probability distributions of failure and repair times are built into the simulation model. Suppose we consider the number of repair stations to be anywhere from one to ten, then $1 \leq y_3 \leq 10$. If we consider that the other two variables are also expressed in a range, we see that an enormous amount of simulation experiments must be conducted to completely study all the possible input combinations of these three factors. Imagine what will happen if the number of independent variables is significantly increased. In fact, in most real-life applications, considerable number of independent variables are often used. If we let $v_i = b_i - a_i + 1$ where each of the independent factors y_i is expressed in an integral range, then the total number of experiments required to completely study each combination of these input variables is $\Pi_{i=1}^{m} v_i$ where $i = 1, 2, \ldots, m$ and there are m independent variables. Notice that this particular design calls for varying only one of the experimental factors at a time while the others are held constant. This particular procedure is known as the one-factor-at-a-time method. It was originally thought to be the only correct way to conduct this type of experiment [2]. More efficient designs have been developed. One of them is known as the full factorial design. With this design, an input variable is studied only at specific levels. For example, a 2^m design will imply that each of the m independent variables will be studied only at two levels—say the upper and lower limits—of these variables. These designs are based on the concept of obtaining a *balanced* design. We shall, however, defer the explanation of this emphasized term to later chapters. Although full factorial designs are more efficient than the one-factor-at-a-time design, they are also problematic when large numbers of variables are involved. It has, however, been shown that fruitful results can be obtained even with a fraction of the full design. This is referred to as the fractional factorial design. Due to the importance of these designs, they are presented in more detail in later chapters.

SIMULATION RUNS WITH THE DESIGN POINTS

The number of experimental conditions under which the system can be studied was determined in the section on the design of the experiment. The appropriate levels of these independent variables established in that section can now be incorporated into the model. Thus, the system is evaluated under different experimental conditions. However, since the outputs realized from simulation are subject to random fluctuations, it is desirable that several replications of each experimental run be conducted and the average yield be used to represent the outcome of that particular run. There exist statistical models for determining the number of replications in an experiment. This, of course, depends on the level of confidence and the precision desired by the modeler. We shall also discuss this issue in future chapters.

Also, notice that before this relatively large number of runs is conducted, the simulation model must have been already validated and verified. If this is not done by this time, the modeler faces the risk of wasting both time, resources, and a great number of simulation runs if the model fails any of these tests.

DEVELOPMENT OF METAMODELS

This stage is really optional. Simulation models are merely descriptive. However, metamodels are auxiliary or supplementary models that are used in the interpretation of more detailed models such as simulation [3,4,10]. Most of the developments of metamodels are based on the use of ordinary least square regression models [3,4,8,10]. They have been found useful in "model simplification, enhanced exploration and interpretation of the model, generalization to other models of the same type, sensitivity analysis, optimization, answering inverse questions [3]." The modeler can, therefore, use metamodels to better understand the system and the interaction among the system's variables.

EVALUATION OF ALTERNATIVES, SENSITIVITY ANALYSIS, AND OPTIMIZATION

Before a decision is made, several alternatives need to be evaluated on the same basis. With the use of simulation, each evaluation will involve running the model with the new input values for the independent variables. Also, the reaction of the system performance measures to changes in the values of the key parameters that we refer to as sensitivity or "what if" analysis can also be conducted. It is apparent from the definition of metamodels that such investigations can be conducted without having to rerun the simulation. If an efficient metamodel is developed, such metamodels will offer a useful means of evaluating the model under different conditions of the input parameters. The metamodel, however, is only valid within the boundaries defined for its independent variables. Again, it is necessary to adequately validate the metamodel itself before it is used in making inferences about the system. In many decision analyses, we are often concerned with finding the optimal decision whether in terms of minimizing or maximizing a particular function. Although optimization is not possible with simulation due to the random fluctuations observed with its outputs, the use of metamodels that are really prescriptive or normative can help to obtain near optimal solutions. Thus, rather than using the simulation outputs only for descriptive purposes, we can in fact apply analytic models in conjunction with simulation outputs to obtain near optimal solutions to ill-structured and complex problems.

DECISION MAKING AND IMPLEMENTATION

The essence of this experimentation is to be able to make an informed decision. Simulation modeling is incomplete without the ability to make decisions and implement the results observed. If we go back for the final time to the machine repair shop problem, we observe again that three objectives were identified, namely: minimize average waiting time of machines, minimize the proportion of idle time of the repair stations, and minimize the cost of operating the repair shop. We have already discussed the interrelationships and the interdependencies between these objectives. At the end of this experiment, we ought to be able to provide enough information so that the decision maker can make an informed judgment. We may, for example, use the metamodel approach to determine the near optimum number of repair stations. We can also present to the decision maker specific information on how the average waiting time, proportion of idle time, and the cost will change if the optimum number of repair stations is incremented, decreased, doubled, and so on. On the other hand, the decision maker may want to find some other information that this model should be able to provide. An accepted decision is then implemented. Until the results of the simulation are implemented, this process should not be considered completed [9].

REFERENCES

1. Banks, J., J. S. Carson II, and J. Ngo Sy. *Getting Started with GPSS/H*. Annandale, VA: Wolverine Software Corporation, 1989.
2. Box, G.E.P., W. G. Hunter, and J. S. Hunter. *Statistics for Experimenters—An Introduction to Design, Data Analysis, and Model Building*. New York: Wiley, 1978.
3. Friedman, L. W., and I. Pressman. "The Metamodel in Simulation Analysis: Can It

Be Trusted?" *Journal of Operational Research Society* 39 (10) (1988): 939–948.

4. Gardenier, T. K. "Pre-Prim as a Pre-processor to Simulations: A Cohesive Unit." *Simulation* (1990): 65–70.

5. Gordon, G. *The Application of GPSS V to Discrete System Simulation.* Englewood Cliffs, NJ: Prentice-Hall, 1975.

6. Hoover, S. V., and R. F. Perry. *Simulation: A Problem-Solving Approach.* Reading, MA: Addison-Wesley Publishing Company, 1989.

7. Keeney, R. L., and H. Raiffa. *Decisions with Multiple Objectives: Preferences and Value Tradeoffs.* New York: Wiley, 1976.

8. Kleijnen, J.P.C. *Statistical Techniques in Simulation,* Parts I and II. New York: Marcel Dekker, 1987.

9. Law, A. M., and W. D. Kelton. *Simulation Modeling and Analysis.* New York: McGraw-Hill Book Company, 1982.

10. Madu, C. N. "Simulation in Manufacturing: A Regression Metamodel Approach." *Computers and Industrial Engineering* 18 (3) (1990): 381–389.

11. Nance, R. "Model Representation in Discrete Event Simulation: The Conical Methodology." Technical Report CS81003-R, Department of Computer Science, Virginia Polytechnic Institute and State University, March 1981.

12. Saaty, T. L. *The Analytic Hierarchy Process.* New York: McGraw-Hill Book Company, 1980.

13. Shannon, R. E. *Systems Simulation: The Art and Science.* Englewood Cliffs, NJ: Prentice-Hall, 1975.

14. Solomon, S. L. *Simulation of Waiting-Line Systems.* Englewood Cliffs, NJ: Prentice-Hall, 1983.

Chapter 3

DATA COLLECTION AND ANALYSIS USING DESCRIPTIVE STATISTICS

INTRODUCTION

Data collection and analysis is the most important task in developing a discrete-event simulation model. The validity of all the subsequent steps, as outlined in Chapter 2, depends on data collection and analysis. If the data is improperly collected and analyzed, the resulting model would be unreliable and would not represent the real system being modeled. It is perhaps the most tedious task in building a simulation model. It requires a lot of routine tasks and is prone to human error as a result of repetitive recording of similar types of data. The data gatherer must exercise patience, be very attentive, and be careful to ensure that the right data are collected.

Because data collection forms a major core of simulation modeling, the process to collect the data must be precisely planned and clearly stated before the actual observations are recorded. In some cases, the data are easily recorded. For example, the arrivals and departures of aircraft are often meticulously recorded [3]. Also, the timing of telephone calls is digitally recorded, as are emergency medical services operations such as ambulatory care services. In all these cases, historical data may be used to analyze a particular system. There are however, many cases where the system may have to be observed to obtain the needed information. Some examples include a bank or a fast-food restaurant's drive-in services. In such cases, data may not exist for analyzing the efficiency of such services. Data must be collected in other ways to analyze such systems. We may also have instances where the operation that is to be studied is currently not in existence. Data collection in these cases may rely on design specifications or postulations based on similar systems that are in existence.

Human collection of data often requires more than one person. The tasks that must be included involve the observation of the system to see how it interacts with its environment. For example, in a drive-in operation are the servers idle when there is no available customer to serve, or do they engage in other activities, such as serving customers that are inside the facility? Other tasks involve the recording of times that events take place, such as the customers' arrival times and the beginning and ending times of services. Thus, to improve the precision and the accuracy of the data collected and to reduce the errors involved, these tasks may have to be redistributed to different people.

Of course, data collection would be meaningless if the wrong data are collected. For example, in analyzing an inventory system, data on demand pattern and lead times would be very necessary. In project scheduling, activity completion times, due dates, leeway on such due dates, and costs of crashing activities are necessary in order to effectively model such systems. Likewise, in queuing or waiting line systems, arrival and service times and the number of service channels are important in analyzing such systems. Thus, it must be clear at the onset what type of data should be collected. The data should provide sufficient insight into the problem that is being solved.

An important question that must be addressed in data collection is how typical is the data? For example, data collected on traffic flow on the George Washington (GW) Bridge—a major bridge between New York and New Jersey—on a Sunday afternoon when there is a pro-football championship game at Giants Stadium is atypical of the traffic flow on the GW Bridge. Likewise, traffic data collected during the rush hours on the New York City highways will not represent the off-peak hours. It is, therefore, necessary to clearly state which periods are of interest. Also, in modeling the behavior of a system during its operational hours it is necessary to collect the data over several periods. By doing this, data on the different times of the day, the different days of the week, and the different months of the year are collected and analyzed. It would be absurd to collect data on a bank's operation, say, on a given Monday and try to generalize such operations to the mid-week (Wednesday) or to Friday. In fact, in many cases, the behavior of the system may vary from hour to hour on different days of the week.

A FAST-FOOD RESTAURANT DRIVE-IN PROBLEM

Consider a fast-food restaurant that maintains a drive-in service. There have been complaints by customers about the waiting time for service. Management would like to evaluate the performance of this service system to determine if alternative service systems should be implemented. Presently, there is only one window that serves all the arriving customers.

In order to address this problem, we have identified the following performance measures:

• Average interarrival times
• Average waiting time in the system (i.e., the time in queue plus the time in service)

- Average waiting time in queue (excludes time in service)
- Average service times
- Average number of customers in queue
- Server's idle time

Observe from the system description that this is a queuing problem. We cannot, however, blindly apply the existing queuing models. We proceed to collect data on this particular system. In order to effectively describe this system, two observers are used. One observer observes the system's interaction with its environment and describes the system's operation while the other, armed with a stop watch, records the arrival times and the starting and ending times for services.

It was predetermined that these three sets of data are sufficient to obtain the performance measures already stated. Also, it was decided to record the operation of this system only for four hours starting from 8:00 AM to 12:00 noon. We will assume that this four-hour period is indicative of the operation of this fast-food restaurant because this problem is only illustrative. More data collection would be necessary to adequately analyze this problem. Table 3.1 presents the recorded data over this observation period. To simplify the data collection, the time has been converted to seconds and is recorded from 0 to 14,400 seconds. The observers were present at the facility before the opening of business.[1] Within the period covered, a total of 111 customers went through the drive-in service. Table 3.1 has four columns. Column 1 represents the arrivals observed; column 2 represents the arrival times of customers; column 3 represents the start times for service; and column 4 represents the service end times. For example, customer 1 arrives at the drive-in service at time 37.8139 seconds (e.g., 37.8139 seconds after 8:00 AM). Since this is the first arrival in the system, service commences immediately. The service ends at time 416.8147 seconds. Notice, therefore, that the server is idle for the first 37.8139 seconds until this arrival occurs. Also, the service time for the first arrival is 379.0008 seconds (416.8147 − 37.8139). Customer 2 arrives at time 120.8366 seconds. The time between his/her arrival and customer 1's arrival is 83.0227 seconds (120.8366 − 37.8139). In fact, this time between successive arrivals is referred to as the *interarrival time*. Also, notice that, while customer 2 arrives at time 120.8366 seconds, he/she has to wait since customer 1 is still being served. The waiting time for customer 2 is 295.9781 seconds (416.8147 − 120.8366). That is, customer 2 does not start service until customer 1 has completed service. It takes 53.0854 seconds to service customer 2 (469.9001 − 416.8147). Notice also that when customer 2 arrives, he/she observes customer 1 in service, so the queue length is 1. If you notice the time of arrival of customer 5, you notice a queue length of 4 where

---

[1]Caution is often exercised in collecting this type of data to ensure that the server being observed is not distracted since this may skew the data. It is perhaps better to collect the data without making the server aware that he/she is being observed.

Table 3.1
Waiting Line Data

Arrival Number	Arrival Time	Beginning Service	Ending Service	Interarrival	Waiting(S)	Waiting(Q)	Idle Time	Queue L	Service T
1	38	38	417		379	0	0		379
2	121	417	470	83	349	296	0	1	53
3	282	470	571	161	289	188	0	2	101
4	310	571	626	28	316	261	0	3	55
5	325	626	787	15	462	300	0	4	162
6	501	787	861	176	360	287	0	3	74
7	570	861	952	70	381	291	0	4	91
8	806	952	1038	235	232	146	0	2	86
9	995	1038	1328	189	334	44	0	1	290
10	1006	1328	1355	12	349	322	0	2	27
11	1014	1355	1413	8	398	340	0	3	58
12	1039	1413	1422	25	383	374	0	3	9
13	1088	1422	1471	49	383	333	0	4	50
14	1353	1471	1723	265	370	118	0	4	252
15	1512	1723	1840	159	328	211	0	1	117
16	1547	1840	1991	35	444	293	0	2	150
17	1744	1991	2355	198	611	246	0	2	365
18	1883	2355	2535	138	653	472	0	2	180
19	1968	2535	2540	85	572	568	0	3	4
20	2108	2540	2552	141	444	431	0	3	12
21	2249	2552	2696	141	446	303	0	4	143
22	2324	2696	2725	74	401	372	0	5	30
23	2533	2725	2756	210	223	192	0	5	31
24	2546	2756	2759	12	213	210	0	4	3
25	2702	2759	2776	156	74	57	0	3	17
26	2803	2803	2912	101	109	0	27	0	109
27	2849	2912	3000	46	151	64	0	1	88
28	2924	3000	3345	75	421	76	0	1	345
29	3275	3345	3402	351	127	70	0	1	57
30	3394	3402	3426	118	32	0	74	1	23
31	3499	3499	3532	106	33	0	0	0	33
32	3905	3905	3919	406	14	0	373	0	14
33	4196	4196	4211	291	14	0	278	0	14
34	4203	4211	4301	7	98	8	0	1	91
35	4628	4628	4678	425	49	0	327	0	49
36	4760	4760	4879	131	119	0	82	0	119

32

Arrival Number	Arrival Time	Beginning Service	Ending Service	Interarrival	Waiting (S)	Waiting (Q)	Idle Time	Queue L	Service T
37	4790	4879	4882	30	92	89	0	1	3
38	4969	4969	5056	179	87	0	87	0	87
39	5009	5056	5092	39	83	47	0	1	36
40	5059	5092	5255	50	196	33	0	1	163
41	5178	5255	5532	120	354	76	0	1	278
42	5400	5532	5548	222	148	132	0	1	16
43	5418	5548	5825	18	407	130	0	2	277
44	5504	5825	5831	85	328	321	0	3	6
45	5568	5831	5843	64	275	264	0	2	11
46	5693	5843	6166	125	473	150	0	3	323
47	5720	6166	6292	27	572	446	0	4	126
48	5855	6292	6394	136	539	437	0	2	102
49	5867	6394	6422	12	555	527	0	3	28
50	5889	6422	6520	22	631	533	0	4	98
51	5943	6520	6596	54	653	577	0	5	76
52	6174	6595	6660	231	485	422	0	5	64
53	6353	6660	6867	179	514	307	0	5	208
54	6453	6867	6883	100	430	414	0	4	16
55	6759	6883	6963	306	204	124	0	2	79
56	6867	6963	7115	107	249	96	0	2	152
57	6878	7115	7210	11	333	238	0	3	95
58	7261	7261	7265	383	4	0	51	0	4
59	7359	7359	7423	98	64	0	94	0	64
60	7392	7423	7627	33	234	31	0	1	204
61	7519	7627	7659	127	140	108	0	1	32
62	7528	7659	7666	9	138	131	0	2	7
63	7561	7666	7704	33	143	105	0	3	38
64	7712	7712	7719	151	7	0	8	0	7
65	8222	8222	8576	509	354	0	503	0	354
66	8282	8576	8673	61	391	294	0	1	97
67	8376	8673	8731	94	355	297	0	2	58
68	8404	8731	8760	28	356	328	0	3	29
69	8418	8760	8926	14	508	342	0	4	166
70	8503	8926	9089	86	585	423	0	5	162
71	8667	9089	9136	164	469	421	0	5	48
72	8728	9136	9139	61	411	409	0	5	2

(continued)

33

Table 3.1 (continued)

Arrival Number	Arrival Time	Beginning Service	Ending Service	Interarrival	Waiting (S)	Waiting (Q)	Idle Time	Queue L	Service T
73	8767	9139	9168	39	401	372	0	4	29
74	8817	9168	9268	50	451	351	0	5	100
75	8888	9268	9342	72	453	379	0	6	74
76	8902	9342	9366	13	464	440	0	7	24
77	9020	9366	9535	118	515	346	0	7	169
78	9130	9535	9554	110	424	405	0	7	19
79	9164	9554	9564	34	399	390	0	6	10
80	9217	9564	9637	53	420	346	0	6	74
81	9297	9637	9762	80	465	340	0	6	125
82	9405	9762	9870	108	465	357	0	5	107
83	9776	9870	9960	371	184	94	0	1	90
84	9786	9960	10072	10	287	175	0	2	112
85	9792	10072	10161	7	369	280	0	3	88
86	9914	10161	10163	122	249	247	0	3	2
87	10172	10172	10203	258	31	0	9	0	31
88	10329	10329	10452	157	123	0	127	0	123
89	10561	10561	10786	231	226	0	108	0	226
90	10570	10786	10794	9	224	216	0	1	7
91	10581	10794	10797	11	216	213	0	2	3
92	10690	10797	10960	109	270	107	0	3	163
93	10871	10960	10962	181	91	89	0	1	2
94	11262	11262	11274	390	12	0	299	0	12
95	11310	11310	11450	48	140	0	36	0	140
96	11511	11511	11610	202	99	0	62	0	99
97	11570	11610	11654	58	85	40	0	1	45
98	11670	11670	11694	100	24	0	15	0	24
99	11793	11793	11819	123	26	0	99	0	26
100	11872	11872	11992	79	120	0	53	0	120
101	11924	11992	12026	51	102	68	0	1	34
102	12178	12178	12235	255	57	0	153	0	57
103	12330	12330	12716	151	386	0	95	0	386
104	12410	12716	12736	80	326	306	0	1	20
105	12549	12736	12855	139	306	188	0	2	118
106	12551	12855	12908	2	357	304	0	3	53
107	12743	12908	12914	192	171	165	0	2	6
108	13146	13146	13192	403	46	0	232	0	46

Arrival Number	Arrival Time	Beginning Service	Ending Service	Interarrival	Waiting (S)	Waiting (Q)	Idle Time	Queue L	Service T
109	13293	13293	13368	147	75	0	101	0	75
110	13488	13488	13531	195	43	0	119	0	43
111	14076	14076	14104	588	28	0	545	0	28
Averages				128	283	194	36	2	88
Variance				13512	31585	27751	9250	4	7753
Standard Deviation				116	178	167	96	2	88

Table 3.2
Summary Statistics for Waiting Line Data

		Interarrival	Waiting(S)	Waiting(Q)	Idle Time	Queue L	Service T
Average		128	283	194	36	2	88
Variance	—	13512	31585	27751	9250	4	7753
Standard Deviation		116	178	167	96	2	88

customer 1 is in service and customers 2, 3, and 4 are waiting in line for service. But, when customer 6 arrives at time 500.7506 seconds, the queue length is only three because customers 1 and 2 finished services at times 416.8147 and 469.9001 respectively and have departed the system. We also observe that the total time a particular customer spends in the system is equal to the sum of his/her waiting time and service time. Thus, customer 2 spent a total of 349.0635 seconds in this system (469.9001 − 120.8366). We also observe that some customers did not have to wait in order to receive service. For example, customer 31 completed service at time 3531.7545 seconds, but customer 32 did not arrive until time 3904.9258 seconds. Thus, the server was idle for 373.1713 seconds (3904.9258 − 3531.7545).

We see that all the performance measures stated previously can be computed directly from Table 3.1. We need to find the averages, however. Table 3.1 also presents the computed performance measures for each transaction. From this, we can compute the averages shown in Table 3.2.

COMPUTATION OF PERFORMANCE MEASURES

Suppose we define the terms presented in Tables 3.1 and 3.2 as variables. Thus, we shall have

X_n = Arrival time of the nth customer

S_n = Service time of the nth customer

$W_n^{(q)}$ = Waiting time of the nth customer in queue

L_n = Queue length observed by the nth customer

A_n = Interarrival time of the nth customer

W_n = Waiting time of the nth customer in the system (includes time in service)

I_n = Idle time of server at the time of nth arrival

$I_n^{(s)}$ = Service start time of the nth customer

$T_n^{(e)}$ = Service end time of the nth customer

$T_n^{(s)}$ = Service start time of the nth customer

These definitions help us to obtain simple and general models for data collection that follow this format. Notice also that the large number of problems we model using discrete-event simulation are amenable to the queuing system.

We can state the formulas as follows:

$$S_n = T_n^{(e)} - T_n^{(s)} \tag{3.1}$$

$$A_n = X_n - X_{n-1} \tag{3.2}$$

$$W_n = T_n^{(e)} - X_n \tag{3.3}$$

$$W_n(q) = \begin{cases} 0; X_n \geq T_{n-1}^{(e)} \\ T_{n-1}^{(e)} - X_n; X_n < T_{n-1}^{(e)} \end{cases} \tag{3.4}$$

$$I_n = \begin{cases} X_n - T_{n-1}^{(e)}; X_n \geq T_{n-1}^{(e)} \\ 0; X_n < T_{n-1}^{(e)} \end{cases} \tag{3.5}$$

L_n can be easily obtained qualitatively by counting the number of cases where the arrival time is greater than the service end time.

Suppose we want to compute the performance measure for customer 25. We can apply equations (3.1) through (3.5) as follows:

$$S_{25} = T_{25}^{(e)} - T_{25}^{(s)}$$

$$= 2775.8608 - 2758.6410$$

$$= 17.2198 \; seconds$$

$$A_{25} = X_{25} - X_{24}$$

$$= 2701.8880 - 2545.6801$$

$$= 156.2079 \; seconds$$

$$W_{25} = T_{25}^{(e)} - X_{25}$$

$$= 2775.8608 - 2701.8880$$

$$= 73.9728 \; seconds$$

$$W_{25}^{(q)} = T_{24}^{(e)} - X_{25}; X_{25} < T_{24}^{(e)}$$

$$= 2758.6410 - 2701.8880$$

$$= 56.753 \; seconds$$

$I_{25} = 0; X_{25} < T_{24}^{(e)} L_{25} = 3$; notice that customer 22 was in service until time 2725.3163 seconds. Customers 23 and 24 were also in the system before customer 25 arrived. Therefore, three customers were in the system when customer 25 arrived.

These formulas offer an expedient way to compute the performance measures presented in Table 3.2. We can further extend equations (3.1) through (3.5) to compute the averages. Thus, the averages are obtained as:

$$\bar{S}_n = \sum_{n=1}^{N} S_n/N \tag{3.6}$$

$$\bar{A}_n = \sum_{n=1}^{N-1} A_n/N \tag{3.7}$$

$$\bar{W}_n = \sum_{n=1}^{N} W_n/N \tag{3.8}$$

$$\bar{W}_n^{(q)} = \sum_{n=1}^{N} W_n^{(q)}/N \tag{3.9}$$

$$\bar{I}_n = \sum_{n=1}^{N} I_n/N \tag{3.10}$$

$$\bar{L}_n = \sum_{n=1}^{N} L_n/N \tag{3.11}$$

We have used the "bar" to differentiate individual observations from the averages. Notice that we are not able to obtain the interarrival time from the first customer since no other arrival occurred before it.

DATA ANALYSIS

Data analysis is primarily conducted through the application of statistics. Statistics is used to identify known characteristics that may be present in the data set. It is, for example, easy to represent the data if it is observed that the data follow any of the known probability density functions. However, there are no guarantees that these well-established attributes may be observed. In such cases the empirical data may be used.

We can classify statistics as either descriptive or inferential. Descriptive statistics uses a set of descriptors such as the mean, median, standard deviation, and so on to analyze the data set. However, descriptive statistics cannot test hypotheses about some important statistical properties of the data set. For example, it is not possible to test the probability density function of the data set through the use of descriptive statistics. Inferential statistics is, therefore, useful under such conditions because it is able to test the theoretical distributions of the data set. Moreover, generalizations about the system's behavior are possible only through inferential statistics. Since the probability distributions of the data sets are often unknown (and they are the subject of statistical tests presented here), the statistical tests used are nonparametric. These tests are particularly useful because they do not require the specification of any probability distribution and because they do not make stringent assumptions about the parameters of the distribution. Nonparametric statistics, which is often referred to as "distribution-free," is applicable irrespective of the shape of the population(s) [2].

DESCRIPTIVE ANALYSIS

In the fast-food restaurant drive-in problem presented earlier in this chapter, 200 random samples on the arrival times and service times were observed. From Table 3.1 the performance measures presented in Table 3.2 were derived. Some of the descriptive statistical analysis of these data has already been done. Equations 3.6 to 3.11 present the averages that are, in fact, the measures of the central tendency of the data. In this section, we extend the discussion to compute the median, mode, spread, and shape of the data. We shall present two approaches: ungrouped and grouped data.

Ungrouped Data

Suppose we want to compute the descriptors stated in Table 3.2 for the waiting times. We can state these descriptors as follows:

$$\bar{W} = \frac{\sum_{n=1}^{N} W_n}{N} \tag{3.12}$$

where $\bar{W}$ is the average waiting time. The median can be computed by arranging the data in an ascending order and then selecting the data point that falls at the center of the data set. Thus, when N is odd, the median (W_m) can be computed as

$$W_m = W_{(N+1)/2} \tag{3.13}$$

where the data set $\{W_n\}$ has already been sorted in an ascending order. Also, when N is even, the median can be computed as

$$W_m = \frac{W_{N/2} + W_{(N/2)+1}}{2} \tag{3.14}$$

The mode can also be computed as the data with the highest frequency or the sample that occurs most frequently. So mode (W_d)

$$W_d = W_n \tag{3.15}$$

Notice that the mean, median, and mode are all measures of central tendency, however, the mean and median are referred to as *unbiased estimators* of the population mean.

Unbiasedness implies that the expected value of a sample statistic is equal to the population statistic. Note that the statistic is an estimator of the population. In other words, if μ is the parameter to be estimated, and $\bar{W}$ is the statistic, then $E(\bar{W})$, where $E(.)$ is the expected value, is an unbiased estimator of μ if $E(\bar{W}) = \mu$.

In measuring spread, we use range, mean absolute deviation, and standard deviation

$$Range\ (R_w) = \max\ (w_n) - \min\ (w_n) \tag{3.16}$$

where w refers to the performance measure for waiting time.

$$Mean\ absolute\ deviation\ (MAD) = \frac{\sum_{n=1}^{N} |W_n - \bar{W}|}{N} \tag{3.17}$$

$$Variance\ (S_w^2) = \frac{\sum_{n=1}^{N} (W_n - \bar{W})^2}{N - 1} \tag{3.18}$$

At times, we may need to compare a set of data to another set that may be expressed in different units. Even when the data sets are in the same units, they may have different means and standard deviations. Coefficient of variation (CV) is a relative measure of the dispersion in data sets and can be expressed as

$$CV = \frac{S_w}{\bar{W}} \tag{3.19}$$

The CV is often expressed in percentages.

Finally, we present models to compute skewness and kurtosis. Skewness is a measure of symmetry or lack of symmetry in the shape of the frequency distribution. This property is important in validating the use of measures such as the mean in measuring the central tendency. A particular frequency distribution may be symmetric (bell-shaped curve); skewed to the left (negative skewness); or skewed to the right (positive skewness). Equation 3.20 measures skewness.

$$n_w = \frac{\sum_{n=1}^{N} (w_n - \bar{W})^3 / N}{S_w^3} \tag{3.20}$$

If n_w approaches 0, then the frequency distribution is symmetric; if n_w is negative, the data is skewed to the left; and if n_w is positive, the data is skewed to the right.

Kurtosis is a measure of the peakness or the flatness of a distribution.

$$\theta_w = \frac{\sum_{n=1}^{N} (w_n - \bar{W})^4 / N}{s^4} \tag{3.21}$$

When $E(n_w) = 0$ and $E(\theta_w) = 3$, the frequency distribution is normally distributed.

We can now use Table 3.1 to compute these descriptors.

Grouped Data

Grouping may be used to describe and summarize data. Oftentimes, the data set may be so large that it would be difficult to estimate the descriptors by listing out the data. Thus, data are grouped into classes, such as according to numerical size. The resulting grouping is referred to as numerical or quantitative distribution. With numerical distributions, class intervals are expressed in numerical forms. In some cases, numerical classification of data may not be possible, and categorical or qualitative distributions are constructed.

The steps in constructing numerical distributions involve (1) choosing classes, (2) sorting (or tallying) the data into these classes, and (3) counting the number of items in each class. The following guidelines may, therefore, be followed in constructing class intervals:

1. Compute the range for the data set using equation 3.16. Divide the range by the approximate number of class intervals desired. It is preferable to maintain a class interval of between five and twenty. Each data point must fall in one and only one class interval.

2. The number obtained from (1) after the range is divided by the desired number of class intervals should be rounded off to a unit that is easy to work with and is convenient. This unit is referred to as the common width of the class intervals or the class width. If possible, the same class width should be used.

3. Select the first class interval so that the smallest measurement in the data set falls into this class interval. The intervals should also be chosen so that no measurement falls in the point of division between two class intervals. This eliminates double counting of a single measurement.

We shall now illustrate this procedure and show how the descriptors can be computed for grouped data. From Table 3.1, there are 110 observations for the interarrival times. These observations range from 2 seconds to 588 seconds. Let us compute the mean, median, mode, and standard deviation for this data. We first compute the *Range* = 588 − 2 = 586. We intend to create ten classes, so

$$Range = \frac{588 - 2}{10} = \frac{586}{10} = 58.6$$

A convenient roundoff will be 60. We can, therefore, construct a frequency distribution as presented in Table 3.3.

$$\bar{A} = \frac{\Sigma fA}{\Sigma f} = \frac{14220}{110} = 129.27 \ seconds \tag{3.22}$$

$$VAR(\bar{A}) = \frac{\Sigma (A - \bar{A})^2 f}{\Sigma f - 1} = \frac{1325874.1}{110 - 1} = 12163.983 \tag{3.23}$$

Std Dev $(A) = \sqrt{12163.983} = 110.29$

Table 3.3 shows a tally count of all the observed interarrival times. Observe from this table that each observed value falls into one of the mutually exclusive class intervals that have been constructed. Since we started with a total of 110 observed interarrival times, the sum of the frequencies of all the class intervals should be 110.

The calculations presented in Table 3.4 show that we need to determine the mid-points (A) of each of the class intervals in order to compute both the mean and the variance. The formulas for the mean and variance of grouped data are given as equations 3.22 and 3.23. Application of these equations gives a mean

Table 3.3
Tally Count for Interarrival Times

A	f	
0 and under 60	////////////////////////////////////	37
60 and under 120	///////////////////////////	27
120 and under 180	/////////////////////	21
180 and under 240	///////////	11
240 and under 300	////	4
300 and under 360	//	2
360 and under 420	/////	5
420 and under 480	/	1
480 and under 540	/	1
540 and under 600	/	1

Table 3.4
Frequency Distribution for Interarrival Times

	f	A	f.A	$(A-\bar{A})^2 f$
0 and under 60	37	30	1110	$(30-129.27)^2.37 = 364,617.72$
60 and under 120	27	90	2430	$(90-129.27)^2.27 = 41,637.59$
120 and under 180	21	150	3150	$(150-129.27)^2.21 = 9,024.39$
180 and under 240	11	210	2310	$(210-129.27)^2.11 = 71,690.66$
240 and under 300	4	270	1080	$(270-129.27)^2.4 = 79,219.73$
300 and under 360	2	330	660	$(330-129.27)^2.2 = 80,585.07$
360 and under 420	5	390	1950	$(390-129.27)^2.5 = 339,900.66$
420 and under 480	1	450	450	$(450-129.27)^2.1 = 102,867.73$
480 and under 540	1	510	510	$(510-129.27)^2.1 = 144,955.33$
540 and under 600	1	570	570	$(570-129.27)^2.1 = 194,242.93$
Total	110		14220	4,607,434.1

interarrival time of 129.27 seconds and a standard deviation of 110.29 seconds. These results are slightly different from the mean and standard deviation of 127.619 seconds and 116.245 seconds obtained from ungrouped data. Thus, when frequency distributions rather than ungrouped data are used in computing these descriptors, there is a slight loss of accuracy. Also, notice that once the data are grouped, it becomes difficult if not impossible to keep track of the interarrival time of a particular customer or transaction. For example, with the ungrouped data of Table 3.1, we can easily see that the second sequential customer arrived at this facility 83 seconds after the first transaction. This information is lost when the data are grouped. Grouping may, therefore, be used effectively to hide the identity of transactions.

In the section on ungrouped data we discussed the use of median as a measure of central tendency. It is much easier to compute the median of ungrouped data. In this section, we shall present a method for computing the median of grouped data.

In our example, we have 110 interarrivals. So, the median should lie between the fifty-fifth and the fifty-sixth interarrival times. We observe from Table 3.4 that 37 interarrival times were observed prior to the class "60 and under 120." The sum of this frequency of 37 to the frequency of the class "60 and under 120," which is 27, equals 64. This class interval is more likely to contain the median since the fifty-fifth and the fifty-sixth interarrival times are contained in this interval. If we assume that these 27 interarrival times are evenly distributed in the interval "60 and under 120," we can determine the median interarrival time by interpolation. We show how this is accomplished by presenting a formula.

$$M_d = L_{m_d} + \left(\frac{\Sigma f/2 - \Sigma f\rho}{f_{M_d}}\right) i \qquad\qquad (3.24)$$

where

M_d = The median

L_{m_d} = The lower limit of the class containing the medium

Σf = The sum of the frequencies for all the classes

Σf_ρ = The sum of all the frequencies of the classes prior to the one containing the median

f_{M_d} = The frequency of the class containing the median

i = The size of the class interval

The median interarrival time can then be calculated as

$$M_d = 60 + \left(\frac{110/2 - 37}{27}\right) (60) = 100 \; seconds$$

Indeed, what we have done is to determine the interarrival time that lies halfway between the fifty-fifth and fifty-sixth observations on the premise that these items are evenly distributed in the class that contains the median.

Another measure of central tendency is the mode. With grouped data, we can determine the *modal class*. This is the class with the highest frequency. The classes, however, must be of the same size. From Table 3.4 we see that the modal class is "0 and under 60" with a frequency of 37.

There are shortcut formulas to compute these descriptors when the class intervals are equal in size. This approach is known as the *step-deviation* method [1]. Basically, it involves the coding of the data. We shall illustrate with the present data only in computing the mean and standard deviation.

Step-Deviation Method

The following steps are taken in using this approach:

1. Arbitrarily assume a mean after the frequency distribution has been constructed.
2. Calculate the average deviation from the assumed mean.
3. Add the average deviation to the assumed mean in order to obtain the true mean. This average deviation is positive if the assumed mean is below the true mean and negative if it is above.

To illustrate this procedure, we select a midpoint of a class that is near the center and assume it to be the mean. This choice is arbitrary as stated in step 1. Subsequently, the deviations of the other class intervals are determined from this point. We decided to assign consecutive negative numbers to the deviations above the assumed mean and consecutive positive numbers to those below the mean. We present the following formulas for the step-deviation method.

$$\bar{A} = \bar{A}_a + \left(\frac{\Sigma fd}{\Sigma f}\right)(i) \qquad\qquad (3.25)$$

$$s = (i)\sqrt{\frac{\Sigma fd^2 - \dfrac{(\Sigma fd)^2}{\Sigma f}}{\Sigma f - 1}} \qquad\qquad (3.26)$$

where

$\bar{A}_a$ = The assumed mean

d = Deviations of midpoints from the assumed mean in the class interval

The other terms have already been defined. Table 3.5 provides the calculation of the arithmetic mean and standard deviation with this procedure.

$$\bar{A} = 150 + \left(\frac{-38}{110}\right)(60) = 150 - 20.7272 = 129.27$$

$$S = (60)\sqrt{\frac{410 - \dfrac{(-38)^2}{110}}{110 - 1}} = 60(1.908) = 114.49$$

Notice that the results obtained are similar. Observe, too, that we did not choose the center of the constructed class intervals as our assumed mean. It is

Table 3.5
Calculation of Mean and Standard Deviation of Grouped Data Using the Step-Deviation Method

Interarrival times	f	A	d	fd	fd²
0 and under 60	37	30	-2	74	148
60 and under 120	27	90	-1	-27	27
120 and under 180	21	150	0	0	0
180 and under 240	11	210	1	11	11
240 and under 300	4	270	2	8	16
300 and under 360	2	330	3	6	18
360 and under 420	5	390	4	20	80
420 and under 480	1	450	5	5	25
480 and under 540	1	510	6	6	36
540 and under 600	1	570	7	7	49
Total	110			-38	410

Figure 3.1
Histogram for Interarrival Times

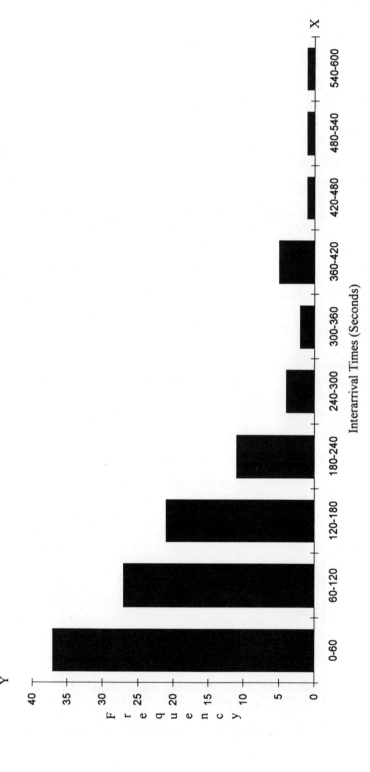

rather obvious by inspecting Table 3.5 that most of the observed data fall in the class intervals of "0 to 180." In fact, these three class intervals account for about 77% of the observed data. We, therefore, notice that these data are skewed. Also, the sparse distribution of the data as we progress to higher class intervals shows that the skewness is to the right. We must, however, state that the choice of the assumed mean is immaterial in the sense that, if you had chosen a different assumed mean, you would have observed similar results. You should try this to get a feeling of the step-deviation method. Clearly, with this approach you are able to work with manageable data, and oftentimes you may be able to estimate both the mean and standard deviation without the help of calculators.

Histogram

A histogram is a graph that is used to display the frequency distribution of data. Each class is represented by a rectangle or bar. Histograms can provide useful information about the shape of the probability distribution; however, further tests using inferential statistics will be necessary to determine if such shapes are due to chance occurrence. In Figure 3.1 we plot the histogram for the interarrival times using the frequency distribution table presented in Table 3.4. It is obvious from the diagram that there is no symmetry and also that the interarrival times have a positive skewness or it is skewed to the right. Some of you may have already suspected some probability distributions that may be used to define our data based on the shape of the frequency distribution of Figure 3.1 and the fact that the mean and standard deviation computed for the interarrival times are almost equal. In Chapter 4 we shall discuss inferential statistical analysis.

REFERENCES

1. Hamburg, M. *Statistical Analysis for Decision Making*, 5th ed. New York: Harcourt Brace Jovanovich, 1989.
2. Siegel, S. *Nonparametric Statistics for the Behavioral Sciences*. New York: McGraw-Hill Book Company, 1956.
3. Solomon, S. L. *Simulation of Waiting-Line Systems*. Englewood Cliffs, NJ: Prentice-Hall, 1983.

Chapter 4

DATA ANALYSIS USING INFERENTIAL STATISTICS

INTRODUCTION

In this chapter, we shall discuss the statistical analysis of the distribution of the interarrival times presented in Table 3.1, and we will want to determine if these data follow a particular pattern. If it is possible to establish such a pattern and define it with a known probability distribution, we can easily extrapolate to other values that were not explicitly observed in our limited observations. In addition, in terms of simulating, data management is simplified since reference to our data can now be made to the identified probability distributions and their parameters thereof. Before we continue this discussion, we must point out that there are two forms of probability distributions: discrete and continuous.

With discrete probability distributions, we deal with random variables that can assume only finite or countable numbers. For example, if we are interested in the *number* of customers arriving in the fast-food restaurant every hour, we are dealing with a discrete random variable. On the other hand, if we deal with a variable that can assume any value in an interval and can only be expressed in a continuum, then we are dealing with a *continuous* random variable. With continuous random variables, variations occur along a continuum. Therefore, a major distinction between the discrete and continuous random variables is that discrete variables are countable while continuous variables are not and can only be measured with some degree of accuracy.

In addition, we shall discuss only the popular statistical distributions that are often used to characterize the interarrival times. These distributions are also applicable to service times. The Poisson distribution is a discrete probability distribution that has been used widely in representing the number of occurrences of an event per interval of time or space. Thus, this distribution has a single parameter known as *rate*. For example, we may be interested in the rate of arrival or the rate of service. In other words, how many customers arrive per hour and so on. There are, however, several continuous probability distributions that have been used in describing either the interarrival times or the service times. These include the following distributions: uniform, normal, negative exponential, erlang, gamma, truncated normal, and lognormal. We shall discuss only the uniform, normal, and negative exponential since these are more widely used.

GOODNESS-OF-FIT TESTS

In many analytic models, it is often assumed that the probability distribution of the random variable is known. For example, in solving a queuing problem we may make an assumption that interarrival and service times follow the negative exponential distribution. Based on that assumption, we can apply some of the well-known queuing models. In reality, we can only detect the probability distribution by testing a hypothesis that specifies a particular probability distribution for the random variable being sampled against the alternative that the sample does not follow that probability distribution. If the sample does not follow the specified distribution, it is possible that it may follow any of the untested probability functions.

The goodness-of-fit test is a method for testing the distributional hypotheses. There are two types of goodness-of-fit tests we shall discuss here, namely the χ^2 goodness-of-fit test and the Kolmogorov-Smirnoff (*K-S*) test. They are also known as one-sample tests. The χ^2 does not require that the values of the parameters of the distribution be specified. In order to test for a particular distribution, the sample data are used to estimate the parameters of the distribution. However, we compensate for the use of sample statistics by using one degree of freedom for each parameter that is estimated. It is necessary that expected frequency in each class be at least five in order to effectively use the χ^2 goodness-of-fit test. If the class intervals are equal, those classes with expected frequencies of less than five should be combined with the closest classes to satisfy this requirement.

The *K-S* test compares the cumulative frequency distribution of the theoretical distribution to the observed cumulative frequency distribution and determines the point where these two distributions have the highest divergence. This large divergence is then tested to see if it is due to chance. With the *K-S* goodness-of-fit test, it is assumed that the distribution parameters are estimable from sources other than the observed sample data.

GOODNESS-OF-FIT TEST FOR THE UNIFORM DISTRIBUTION

A random variable X is said to be uniformly distributed on the interval (a,b) if the range of X is in that interval and the probability density function of X, known as f(x), is constant in that interval.

If we consider the interarrival time data of Table 3.1, we have a range of 2 to 588. So, the interarrival times will be uniformly distributed on the interval $2 \leq A \leq 588$ and the probability density function of A can be defined as

$$f(A) = \begin{cases} \dfrac{1}{588-2} = \dfrac{1}{586}, & 2 \leq A \leq 588 \\ = 0, & otherwise \end{cases}$$

The area under the uniform distribution could be expressed as

$$\int_2^{588} \frac{1}{586} \, dA = 1.$$

Please note that in general,

$$\int_a^b x^n dx = \frac{x^{n+1}}{n+1} \bigg|_a^b \tag{4.1}$$

We shall define our hypotheses as follows:

H_0: The interarrival time follows the uniform distribution

H_1: The interarrival time does not follow the uniform distribution

H_0: Referred to as the null hypothesis and it is the hypothesis we would like to retain unless there is enough evidence to contradict it

H_1: Referred to as the alternative or research hypothesis. This hypothesis is adopted when a decision is made to reject H_0

We shall also define the χ^2 statistic as

$$\chi^2 = \sum_{i=1}^k \frac{(f_i - n\rho_i)^2}{n\rho_i} \tag{4.2}$$

where

f_i = An observed frequency for class $_i$

n = The number of observations

ρ_i = The relative frequency of class $_i$

k = Number of classes

$n\rho_i$ = The expected or theoretical frequency of class

Using our interarrival time data, we can develop a table for the goodness-of-fit of the uniform distribution for interarrival times. This is presented as Table 4.1.

Table 4.1
Test for Uniform Distribution

i	Interarrival times	$A=f_i$	ρ_i	$n\rho_i$	$\chi^2 = \dfrac{(f_i - n\rho_i)^2}{n\rho_i}$
1	0 and under 60	37	0.100	11	61.45
2	60 " 120	27	0.100	11	23.27
3	120 " 180	21	0.100	11	9.09
4	180 " 240	11	0.100	11	0.00
5	240 " 300	4	0.100	11	4.45
6	300 " 360	2	0.100	11	7.36
7	360 " 420	5	0.100	11	3.27
8	420 " 480	1	0.100	11	9.09
9	480 " 540	1	0.100	11	9.09
10	540 " 600	1	0.100	11	9.09
	Totals	110	1.000	110	136.16

Notice from Table 4.1 that we have a constant probability for each class since the interarrival times will be equally distributed in these classes if the distribution is uniform. Thus, the expected frequencies are at least five. The computed $\chi^2 = 136.16$. We mentioned above that the χ^2 compensates for the use of sample statistics by losing one degree of freedom for each parameter that is estimated. With the uniform distribution, we discount one degree of freedom for the use of sample size (n) in computing the expected frequency $(n\rho_i)$. We can, therefore, express the degrees of freedom for the χ as $k - r$ where k is the number of classes and r is the number of parameters that is estimated with sample statistics. In this example, $k = 10$ and $r = 1$, so the degree of freedom is nine. We must also specify the level of confidence that is desired in the use of χ^2. The computed χ^2 value is to be compared to the $100\,(1 - \alpha)$ percentile of the χ^2 distribution with $k - r$ degrees of freedom. α is referred to as the probability of the type I error or, rather, the probability of rejecting H_0 when in fact it is true. Typical values of α are 0.01, 0.05, and 0.10. In this book we shall use a 95% confidence level or an $\alpha = 0.05$. From the χ^2 table, we obtain the $\chi^2_{1-\alpha}$, $k - r = \chi^2_{0.95,9} = 16.919$. This value of χ^2 is called the critical value. Since the computed value of $\chi^2 = 136.16$ is greater than this critical value of 16.919, we shall reject H_0. A rejection of H_0 implies an acceptance of H_1. Thus, we conclude that the interarrival times are not uniformly distributed. We can graphically show that if we plot the χ^2 distribution

Figure 4.1
χ^2 Distribution

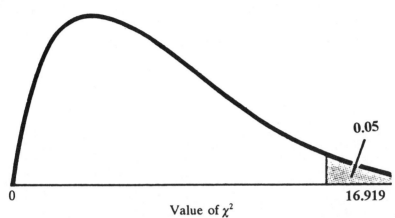

the computed value will fall in the rejection region. Figure 4.1 shows the distribution.

Since the interarrival times are not uniformly distributed, we choose to try another continuous probability distribution since interarrival time is expressed in a continuum and is not countable. A logical probability distribution to consider is the normal distribution also known as the Guassian distribution.

GOODNESS-OF-FIT TEST FOR THE NORMAL DISTRIBUTION

The hypotheses already presented are still valuable in conducting this test. There is some important information we should know about the normal distribution. The normal distribution is, perhaps, the most widely used probability distribution. It is a symmetric distribution with a bell-shaped curve. It also has two major parameters—mean and standard deviation. Also, one of the most important theorems in statistical inference, known as the *Central Limit Theorem*, refers directly to the normal distribution.

The *Central Limit Theorem* states that if a random variable X has a mean *u* and a finite standard deviation σ, then the probability distribution of X approaches the normal distribution as the sample size (*n*) increases without limit.

Note that the *Central Limit Theorem* is a statement about sampling distributions and is applicable to both discrete and continuous random variables. Based on this theorem, samples drawn from nonnormal distributions will approach the normal distribution as *n* increases without limit.

With the normal distribution, the random variable X can be expressed in an interval $-\infty < X < \infty$. Therefore, in using the normal distribution for interarrival times, it is better to use what is known as the *Truncated Normal Distribution* to truncate of the negative values of the normal distribution since the interarrival times cannot be negative. The *z-score* is commonly used in determining the probabilities of areas under the normal curve. The *z-score* is a measure of the number of standard deviations from the mean and can be expressed as

$$z = \frac{x - u}{\sigma} \tag{4.3}$$

Let us apply this information to our test for the distribution of interarrival times. We can restate the frequency distribution with new expected frequencies computed for the normal distribution. This is presented as Table 4.2.

In order to compute ρ_i, ρ_2, . . . , ρ_{10}, we need to know the mean and standard deviation of the normal random variable. We, therefore, use the sample to compute estimates of u and σ. This we accomplished in Chapter 3 where we determined that $\bar{A} = 129.27$ seconds and *Std. Dev. (A)* $= 110.29$ seconds. We can, therefore, use the standard normal table to find the probabilities. For example, if we consider class 1, we want to find the probability that A is in the interval 0 and 60. That probability we denote as ρ_1. Since we are assuming normal

Table 4.2
Test for Normal Distribution

i	Interarrival times	f_i	ρ_i	$n\rho_i$
1	under 60	37	0.2643	29.073
2	60 and under 120	27	0.2038	22.418
3	120 and under 180	21	0.2091	23.001
4	180 and under 240	11	0.1641	18.051
5	240 and under 300	4	0.0981	10.791
6	300 and under 360	2	0.0423	4.653
7	360 and under 420	5	0.0142	1.562
8	420 and under 480	1	0.0031	0.341
9	480 and under 540	1	0.0009	0.099
10	540 and under 600	1	0.0001	0.011
	Total	110	1.000	

distribution, we can compute the probability as follows: Since the random variable x can assume negative value, we notice that $P(x < 0) = 0.12$. To simplify our calculation, we shall redefine class 1 as an open-ended interval to include the $P(x < 60) = 0.2643$. By doing so, we satisfy an important probability axiom that the sum of probabilities is 1. As suggested earlier, in dealing with interarrival times it is often preferable to truncate the negative values.

We want to find the probability of the shaded region. Again, the sample estimates of the mean and standard deviation are used since we do not have the population values. Using z, we obtain

$$z_1 = \frac{0 - 129.27}{110.29} = -1.17$$

$$z_2 = \frac{60 - 129.27}{110.29} = -0.63$$

We now go to the standard normal table where we obtain that the probabilities are 0.3790 and 0.2357 when $z = -1.17$ and -0.63 respectively. Therefore, $P(0 < A < 60) = 0.3790 - 0.2357 = 0.1433$. However, $P(A < 60) = 0.2643$. Once the probabilities are computed, the procedure for computing χ^2 is the same, and we leave it as an exercise to the reader to verify Table 4.2.

Observe from Table 4.2 that the expected frequencies obtained for classes six to ten are all less than five. Thus, the χ^2 approximation may not be good without some adjustments. So, to take care of this problem, we combined all those classes with expected frequencies less than five. Table 4.3 is therefore constructed.

By combining the frequencies, we have effectively six classes that are used. In order to determine the critical value of the χ^2 distribution, we note that the

Table 4.3
Modified Table for Testing the Normal Distribution

i	interarrival times	f_i	p_i	πp_i	$\chi^2 = \frac{(f_i - np_i)}{np_i}$
1	under 60	37	0.2643	29.073	2.1614
2	60 and under 120	27	0.2038	22.418	0.9365
3	120 and under 180	21	0.2091	23.001	0.1741
4	180 and under 240	11	0.1641	18.051	2.7542
5	240 and under 300	4	0.0981	10.791	4.2737
6 to 10	300 and more	10	0.0606	6.666	1.6675
		110	1.0000		11.9674

sample size (n), and the estimates for the mean and standard deviation are required to test for the normal distribution. Thus, using our expression of the degrees of freedom as $k - r$, we have $6 - 3$ where one degree of freedom accounts for each of the three parameters n, u, and σ. Thus, $\chi^2_{0.95,3} = 7.815$. Since our computed $\chi^2 = 11.9674$ is greater than 7.815, we reject H_0. Thus, the interarrival time is not normally distributed.

GOODNESS-OF-FIT TEST FOR THE NEGATIVE EXPONENTIAL DISTRIBUTION

The negative exponential distribution has only one parameter, which we denote here as μ. Its mean is equal to its standard deviation. Also, it is typically used to represent the time of occurrence of events. Time is continuously and positively measured. A continuous random variable expressed with the negative exponential distribution must, therefore, assume only positive numbers. If a random variable X is negative exponentially distributed, its probability density function can be expressed as

$$f_x(t) = \frac{1}{\mu} e^{-t/\mu}, \quad t > 0$$

$$= 0, \quad \text{otherwise} \tag{4.4}$$

Its cumulative density function can easily be obtained by integration as

$$F_x^{(t)} = 0, \quad t < 0$$
$$= 1 - e^{-t/\mu}, \quad t > 0 \tag{4.5}$$

where μ is the mean time.

A unique and important property of the exponential distribution is that its random variables are said to be *memoryless*. For example, suppose that a customer at the fast-food restaurant example had already spent twenty minutes while waiting for service, the probability that the same customer will spend at least ten more minutes given that he/she had already spent twenty minutes will be equal to the probability that a new customer arriving at this restaurant will spend at least ten minutes before being served. The exponential distribution does not keep track of history so it does not remember that this customer had already waited twenty minutes.

If we look closely at our interarrival time data, we observe that the mean of 129.27 seconds is very close to the standard deviation of 110.29 seconds. Also, the histogram in Figure 3.1 that showed the positive skewness of this data is similar in shape to that of the negative exponential. These early indicators observed from our use of descriptive statistics may have saved us time if we tried the more likely distribution for goodness-of-fit. We shall proceed to test if these

early observations confirm that the interarrival times follow the negative exponential or are due to chance occurrence. We will now use some concepts from
calculus to derive the probabilities for the exponential distribution.

$$P_1 = \int_0^{60} f_x(t)dt = \int_0^{60} .0077e^{-.0077t}$$

If we let $\mu = -0.0077\, t$

$$\frac{d\mu}{dt} = -0.0077$$

$$-\frac{d\mu}{.0077} = dt$$

Notice that $\dfrac{1}{\mu} = \dfrac{1}{129.27} = 0.0077$

Therefore, by substitution $-1/.0077\int .0077\, e^{\mu}_\mu d\mu = -e^{\mu}$

Since $d\mu = -.0077dt$, we can substitute back in terms of t so that we can
evaluate the integral with respect to t. So,

$$-e^{-.0077t}\big|_0^{60} = -[e^{-.0077(60)} - e^0] = 1 - e^{-0.464} = 1 - 0.6286 = 0.3714$$

Likewise, we can compute all the other probabilities. We shall try one more.

$$P_2 = \int_{60}^{120} .0077\, e^{-.0077t}dt$$

Again, by substitution, we obtain

$$-e^{-.0077t}\big|_{60}^{120} = -[e^{-0.924} - e^{-0.462}] = -[0.3969 - 0.6300] = 0.2331$$

The rest of the table can easily be filled with these probabilities. From Table
4.4, we observe that the expected frequencies are less than 5 when $i = 6, 7, 8, 9,$
and 10. We decide to combine these cases. Table 4.5 presents the modified table.
Since the negative exponential distribution has only 1 parameter (μ), we can
determine the critical value as $\chi^2_{0.95,4} = 9.488$. Notice that 1 of the 2 degrees of
freedom represents the sample size. Observe that the computed $\chi^2 = 3.2364 <$
9.488. Therefore, we do not reject H_0. We can now state that the negative
exponential distribution provides the best fit for the interarrival time. Our decision is then to accept the null hypothesis.

Table 4.4

The Test for Negative Exponential Distribution

i	interarrival times	f_i	ρ_i	$n\rho_i$
1	0 and under 60	37	0.3713	40.85
2	60 and under 120	27	0.2331	25.64
3	120 and under 180	21	0.1423	15.65
4	180 and under 240	11	0.0970	10.67
5	240 and under 300	4	0.0582	6.402
6	300 and under 360	2	0.0368	4.048
7	360 and under 420	5	0.0231	2.541
8	420 and under 480	1	0.0146	1.606
9	480 and under 540	1	0.0092	1.012
10	540 and more	1	0.0146	1.606
	Total	110	1.0000	

Table 4.5

Modified Test for Negative Exponential Distribution

i	interarrival times	f_i	ρ_i	$n\rho_i$	$\chi^2 = \dfrac{(f_i - n\rho_i)^2}{n\rho_i}$
1	0 and under 60	37	0.3713	40.85	0.3629
2	60 and under 120	27	0.2331	25.64	0.0721
3	120 and under 180	21	0.1423	15.65	1.8289
4	180 and under 240	11	0.0970	10.67	0.0102
5	240 and under 300	4	0.0582	6.402	0.9012
6 to 10	300 and more	10	0.0983	10.813	0.0611
		110	1.0000		3.2364

GOODNESS-OF-FIT TEST FOR THE POISSON DISTRIBUTION

A discrete random variable x has a Poisson distribution if

$$P(x) = \frac{\mu^x e^{-\mu}}{x!}, \qquad x = 0, 1, \ldots$$

where $\mu > 0$. Thus, x can be countably finite or infinite. Notice that the Poisson has only one parameter (μ). In contrast to the other distributions already discussed, the Poisson is a discrete-probability distribution. So, rather than testing the probability distribution of interarrival times, we shall test the null hypothesis that the arrival rate of the transactions is Poisson distributed. Rate is the only parameter of this distribution. We shall state some important properties of the Poisson distribution before proceeding with the goodness-of-fit test. These are:

1. The probability of exactly one arrival in each subinterval of time is small and it is constant for each subinterval.

2. The probability of more than one arrival in any small interval is negligible and can be assumed to be zero.

3. The number of arrivals observed in any small interval is not dependent on the location of that subinterval.

4. The number of arrivals in any subinterval is independent of the number of arrivals in any other nonoverlapping subinterval.

Suppose we go back to Table 3.1, where we presented the arrival time data; we can determine the number of arrivals in a specified time interval. We now construct a new frequency distribution but this time we use arrival time data. Table 4.6 is constructed by using the arrival time data in Table 3.1 and determining the number of arrivals in all of the 100 second intervals. For example, the first interval is 0 to 100 seconds. Only one arrival occurred at time 38 seconds. The next interval is 101 to 200 seconds. This time 0 arrival was observed. The third interval is 201 to 300 seconds. Only one arrival was observed at time 282 seconds. After this table has been developed, we count the number of intervals with 0, 1, 2, 3, and 4 arrivals. This forms the frequency distribution presented as Table 4.6. Notice 4 is the maximum number of arrivals obtained in any single interval of 100 seconds.

First of all we determine the expected number of arrivals per 100 seconds. This expected value will be the arithmetic mean or the rate of the Poisson distribution. This mean is expressed as

$$\mu = \frac{\sum_{i=1}^{n} A_i f_i}{\sum f_i} = \frac{(0 \times 63) + (1 \times 59) + (2 \times 17) + (3 \times 4) + (4 \times 1)}{144} = \frac{109}{144}$$

The rate of arrival is, therefore, 0.7569 per 100 seconds.

With the rate of the Poisson determined, we can now use the Poisson distribution to find the probabilities that 0, 1, 2, 3, or 4 arrivals will occur every 100 seconds. These probabilities which will be used to determine the expected frequencies will then be compared to our observed frequencies.

Table 4.6

Test for Poisson Goodness-of-Fit of the Number of Arrivals in Every 100-Second Interval*

i	Number of Arrivals/ 100 seconds	f_i frequency	$A_i f_i$
1	0	63	0
2	1	59	59
3	2	17	34
4	3	4	12
5	4	1	4
	Total	144	109

*Note that the data is collected over a period of 4 hours, which is equivalent to 14,400 seconds. There is, therefore, a total of 144 100-second intervals.

Applying the probability density function for the Poisson, we will have

$$P(x) = \frac{(0.7569)^x e^{-0.7569}}{x!}; \quad x = 0, 1, 2, 3, 4$$

So, $P(0) = 0.4691; P(1) = 0.3508; P(2) = 0.1344; P(3) = 0.0339;$ and $P(4) = 0.0064$.

Table 4.7 presents the χ^2 test for the Poisson distribution.

The computed $\chi^2 = 2.39$. The critical value obtained from the χ^2 table at 95% level confidence and a degree of freedom of $4 - 2 = 2$ is 5.99. Since the computed $\chi^2 = 2.39 < 5.99$, we decide not to reject the null hypothesis that the number of arrivals per 100 seconds or the arrival rates are Poisson distributed.

Table 4.7

χ^2 Goodness-of-Fit Test for the Poisson Distribution*

i	Number of Arrivals/ 100 seconds	f_i	p_i	np_i	$\chi^2 = \frac{(f_i - r}{np}$
1	0	63	.4691	67.55	0.3065
2	1	59	.3508	50.52	1.4234
3	2	17	.1344	19.35	0.2854
4	3 or more arrivals	5	.0457	6.58	0.3794
	Total	144	1.0000		2.3947

*Since the expected frequencies of classes 4 and 5 are less than 5, they have been combined.

This leads us to an important relationship between the Poisson and the negative exponential distribution. When the interarrival times follow the negative exponential distribution, then, the arrival rate must follow the Poisson distribution. So a statement that depicts the interarrival times as a negative exponential distribution implies that the arrival rate is Poisson distributed. Also, the mean of one is the inverse of the mean of the other. The *memoryless* property discussed for the negative exponential is also applicable to the Poisson.

In the next sections, we shall illustrate the use of the Kolmogorov-Smirnoff (*K-S*) goodness-of-fit test.

KOLMOGOROV-SMIRNOFF (K-S) GOODNESS-OF-FIT TEST

The *K-S* test, like the χ^2 test, is a test of goodness-of-fit. The *K-S* compares a theoretical distribution to a set of sample observations. The sample is assessed to determine if it comes from a population having the hypothesized theoretical distribution.

In order to use the *K-S* method the cumulative frequency of the hypothesized theoretical distribution is compared with the cumulative frequency distribution determined for the sample observations. The maximum deviation of the cumulative frequency for the observed and the theoretical distributions is tested to see if such a large divergence occurred due to chance.

The *K-S* test is a more powerful test than the chi-square goodness-of-fit test. We shall briefly contrast the *K-S* and the χ^2 goodness-of-fit tests to get a better feeling of the power of the *K-S* test.

The *K-S one-sample test* allows for the consideration of individual observations. It is not required that observations be grouped into classes as we did with the χ^2 test. When we group observations, we lose information. This problem is, therefore, avoided with the use of the *K-S* test.

We noted in the case of χ^2 that it is required that each class interval contains at least a frequency of 5. When this is not observed, adjacent classes must be added to avoid having classes with smaller frequencies. This is not necessary when the *K-S* test is used. Also, when very small samples are used, the χ^2 test becomes inapplicable. This is not so with the *K-S* test.

STEPS IN USING THE K-S TEST

These steps may be useful in using the *K-S* one-sample test:

1. State the null hypothesis (H_0) specifying the theoretical cumulative distribution.
2. Arrange the sample observations either as individual observations (i.e., when the sample is small) or as grouped observations (i.e., when the sample is large) and compute the sample cumulative distribution.
3. Compute the theoretical cumulative distribution. Pair the observed and the theoretical cumulative distributions for comparable classes or observations.

4. Compute the absolute difference for each pair of the observed cumulative frequency distribution and the theoretical frequency distribution.

5. Use the K-S table to find the critical values for a specified level of significance α and degrees of freedom (n) where n is the sample size. If the computed maximum difference is less than this critical value, do not reject H_0. Otherwise, H_0 should be rejected implying that the theoretical distribution specified under H_0 is not appropriate for fitting the data.

We shall illustrate this procedure by testing the interarrival times distribution. Specifically, we shall test to see if interarrival times follow the normal distribution, exponential distribution, and the Poisson distribution.

Goodness-of-Fit Test for the Normal Distribution

In an earlier section we discussed the goodness-of-fit test for the normal distribution using the χ^2 test. There, we constructed the class intervals and noted from Table 4.2 that the expected frequencies for classes six to ten were less than five. As a result, classes six to ten were combined as shown in Table 4.3. With the use of the K-S test, this process of combining classes with small frequencies is unnecessary.

Step 1: We shall state the hypothesis as follows:
  H_0: The interarrival times are normally distributed.
  H_1: The interarrival times are not normally distributed.

Step 2: We have already grouped the observation on interarrival times as contained in Table 4.2.

Step 3: We shall compute the cumulative frequencies for both the observed and the theoretical distribution by finding the probabilities for each class and taking the successive sums of their probabilities. Table 4.8 presents these results.

Notice that the maximum difference is 0.1138. From the K-S table, the critical value at a level of significance of 0.05 is 0.1297. Since the maximum difference is less than 0.1297, we do not reject H_0. This result seems to contradict our prior test with the χ^2 that rejected the null hypothesis that the interarrival time is normally distributed. However, let us conduct this test for the negative exponential.

Goodness-of-Fit Test for the Negative Exponential Distribution

From Table 4.4, we derive most of our information on the negative exponential distribution. We shall again conduct the K-S test as has already been shown. Table 4.9 presents the results of that test.

The maximum difference between the theoretical and the observed cumulative frequency distribution is 0.0349, which is less than the critical value of 0.1297.

Table 4.8
Test for Normal Distribution (K-S test)

	Interarrival times	t	P_{oi}	F_{oi}	P_{ti}	F_{ti}	$|F_{ti}-F_{oi}|$
1	under 60	37	0.3364	0.3364	0.2643	0.2643	0.0721
2	60 and under 120	27	0.2455	0.5819	0.2038	0.4681	0.1138
3	120 and under 180	21	0.1909	0.7728	0.2091	0.6772	0.0956
4	180 and under 240	11	0.1000	0.8728	0.1641	0.8413	0.0315
5	240 and under 300	4	0.0364	0.9092	0.0981	0.9394	0.0302
6	300 and under 360	2	0.0182	0.9274	0.0423	0.9817	0.0543
7	360 and under 420	5	0.0455	0.9729	0.0142	0.9959	0.0230
8	420 and under 480	1	0.0091	0.9820	0.0031	0.9990	0.017
9	480 and under 540	1	0.0091	0.9911	0.0009	0.9999	0.0088
10	540 and under 600	1	0.0091	1.000	0.0001	1	0.0000
	Σf_i = 110		1.0000		1.0000		

P_{oi} = Probability of class i based on the observed frequency $(f_i/\Sigma f_i)$; P_{ti} = Theoretical probability of class i; F_{oi} = Observed cumulative probability of class i; F_{ti} = Theoretical cumulative probability of class i.

Table 4.9
Test for the Negative Exponential Distribution (K-S test)

i	interarrival times	f_i	P_{oi}	F_{oi}	P_{ti}	F_{ti}	$|F_{ti}-F_{oi}|$
1	0 and under 60	37	0.3364	0.3364	0.3713	0.3713	0.0349
2	60 and under 120	27	0.2455	0.5819	0.2331	0.6044	0.0225
3	120 and under 180	21	0.1909	0.7728	0.1423	0.7467	0.0261
4	180 and under 240	11	0.1000	0.8728	0.0970	0.8437	0.0291
5	240 and under 300	4	0.0364	0.9092	0.0582	0.9019	0.0073
6	300 and under 360	2	0.0182	0.9274	0.0368	0.9387	0.0113
7	360 and under 420	5	0.0455	0.9729	0.0231	0.9618	0.0111
8	420 and under 480	1	0.0091	0.9820	0.0146	0.9764	0.0056
9	480 and under 540	1	0.0091	0.9911	0.0092	0.9856	0.0055
10	540 and more	1	0.0091	1.0000	0.0146	1.0000	0.0000
			1.0000				

This test again suggests that H_0 should not be rejected. It seems like there is a contradiction in our tests since the interarrival time data cannot possibly be described by two different probability distributions. However, we observe that the maximum difference obtained when the negative exponential distribution was hypothesized as the theoretical distribution is very close to zero while the maximum difference obtained under the normal distribution is very close to the critical value. Moreover, since we know that the mean and the standard deviation of the negative exponential must be equal, we suspect that our interarrival time data may in fact be exponentially distributed. This suspicion is, however, not enough to statistically make a judgment on the appropriate theoretical distribution because we know that, if the interarrival time is exponentially distributed, then the arrival rate must also follow the Poisson distribution. It is, therefore, logical to test if the arrival rate is Poisson distributed.

POISSON GOODNESS-OF-FIT TEST

We shall use the results of Table 4.6 to illustrate.

The maximum difference is 0.0316 and the critical value at a 0.05 level of significance is 0.1133. Observe that the maximum difference of 0.0316 shown in Table 4.10 is also closer to zero than to the critical value. We, therefore, decide not to reject the null hypothesis that the arrival rate is Poisson distributed. Likewise, we conclude that the interarrival time is negative exponentially distributed.

So far, we have assumed that one of the known theoretical distributions may provide a good fit to our sample observations. It is also conceivable that none of these distributions may provide a good fit to our set of observations. In such cases, the empirical distribution itself may be used to describe the observed data. Here, the classes are created using the guidelines presented in Chapter 3 in the

Table 4.10
Test for the Poisson Distribution (K-S test)

i	Number of arrival/ 100 seconds	f_i	P_{oi}	F_{oi}	P_{ti}	F_{ti}	$\lvert F_{ti}-F_{oi} \rvert$
1	0	63	0.4375	0.4375	0.4691	0.4691	0.0316
2	1	59	0.4097	0.8472	0.3508	0.8199	0.0273
3	2	17	0.1181	0.9653	0.1344	0.9543	0.0110
4	3	4	0.0278	0.9931	0.0339	0.9882	0.0049
5	4 or more	1	0.0069	1.0000	0.0118	1.0000	0.0000
		144	1.0000				

discussion on grouped data. Subsequently, the relative frequency of each class, as well as the cumulative frequency distributions, are computed. This information is supplied in the simulation model.

In concluding this chapter, we shall point out that the tests performed for the interarrival times should also be conducted for the service time in order to decide its probability distribution. The reader should use the data in Table 3.1 on service times to determine the appropriate theoretical distribution for service times.

Chapter 5

GENERATION OF RANDOM NUMBERS AND RANDOM VARIABLES

INTRODUCTION

In Chapter 4 we discussed statistical procedures for detecting the theoretical probability distributions of random variables. For example, in the fast-food, drive-in restaurant problem, it was shown that the interarrival time is negative exponentially distributed with a mean of 127.62 seconds. If this queuing system is to be analyzed through simulation, we desire to generate interarrival times that have the same characteristics as the specified theoretical distribution. These interarrival times are referred to as *random* since their occurrences are not predictable. They are also random because all the occurrences within the sample space we are drawing from are assumed to be equally likely. The generation of random variables, therefore, refers to the random assignment of numerical values to the random variables for specified probability distributions.

The aim of this chapter is to expose the reader to some of the basic concepts in the generation of random numbers and random variates. Discussions are presented on how to generate and test the random numbers. We shall also discuss the technique used by GPSS/H in generating random numbers.

PSEUDORANDOM NUMBERS

The type of random numbers used in simulation is known as *pseudorandom numbers*. The term "pseudo" means false. This means that our so-called random numbers are not really random. They are close to random but are not random. The lack of randomness with these numbers can be detected from statistical tests that measure the independence between numbers. Pseudorandom numbers often fail such statistical tests. In fact, the sequence of a pseudorandom number is completely reproducible.

The reproducibility of pseudorandom numbers has tremendous value in the context of simulation and that is why they are preferred to "true" random numbers. Some of the values are

1. It is easier to replicate an experiment. For example, alternative systems can be compared under the same experimental conditions.
2. They are useful in debugging a computer program. This allows for the replication of results obtained from a simulation run since the same sequence of random numbers is used in the simulation run. This makes it easier to verify the simulation model for internal consistency.
3. The reproducibility of random numbers also makes it easier to increase the precision of the simulation output.

We shall henceforth refer to these pseudorandom numbers simply as random numbers.

CHARACTERISTICS OF A RANDOM NUMBER GENERATOR

There are some important properties that a good random number generator must possess. Many of these properties can also be statistically tested. It is essential that these statistical properties be satisfied in order to obtain meaningful simulation outputs. Although most simulation programs have inbuilt algorithms for generating random numbers for specified probability distributions, it is necessary to know the concepts behind these algorithms. Also, some of the programs including General Purpose Systems Simulation (GPSS) and GPSS/H are not extensive in terms of the number of probability distributions that can be directly specified by the user. Thus, the user has to generate the random numbers and supply them to the program. These characteristics are discussed in the following sections.

Computational Efficiency

We are all familiar with the use of random number tables for manual simulation. These tables are very extensive and often require a large computer memory if they were to be stored in the computer for usage in simulation. Therefore, random number generators must be computationally efficient in that the processing speed should be relatively fast and the computer storage requirement should be reasonable.

Uniformly Distributed Random Numbers

Random numbers are generated on the premise of equal probability of occurrence in the interval between zero and nine. This interval covers the ten discrete integer numbers. Thus, the random number generated should generate any of the numbers from 0, 1, 2, . . . , 9 with an approximate probability of 0.1.

Statistical Equivalence to the Theoretical Distribution

In Chapter 4, we went to great length to identify the theoretical probability distribution of our sample data. When a theoretical probability distribution is confirmed and is simulated with a random number generator the statistical properties of the simulated random numbers must conform with the properties of the specified theoretical probability distribution. For example, the statistical distribution and the parameters of that distribution should be equivalent to that of the theoretical distribution.

Statistical Independence

The test for statistical independence must be satisfied. For example, if it is known that the interarrival time of the second customer is 83 seconds, it should not be predictable that the next arrival should occur at time 162 seconds. If it is possible to predict without looking at the computer algorithm used in generating these numbers, then the random number will be statistically dependent.

Lack of Trend

The random numbers should not follow a particular pattern. For example, the pattern of change to larger or smaller values should not be apparent.

Long Period

One common property of pseudorandom number stream is that it repeats itself. It is desirable that large numbers of random numbers be generated before the process repeats itself. The maximum number in this sequence before the cycle is repeated is known as the *period* or the *word length* of the generator. A good generator should, therefore, have a very long period or a long cycle length.

GENERATION OF RANDOM NUMBERS

Hull and Dobell [5] traced the origins of random number generation. Until the advent of computers, random numbers were manually generated. Earliest methods for generating random numbers included drawing numbers from a well-stirred urn, throwing dice, dealing out cards, and so on [8]. Many of the lotteries drawn in many of the states in the United States, such as the New York State Lotto, are still based on drawing numbered balls from a "well-stirred urn." Suppose we consider this latter case. An urn is filled with ten numbered balls with values 0, 1, 2, 3, 4, 5, 6, 7, 8, and 9, and the urn is well stirred before drawing. A mechanical device, as used in these lotteries, draws one ball at a time. The number that appears on that ball represents a random number. If the sampling procedure is done with replacement, the ball is put back in the urn and the urn is well stirred again before the next random number is drawn. It is obvious here that each of the ten balls will have equal probability of 0.1 of being drawn. This particular case exemplifies a truly random process since it is impossible to predict the occurrence of drawing any of the ten balls. Moreover, the probability that any of the balls will be drawn is the same in each random drawing. However, this procedure becomes very awkward when large numbers of random numbers are to be drawn, as in the case of simulation. Also, the use of the popular random number tables are inefficient for simulation. Computer-based algorithms that satisfy the desired properties for pseudorandom numbers are used, therefore.

Midsquare Method

The midsquare method is considered to be the first arithmetic generator that was developed. This method was proposed by the venerable mathematician von Neuman and Metropolis in the 1940s. Although the midsquare is very simple, it is statistically inefficient.

In order to generate random numbers, some constants that are referred to as *seeds* must be chosen. These constants influence the size of the random numbers generated.

Suppose we are interested in generating a set of two-digit random numbers— we shall choose a seed with two digits. The seed is squared, and its middle digits are used as the seed for the next random number until we have generated enough random numbers. We shall show with an example the problems of this method. If we start with a seed of 55, we shall obtain Table 5.1. But before we discuss the results of Table 5.1, let us consider another two-digit seed, say 35, and we obtain Table 5.2.

Notice that in Table 5.1, only one random number was generated before this process degenerated into an irretrievable condition. The generation of 00 as a random number implies that all subsequent random numbers will be 00. Table

Table 5.1

Generation of Two-Digit Random Numbers with the Midsquare Method (Starting Seed = 55)

Random Number Seed	Square of the Random Number Seed
55	3025
02	0004
00	

Table 5.2

Generation of Two-Digit Random Numbers with the Midsquare Method (Starting Seed = 35)

Random Number Seed	Square of the Random Number Seed
35	1225
22	0484
48	2304
30	0900
90	8100
10	0100

5.2 has a longer cycle. However, once the random number 10 was generated, the process again degenerates into an irretrievable condition. The midsquare method is, therefore, grossly inefficient in generating random numbers. It lacks the characteristics of a random number generator discussed earlier for good generators. For instance, all good generators must have a means of reseeding when degeneracy occurs. Furthermore, long periods should be present before the sequence is reproduced. In using this method, care must be exercised in choosing the seed (initial number), otherwise serial correlation will be present.

Midproduct Method

Another simple and poor method for generating random numbers is the midproduct method. This particular method requires the specification of two initial seeds. The product of these seeds is taken, and the random number is extracted from the two middle digits. Like the midsquare method, the midproduct method has a very short cycle, although longer than the midsquare, it easily degenerates. This process of multiplication and extraction of middle values also requires considerable computational time and space.

We must, however, note that if the number of digits in the seeds is increased, the cycle length is increased and the chances of degeneracy are significantly reduced. We shall illustrate in Table 5.3 the midproduct method with two seeds, 35 and 65. The product of these two random digits is 2275. The middle digits that are underlined are extracted (27) and multiplied with the second seed (65) to obtain a product of 1755. Again, the middle digits are extracted (75) and multiplied with the last seed. This process continues until the required random numbers have been generated or until degeneracy occurs. Observe that this procedure also degenerates to 00 and that there is no means of coming out of this degeneracy.

Table 5.3
Midproduct Random Number Generation with Two-Digit Seeds

Random Numbers	Product of Random Numbers
35	
65	2275
27	1755
75	2025
02	0150
15	0030
03	0045
04	0012
01	0004
00	0000

Consider a case where the number of digits in the seeds has been increased to four digits. Table 5.4 illustrates this case with two four-digit seeds—4578 and 5675. Notice that the cycle length has significantly increased and the problem of degeneracy is more remote. Even though the increase in the number of digits has increased the efficiency of the generator, it is still inefficient in terms of computational time and space.

Fibonacci and Additive Congruential Method

With this method, two preceding numbers are added and divided by a number called the modulus. The remainder becomes the random number digit. This particular method is referred to as Fibonacci because the concept of adding two preceding numbers is concordant with the recursion defining the Fibonacci series—a popular series in mathematics. Bratley et al. [3] noted some of the drawbacks with this approach. In particular, the random digits generated are often serially correlated. If we define Y_i as the ith number generated and the modulus is m, we can express the Fibonacci method as

$$Y_i = (Y_{i-1} + Y_{i-2}) \; modulus \; m \tag{5.1}$$

Notice that Y_0 and Y_1 are the initial seeds that have to be chosen. We can then determine Y_i for $i > 1$. Suppose $m = 100$, $Y_0 = 2$, and $Y_1 = 2$; then, Table 5.5 presents a partial list of the next sequence of random digits.

Table 5.4
Midproduct Random Number Generation with Four-Digit Seeds

(1)	4578		(25)	6846	05600028
(2)	5675	25980150	(26)	6000	41076000
(3)	9801	55620675	(27)	0760	00456000
(4)	6206	60825006	(28)	4560	00346560
(5)	8250	51199500	(29)	3465	15800400
(6)	1995	16458750	(30)	8004	27733860
(7)	4587	09151065	(31)	7338	58733352
(8)	1510	06926370	(32)	7333	53809554
(9)	9263	13987130	(33)	8095	59360635
(10)	9871	91435073	(34)	3606	29190570
(11)	4350	42938850	(35)	1905	06869430
(12)	9388	40837800	(36)	8694	16562070
(13)	8378	78652664	(37)	5620	48860280
(14)	6526	56674828	(38)	8602	48343240
(15)	6748	44037448	(39)	3432	29522064
(16)	0374	02523752	(40)	5220	17915040
(17)	5237	01958638	(41)	9150	47763000
(18)	9586	50201882	(42)	7630	69814500
(19)	2018	19344548	(43)	8145	62146350
(20)	3445	06952010	(44)	1463	11916135
(21)	9520	32796400	(45)	9161	13402543
(22)	7964	75817280	(46)	4025	36873025
(23)	8172	65081808	(47)	8730	35138250
(24)	0818	06684696	(48)	1382	12064860

A statistical test of this sequence of random digits will detect serial dependence. This implies that Y_{i+1} can be predicted by knowing the Y_i value.

Linear Congruential Methods

Most of the random number generators use the linear congruential generators (LCGs). These generators were introduced by Lehmer [9] in 1951. These generators compute pseudorandom number sequences using a recurcive formula

Table 5.5
Random Number Generation for Fibonacci and Additive Congruential Methods

i	Random Numbers (Y_i)
0	2
1	2
2	4
3	6
4	10
5	16
6	26
7	42
8	68
9	10
10	78
11	88
12	66
13	54
14	20
15	74
16	94
17	68
18	62
19	30
20	92

$$Y_i = (aY_{i-1} + c) \ (\text{mod } m) \tag{5.2}$$

The statistical quality of the generator is determined by the parameters a, c, and m where a is the multiplier, c is the increment, and m is the modulus. Y_0 is the starting value or the seed.

Observe from equation 5.2 that if $c = 0$, the generator becomes multiplicative and is known as a *multiplicative congruential generator*.

$$Y_i = aY_{i-1} \;(\text{mod } m) \tag{5.3}$$

Y_i is, therefore, the remainder when Y_{i-1} is divided by m. It is clear that $0 \le Y_i \le m - 1$. Since the desired random number is uniformly distributed in the interval $(0,1)$, that number $U_i = Y_i/m$ and $i = 1, 2, \ldots$. It is required that a, c, m, and Y_0 be nonnegative integers and also $a < m$, $c < m$, $Y_0 < m$, and $m > 0$. The widely used values for these parameters are $m = 2^{31} - 1 = 2147483647$ and either $a = 16807$ or $a = 630360016$ [3,6].

In fact, the random number streams in GPSS/H are generated using this approach. The use of $m = 2^{31} - 2$ is adopted in GPSS/H. This ensures that over two billion values are generated before the sequence is repeated.

There are also problems with the use of the LCGs. Law and Kelton [8] and Bratley et al. [3] noted that the Y_is generated are not really random. This is a problem that plagues all the pseudorandom number generators. However, with a careful selection of the parameters a, c, m, and Y_0, the U_is obtained will appear to be independent and identically distributed random variables in the interval $(0,1)$. The other objection is the fact the U_is are rational numbers. This influences the probabilities computed for U_i, which seems not to be in conformity with expectations since U_i is uniformly distributed in the interval $(0,1)$.

In ending this discussion, we shall point out that there are various factors that influence the choice of a particular random number generator. One important factor is the hardware and software availability. For example, in using the LCGs, it is necessary to have knowledge of both the hardware limitations, such as the word length of the host computer. The ease of use and the user's confidence are also instrumental in selecting a particular random number generator.

Although there are many other generators, we shall limit the discussion only to those that have been discussed so far. The interested reader should seek more advanced books on simulation [3,8].

GENERATION OF RANDOM VARIABLES

In the fast-food restaurant example presented in Chapter 3, it is observed from Table 3.1 that the interarrival times, service times, etc. take on different numerical values due to chance. Thus, a variable with this characteristic can be referred to as a *random variable*. Many of the random variables are obtained from nonuniform distributions. For example, the statistical tests for goodness-of-fit conducted in Chapter 4 concluded that the interarrival times observed for the fast-food restaurant problem follow the negative exponential distribution. Obviously, the negative exponential distribution is a nonuniform distribution. The question then arises as to how to sample from nonuniform distributions since our previous discussions in this chapter focused on generating random numbers that are independent and identically and uniformly distributed.

Many simulation programs have built-in functions for generating random variables. For example, GPSS/H has built-in functions for generating random variables for the negative exponential, normal, and the triangular distribution. However, a user can specify other functions outside the built-in functions. With GPSS-PC the user specifies the function and enters a string of pairs of finite numbers obtained through the use of random number generators. There are many forms of the user-defined functions. However, we shall concentrate in this section on how to generate random variables for continuous and discrete probability distributions.

INVERSE TRANSFORMATION METHOD

Random numbers are uniformly distributed in the interval (0,1). For a selected random number in this interval the inverse transformation method transforms it to a single random variable. In other words, for any specified probability value, the corresponding value of the random variable can be determined. This is a backward procedure because we would normally know the value of the random variable and then proceed to compute its probability. The inverse transformation method is operationalized through the use of the cumulative density function of the random variable x. Suppose we denote $F(x)$ as the cumulative density function of a probability distribution (discrete or continuous). If $F(x) = r$, then $x = F^{-1}(r)$ where $F(x)$ is a random number between 0 and 1, and x is the corresponding random variable for that random number. Thus, in order to find x, we specify a value of r that is uniformly distributed in the interval 0 and 1. Determination of the random variable x depends on being able to solve the inverse function $F^{-1}(r)$.

DISCRETE PROBABILITY DISTRIBUTIONS

In this section, we shall discuss how to generate the random variables for discrete probability distributions. We shall first describe an application with an empirical discrete distribution.

Empirical Discrete Distribution

Suppose we roll a fair die twice and would like to construct the probability distribution of the sum of numbers that would appear from this experiment; we can identify the sample space as shown in Table 5.6, which represents all the possible outcomes that can be expected from rolling a die twice. Notice that a die has six faces that are numbered 1 through 6. Since we are assuming a *fair die*, each face has equal likelihood of occurrence. Therefore, the probability of observing any of the six faces in a roll of the die is $1/6$. If we define the random variable x as the sum of the two faces observed from rolling two dice, we can, from Table 5.6, deduce that x will take on values from 2 through 12. That is, if in a roll, faces of 1 are observed, the sum becomes $1 + 1 = 2$. On the other hand, if faces of 6 are obtained in a roll, the sum becomes $6 + 6 = 12$. We can proceed to find the probabilities of x. We can, therefore, construct a probability distribution

Table 5.6
Sample Space for the Roll of Two Fair Die

(1,1)	(1,2)	(1,3)	(1,4)	(1,5)	(1,6)
(2,1)	(2,2)	(2,3)	(2,4)	(2,5)	(2,6)
(3,1)	(3,2)	(3,3)	(3,4)	(3,5)	(3,6)
(4,1)	(4,2)	(4,3)	(4,4)	(4,5)	(4,6)
(5,1)	(5,2)	(5,3)	(5,4)	(5,5)	(5,6)
(6,1)	(6,2)	(6,3)	(6,4)	(6,5)	(6,6)

table for this experiment as shown in Table 5.7. The $f(x)$ is computed by counting the number of occurrences of x and dividing that number by the sample space, which is 36 in this example. For example, $x = 7$ will include the following experimental outcomes: *(6,1), (5,2), (4,3), (3,4), (2,5),* and *(1,6).* Thus, there

Table 5.7
Random Number Generation for an Empirical Discrete Probability Distribution

x	f(x)	F(x)	Random Number (r)
2	0.0278	0.0278	.0000-.0278
3	0.0556	0.0834	.0279-.0834
4	0.0833	0.1667	.0835-.1667
5	0.1111	0.2778	.1668-.2778
6	0.1389	0.4167	.2779-.4167
7	0.1667	0.5834	.4168-.5834
8	0.1389	0.7223	.5835-.7223
9	0.1111	0.8334	.7224-.8334
10	0.0833	0.9167	.8335-.9167
11	0.0555	0.9722	.9168-.9722
12	0.0278	1.0000	.9723-.9999
Total	1.0000		

are six outcomes and the probability that $x = 7$ is $6/36 = 0.1667$. The cumulative probability $F(x)$ is obtained by taking the sum of successive probabilities up to and including x. Thus,

$$F(7) = 0.0278 + 0.0556 + 0.0833 + 0.1111 + 0.1389 + 0.1667 = 0.5834$$

$F(x)$ is said to be a nondecreasing function with increasing x. That is to say, that $F(x_i) \leq F(x_{i+1})$ for $x_i < x_{i+1}$. For example, $F(6) \leq F(7)$ because $F(7) = F(6) + f(7)$. It is also apparent that $F(x_i) = F(x_{i+1})$ only when $f(x_{i+1}) = 0$.

A histogram can be used to represent the resulting cumulative density function $(F(x))$ as shown in Figure 5.1.

Suppose that random number r is in the interval 0.0835 and 0.1667; it is easy to see that the value of the random variable is 4. Also, if r is in the interval 0.7224 to 0.8334, then the random variable x is 9. Observe that the random numbers (r) presented in Table 5.7 are designed to fall in mutually exclusive class intervals. This is done to ensure that r is nonoverlapping in these classes. Observe also that the probabilities of x are still maintained. For example, when the value of the random variable x is determined as 5, the probability that $x = 4$ can be computed as $0.2778 - 0.1667 = 0.1111$. These are actually the same probabilities we have computed in Table 5.7. This procedure guarantees the *uniqueness* of the value of x for any given value of r. However, the reverse is not true. It is obvious that the specification of x will not guarantee a unique value of r since the r values are specified in a range. For example, if $x = 5$, all we know is that $0.1668 \leq r \leq 0.2778$. The method illustrated in this example is known as the *table look-up method*, and it is appropriate for use in generating the random variables for any finite discrete probability function. It will generate discrete random variables with the required probability.

The Binomial Distribution

The binomial distribution is perhaps the most widely applied discrete probability distribution. The process that leads to the binomial distribution is known as the Bernoulli trial or Bernoulli process.[1] The Bernoulli process is based on the concept of a series of experimental trials. We shall state the following assumptions that guide the use of the binomial distribution.

1. There are only two mutually exclusive outcomes that can be observed from each trial of the experiment. These experimental outcomes are referred to as "success" and "failure." For example, if we toss a fair coin, there are two mutually exclusive outcomes in each toss. The outcome can be either a head or a tail.

2. The probability of success is constant in each trial of the experiment. If it is denoted as p, then the probability of failure is denoted as $q = 1 - p$.

---

[1]This is named after a Swiss mathematician, James Bernoulli (1654–1705), who contributed significant work on the binomial distribution.

Figure 5.1
Histogram for the Sum of Two Fair Die

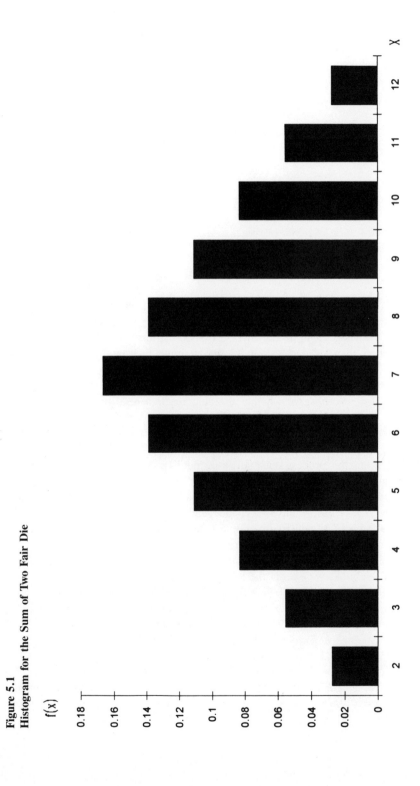

3. Each trial is independent. Therefore, the outcome of any given trial or sequence of trials will not influence the outcomes of subsequent trials.

The probability function for the binomial distribution is expressed as

$$f(x) = \binom{n}{x} p^x (1 - p)^{n-x} \qquad x = 0, 1, 2, \ldots, n \qquad (5.4)$$

where

x = Number of successes in n trials
p = Constant probability of success
n = Number of independent trials

Notice that only two parameters are needed to define the binomial distribution, namely n and p. Thus, the binomial distribution is frequently referred to as $B(n,p)$. We shall illustrate the inverse transformation method for the binomial distribution in a similar fashion as the example presented for the empirical discrete distribution.

Example 5.1. Consider an experiment where we toss a fair coin six times and, in each toss, we observe whether the outcome is a head or tail. Suppose the interest is in the number of heads observed from this experiment. We can, therefore, express our success (x) as the number of heads observed. Then, $x = 0$, *1, 2, 3, 4, 5, 6.*

We see that this process is actually a Bernoulli process. For example, there are two mutually exclusive outcomes—head or tail. Second, since we have a fair coin and the occurrence of a head or a tail is equally likely, the constant probability is *1/2.* Third, each toss is independent. We can, therefore, apply the binomial probability density function presented in equation 5.4 to find the probabilities of *0, 1, 2, 3, 4, 5* or *6* successes. Table 5.8 presents this result.

From the table of uniform random numbers between 0 and 1 presented at the back of the book, we extract the following random numbers *(r): 0.911, 0.082, 0.448, 0.697,* and *0.153.* To determine their corresponding random variables, we refer to Table 5.7. We observe that r of 0.911 is in the range 0.8908 to 0.9844. So, $x = 5$. For $r = 0.082$, we also observe that r is in the range 0.0157 to 0.1094. So, $x = 1$. Similarly, the other values of x can be determined as $x = 3$ when $r = 0.448$; $x = 4$ when $r = 0.697$; and $x = 2$ when $r = 0.153$. Alternatively, we can use the cumulative density function $F(x)$ to determine x directly. Notice, for example, that when $r = 0.911$, that the first value of $F(x)$ that exceeds $r = 0.911$ is 0.9844. So, $x = 5$. Also, when $r = 0.082$, the first value of $F(x)$ that exceeds that value of r is 0.1094. So, $x = 1$.

Table 5.8
Inverse Transformation Method for the Binomial Distribution

x	f(x)	F(x)	Random Number (r)
0	$\binom{6}{0}\left(\frac{1}{2}\right)^{0}\left(\frac{1}{2}\right)^{6}=0.0156$	0.0156	.0000 --- .0156
1	$\binom{6}{1}\left(\frac{1}{2}\right)\left(\frac{1}{2}\right)^{5}=0.0938$	0.1094	.0157 --- .1094
2	$\binom{6}{2}\left(\frac{1}{2}\right)^{2}\left(\frac{1}{2}\right)^{4}=0.12344$	0.3438	.1095 --- .3438
3	$\binom{6}{3}\left(\frac{1}{2}\right)^{3}\left(\frac{1}{2}\right)^{3}=0.3125$	0.6563	.3439 --- .6563
4	$\binom{6}{4}\left(\frac{1}{2}\right)^{4}\left(\frac{1}{2}\right)^{2}=0.2344$	0.8907	.6564 --- .8907
5	$\binom{6}{5}\left(\frac{1}{2}\right)^{5}\left(\frac{1}{2}\right)=0.0937$	0.9844	.8908 --- .9844
6	$\binom{6}{6}\left(\frac{1}{2}\right)^{6}\left(\frac{1}{2}\right)^{0}=0.0156$	1.0000	.9845 --- .9999
Total	1.0000		

Poisson Distribution

The Poisson distribution[2] is also a discrete probability distribution. It is useful in computing the probabilities of occurrences of events that take place in a specified interval of time or space. Like the binomial distribution, certain assumptions have to be satisfied before the Poisson distribution can be applied. These assumptions are

1. The probability of the occurrence of an event in a subinterval is small.

[2]Developed in 1837 by a French mathematician, Simeon Denis Poisson (1781–1840).

2. The probability of an occurrence in a subinterval is the same for all subintervals of equal length.

3. The probability of more than one occurrence is zero in any subinterval.

4. The occurrence or nonoccurrence of an event in any subinterval is independent of the probability of occurrence or nonoccurrence in any other subinterval.

There are many applications of the Poisson distribution. It can be used to represent the arrivals of customers in the fast-food restaurant problem, the demand for services, number of errors in a book, product demand, and so on.

The probability density function of the Poisson distribution is expressed as

$$f(x) = \frac{u^x e^{-u}}{x!}; \qquad x = 0, 1, 2, \ldots . \tag{5.5}$$

where u is the mean number of occurrence per interval, or rather the *rate; x* is the random variable that can represent the number of occurrences of an event; and e is an irrational term that is equal to 2.718. It is sometimes referred to as the exponent or the base of the Naperian or natural logarithm system. We shall present an example to show again how the inverse transformation method can be used to generate Poisson random variables.

Example 5.2. It has been determined that accidents at a major interstate highway occur at the rate of 2.5 per day according to a Poisson distribution. We want to select the random variables from this Poisson distribution with $u = 2.5$ accidents/day. We observe that u is the only parameter that is needed to define the Poisson distribution. The Poisson density function for the number of accidents can be expressed as shown in Table 5.9 where

$$f(x) = \frac{2.5^x e^{-2.5}}{x!}; \qquad x = 0, 1, 2, \ldots \qquad \text{and} \qquad u = 2.5$$

Suppose that from the uniform random number table, we extracted the following random numbers (r): 0.0911, 0.082, 0.448, 0.697, and 0.153. From Table 5.9, we observe that $r = 0.911$ is in the range of 0.8912 and 0.9579. So, $x = 5$. Alternatively, the first value of $f(x)$ that exceeds $r = 0.911$ is 0.9579. So, $x = 5$. Also, we see that $r = 0.082$ is in the interval .0000 and .0821. So, $x = 0$. Also, the first value of $f(x)$ that exceeds $r = 0.0820$ is 0.0821. We can, therefore, find the rest of the random variables as $x = 2$ when $r = 0.448; x = 3$ when $r = 0.697;$ and $x = 1$ when $r = 0.153$.

Similarly, the random variables for other discrete probability distributions can be generated easily. We limit our discussion only to the three cases already discussed since they are widely used. We shall now discuss the generation of random variables for continuous probability distributions.

Table 5.9
Inverse Transformation Method for the Poisson Distribution

x	f(x)	F(x)	Random Number (r)
0	0.0821	0.0821	.0000 - 0.821
1	0.2052	0.2873	.0822 - .2873
2	0.2565	0.5438	.2874 - .5438
3	0.2137	0.7575	.5349 - .7575
4	0.1336	0.8911	.7576 - .8911
5	0.0668	0.9579	.8912 - .9579
6	0.0278	0.9857	.9580 - .9857
7	0.0099	0.9956	.9858 - .9956
8	0.0031	0.9987	.9957 - .9987
9	0.0022	1.000	.9988 - .9999

CONTINUOUS PROBABILITY DISTRIBUTIONS

In this section, we shall use the inverse transformation method to generate random variables for continuous probability distributions.

Uniform Distribution

If a continuous random variable x assumes all values in the interval $[a,b]$, where both a and b are finite, its probability density function is stated as

$$f(x) = \begin{cases} \dfrac{1}{b-a}, & a \le x \le b \\ 0, & \text{elsewhere} \end{cases} \qquad (5.6)$$

The variable x is said to be uniformly distributed over the interval $[a,b]$. We can represent the probability density function for the uniform distribution using Figure 5.2; x is equally distributed in the interval $[a,b]$. Since x is a continuous random variable, we can obtain its cumulative density function by means of integration as

$$f(x) = \int_a^x \frac{1}{b-a}\, dt = \frac{x-a}{b-a} \qquad (5.7)$$

Figure 5.2
Uniform Distribution Table

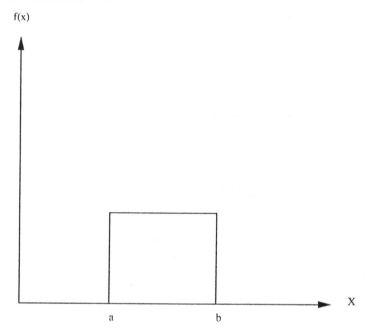

Suppose we let $f(x) = r$, then,

$$r = \frac{x - a}{b - a}$$

and

$$x = a + (b - a) r \tag{5.8}$$

Again, we can determine the value of x if r is specified. Suppose that x is uniformly distributed in the interval [30,80], and $r = 0.666$. Then

$$x = 30 + (80 - 30)(0.666) = 63.3$$

Thus, for a uniformly distributed random number between 0 and 1, the corresponding numerical assignment to the random variable can easily be determined by method of inverse transformation.

Negative Exponential Distribution

The negative exponential distribution has a probability density function given as

$$f(x) = \begin{cases} \alpha\, e^{-\alpha x}, & x > 0 \\ 0, & elsewhere \end{cases} \tag{5.9}$$

and α is the only parameter for this distribution. It has a mean of $1/\alpha$. The probability density function for the negative exponential is given in Figure 5.3. The cumulative density function for the negative exponential distribution is also obtained by means of integration as

$$f(x) = \alpha \int_0^x e^{-\alpha t}\, dt \tag{5.10}$$

Let

$$u = -\alpha t$$

$$\frac{du}{dt} = -\alpha$$

$$du = -\alpha dt$$

$$dt = -\frac{1}{\alpha}\, du$$

Figure 5.3
Exponential Density Function

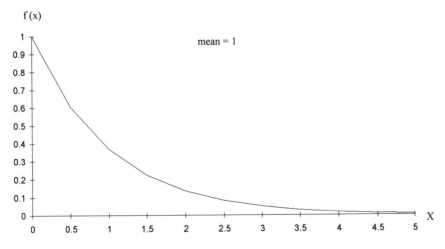

By substitution, $-\alpha(1/\alpha)\int e^u du = -e^u$. We can now substitute back $-\alpha t$ for u. So

$$-e^{-\alpha t}\big|_0^x = -[e^{-\alpha x} - e^0] = 1 - e^{-\alpha x}$$

Therefore,

$$f(x) = 1 - e^{-\alpha x}; \; x > 0 \tag{5.11}$$

Again, if we let $r = f(x)$, then

$$r = 1 - e^{-\alpha x} \tag{5.12}$$

$$1 - r = e^{-\alpha x} \tag{5.13}$$

$$\ln(1 - r) = -\alpha x \tag{5.14}$$

$$x = -\ln\frac{(1 - r)}{\alpha} \tag{5.15}$$

ln is the natural logarithm, and it is equivalent to $\log_e$. Due to the symmetry exhibited by the uniform distribution, it is computationally more efficient to replace $1 - r$ by r. So equation 5.15 can be rewritten as

$$x = \frac{-\ln r}{\alpha} \tag{5.16}$$

Suppose that the demand rate for a particular product is 10 units per hour. This is equivalent to saying that there will be a demand for this product every 6 minutes. If $r = 0.8$, then $x = [-\ln(0.8)]$ (6) where $1/\alpha = 6$ *minutes*. So, $x = 1.34$ *minutes*.

THE COMPOSITION METHOD

The composition method is useful when the probability function can be expressed as a combination of other probability distributions with different weights. For example, the probability density function $f(x)$ can be expressed as

$$f(x) = \sum_{i=1}^{\infty} P_i f_i(x) \tag{5.17}$$

where $P_i \geq 0$ and $\sum_{i=1}^{\infty} P_i = 1$. However, as this series increases, it is possible to observe cases where $P_i = 0$ for $i > j$. Such conditions will make equation 5.17 finite. Thus,

$$f(x) = \sum_{i=1}^{n} P_i f_i(x) \tag{5.18}$$

where $P_i > 0$, for $i = 1, 2, \ldots, n$ and $\Sigma_{i=1}^{n} P_i = 1$. Since a combination of probability functions are presented in equations 5.17 and 5.18, more than one random number has to be specified in order to generate a single random variable.

The Gamma Distribution

A random variable x has a Gamma probability distribution if

$$f(x) = \begin{cases} \dfrac{\alpha}{\Gamma(n)} (\alpha x)^{n-1} e^{-\alpha x}, & x > 0 \\ 0, & \text{elsewhere} \end{cases} \tag{5.19}$$

Notice that there are two parameters in equation 5.19, namely α and n. Also,

$$\begin{aligned} \Gamma(n) &= (n - 1)\, \Gamma(n - 1) \\ &= (n - 1)\,(n - 2)\, \Gamma(n - 2) = \ldots \\ &= (n - 1)\,(n - 2) \ldots \Gamma(1) \end{aligned}$$

Therefore, $\Gamma(n) = (n - 1)!$ where n is a positive integer. The symbol $\Gamma(.)$ is known as a gamma function. Notice also that if $n = 1$, equation 5.19 reduces to

$$f(x) = \alpha e^{-\alpha x}, \; x > 0 \tag{5.20}$$

This is the popular case of the negative exponential distribution.

The Erlang Distribution

The Erlang distribution is derived as the sum of independent random variables that are exponentially distributed with a mean $1/n\alpha$ where n is the number of phases in the Erlang distribution; n also determines the shape of the Erlang distribution.

In our discussion of negative exponential distribution we showed that the random variable for the negative exponential can be expressed using equation 5.16.

If we apply the composition method to generate the random variable for the Erlang with a mean of $1/n\alpha$, we shall have

$$x = -\frac{\ln r_1}{n\alpha} - \frac{\ln r_2}{n\alpha} - \frac{\ln r_3}{n\alpha} + \cdots - \frac{\ln r_n}{n\alpha} \tag{5.21}$$

So,

$$x = \frac{-1}{n\alpha} \sum_{i=1}^{n} \ln r_i \tag{5.22}$$

We observe that $\ln r_1 + \ln r_2 + \ldots + \ln r_n = \ln(r_1, r_2, \ldots, r_n)$. This follows from a general property of logarithms. This property increases the computational efficiency of the model since the summation sign can be replaced by a multiplicative sign. Thus,

$$x = -\frac{1}{n\alpha} \ln \left(\prod_{i=1}^{n} r_i \right) \tag{5.23}$$

Observe, however, that in order to generate the random variable x, a total of n random numbers must be specified. For example, if $n = 2$, $r_1 = 0.5$, $r_2 = 0.8$, and $1/\alpha = 6$, x can be generated as

$$x = -\frac{1}{2} \ln[(0.5)(0.08)].6 = 2.749$$

THE METHOD OF CONVOLUTIONS

The method of convolution is applicable when a random variable x can be expressed as a linear combination of n independent variables. Thus,

$$x = \sum_{i=1}^{n} a_i x_i \tag{5.24}$$

With this method, n independent random numbers $(r_1, r_2, \ldots, r_n)$ have to be selected and used in generating the n random variables $(x_1, x_2, \ldots, x_n)$. The efficiency of this method depends on the efficiency of sampling from the distributions $f_i(x)$.

We shall apply the method of convolutions to generate the random variables for the normal distribution.

The Normal Distribution

The normal distribution is perhaps the most popular probability distribution. Several methods for generating its random variates exist [2,7,10]. We shall illustrate the use of the convolution method. This approach generates random variates that are approximately normally distributed, however, it is computationally very efficient. Suppose we take a sum of N independent and identically distributed random variables with mean u_i and standard deviation σ_i, we notice from the central limit theorem that as N increases without bound, this sum will become normally distributed with a mean u and a variance σ^2 that can be expressed as

$$u = \sum_{i=1}^{N} u_i \quad \text{and} \quad \sigma^2 = \sum_{i=1}^{N} \sigma_i^2$$

For a uniform random variable in the interval $(0,1)$, it is easy to see that its mean and variance are given as $\frac{1}{2}$ and $\frac{1}{12}$ respectively (i.e., $E(X) = \int_0^1 x dx$ and $VAR(X) = \int_0^1 (x - E(x))^2 f(x)$).

Since we are taking the sum of N random variables, then $E(\sum_{i=1}^{N} r_i) = N/2$ and $VAR(\sum_{i=1}^{N} r_i) = N/12$.

This algorithm generates the random variable for a standard normal variate with $u = 0$ and $\sigma = 1$. This can then be easily transformed to the case where x is normally distributed with mean u and standard deviation σ by using the *z-score*, so

$$z = \frac{x - u}{\sigma} \tag{5.25}$$

By substitution, we obtain that

$$z = \frac{\sum_{i=1}^{N} r_i - \frac{N}{2}}{\sqrt{N/12}} \tag{5.26}$$

Observe from equation 5.26 that if $N = 12$, then the denominator is 1, thus reducing equation 5.26 to

$$z = \sum_{i=1}^{12} r_i - 6 \tag{5.27}$$

This significantly enhances the computational speed. As a result $N = 12$ is commonly used. However, the general rule is that N should be larger than, or at least equal to, 6.

Although this approximation is quite reliable around the central tendency of the normal distribution, it is inaccurate around the extremes of the tails.

ACCEPTANCE/REJECTION METHOD

Von Neumann [13] largely developed the acceptance/rejection method. This method involves two steps. In step 1, a sample is drawn from a probability distribution $y(x)$. In step 2, a second sample is drawn from a uniform distribution with the interval $(0,1)$. The decision on whether to accept or to reject x is based on the second sample. If $0 \leq g(x) \leq 1$ for all x, then $f(x)$ is defined as $f(x) = Ay(x)g(x)$, where $A \geq 1.0$.

$y(x)$ is a probability density function, and its inverse can be determined. From the above definition we get $Ay(x) \geq f(x)$ for all x. $Ay(x)$ is known as the majorizing function. In using the acceptance/rejection method the majorizing function must be specified. Aherns and Deiter [1] have used this method in generating the random variates for some special cases of the gamma distribution. More efficient algorithms for the Erlang cases were also introduced by Tadikamalla [11,12]. Since this method is considerably more difficult and requires knowledge of calculus, we shall refer the interested reader to books that treat this method adequately [4,8].

REFERENCES

1. Ahrens, J. H., and U. Dieter. "Computer Methods for Sampling from Gamma, Beta, Poisson and Binomial Distributions." *Computing* 12 (1974): 223–246.
2. Box, G.E.P., and M. E. Muller. "A Note on the Generation of Random Normal Deviates." *Annals of Math. Statistics* 29 (1958): 610–611.
3. Bratley, P., B. L. Fox, and L. E. Schrage. *A Guide to Simulation.* New York: Springer-Verlag, 1983.
4. Hoover, S. V., and R. F. Perry. *Simulation: A Problem-Solving Approach.* Reading, MA: Addison-Wesley Publishing Company, 1989.
5. Hull, T. E., and A. R. Dobell. "Random Number Generator." *SIAM Rev.* 4 (1962): 230–254.
6. Katzan, H., Jr. *APL User's Guide.* New York: Van Nostrand Reinhold, 1971.
7. Kinderman, A. J., and J. G. Ramage. "Computer Generation of Normal Random Variables." *Journal of the American Statistical Association* 71 (1976): 893–896.
8. Law, A. M., and W. D. Kelton. *Simulation Modeling and Analysis.* New York: McGraw-Hill Book Company, 1982.
9. Lehmer, D. H. "Mathematical Methods in Large-Scale Computing Units." *Ann. Comput. Lab.* [Harvard Univ.] 26 (1951): 141–146.
10. Marsaglia, G., and T. A. Bray. "A Convenient Method for Generating Normal Variates." *SIAM Review* 6 (1964): 620–624.
11. Tadikamalla, P. R. "Computer Generation of Gamma Random Variables I." *Comm. ACM* 21 (1978): 419–422.
12. Tadikamalla, P. R. "Computer Generation of Gamma Random Variables II." *Comm. ACM* 21 (1978): 925–928.
13. Von Neumann, J. *Various Techniques Used in Connection with Random Digits.* U.S. Nat. Bur. Stand. Applied Math. Ser. No. 12 (1951): 36–38.

Chapter 6

TESTS FOR THE GOODNESS-OF-FIT OF RANDOM NUMBER GENERATORS

INTRODUCTION

In Chapter 5 we discussed the important properties that a good random number generator must possess. Among the six properties outlined are uniformity and statistical independence and randomness. This chapter focuses on testing the goodness-of-fit of random number generators. Specifically, the random numbers generated in Chapter 5 using the different techniques are tested to see if they satisfy these statistical properties.

TEST FOR UNIFORMITY

The premise of random number generation is that the random numbers are generated from a uniform distribution. It is, therefore, necessary to test the random numbers generated to ascertain that they are uniformly distributed. Chapter 4 discussed the use of χ^2 and the Kolmogorov-Smirnoff $(K$-$S)$ tests in detecting the theoretical distributions of random variables. These tests are also applicable in this section since the data generated through a random process are tested to see if they are drawn from a uniform distribution. Indeed, the examples presented in that chapter are sufficient to understand how this test works. For the sake of completeness, however, we shall present examples with the data generated by a random number generator.

Table 5.5 presented a series of random numbers generated by the Fibonacci and additive congruential methods. We shall first construct the frequency distribution for this set of data. Observe that the minimum and maximum values in this data set are 2 and 94, respectively. Using information from Chapter 3 on how to group data, we will see that if we decide to have five class intervals, then the

Table 6.1

Uniform Distribution Test for Random Numbers Generated by Fibonacci and Additive Congruential Methods

i	Random Number	Frequency	Observed Cumulative Probability	P_i	np_i	Expected Cumulative Probability	Absolute Difference
1	0 and under 19	7	0.333	0.2	4.2	0.2	0.133
2	19 and under 38	3	0.476	0.2	4.2	0.4	0.076
3	38 and under 57	2	0.571	0.2	4.2	0.6	0.029
4	57 and under 76	5	0.809	0.2	4.2	0.8	0.009
5	76 and under 95	4	1.000	0.2	4.2	1.0	0.000
		21					

class width should be $(94 - 2)/5 = 18.4$. The size of the class interval is rounded off to a convenient size, which is nineteen. The class intervals are, therefore, constructed as presented in Table 6.1.

The hypothesis under testing is stated as follows:

H_0: The random numbers are uniformly distributed.

H_1: The random numbers are *not* uniformly distributed.

Since the expected frequencies obtained for the five classes are below five, it is apparent that the χ^2 goodness-of-fit test will not be appropriate. The more powerful *K-S* test is used. The cumulative probabilities are, therefore, computed. It is observed that the maximum absolute difference is 0.133. The critical value obtained from the *K-S* one-sample test at a level of significance of 0.05 is 0.294. Since the maximum absolute difference of 0.133 is less than 0.294, we decide not to reject H_0. It is, therefore, likely that this set of random numbers generated by the Fibonacci and additive congruential methods are uniformly distributed.

We had discussed earlier the advantages of the K-S method over the χ^2 goodness-of-fit test. This example also highlights one of the problems with the use of the χ^2 test when the expected frequencies are below five. We, therefore, *strongly* recommend the use of the *K-S* test.

TEST FOR SERIAL CORRELATION OR AUTOCORRELATION

A set of random numbers that exhibit a "*natural* sequential order" [1] is said to be autocorrelated.[1] In other words if it is possible to predict the $(N + 1)^{th}$ random

---

[1]Another name for autocorrelation is serial correlation, and they are used interchangeably in this book.

number from knowledge of the Nth random number without examination of the algorithm used in generating these numbers, then this random number generator will generate serially or autocorrelated random numbers. For example, if a sequence of numbers is projected as $-10, -9, -8, -7, -6, -5, \ldots$ it is obvious that, if this sequence is maintained, the series observed will be autocorrelated. We can, for example, deduce that if the number -8 occurs, the next number in sequence will be -7, and so on. There are reasons why it is desirable that random numbers used in simulation should not be serially correlated. The following are some of the reasons:

1. When autocorrelation is present, estimates obtained through the use of least square deviation methods are not efficient even though they may be unbiased. Efficiency relates to the variance of unbiased estimators. If two unbiased estimators are compared in terms of relative efficiency, the one with the minimum variance will be the most efficient. For example, sample mean ($\bar{x}$) and median (M_d) are both unbiased estimators of central tendency. However, the variance of $M_d(\sigma_{md}^2)$ is larger than the variance of the sample mean ($\sigma_{\bar{x}}^2$). In other words, $\sigma_{md}^2/\sigma_{\bar{x}}^2 > 1$ implying that $\sigma_{\bar{x}}^2 < \sigma_{md}^2$, so $\bar{x}$ is relatively more efficient than M_d. However, when autocorrelation is present the estimates observed for the parameters of interest may not have minimum variance and are, therefore, not efficient.

2. Simulation outputs are subject to random variations. With the presence of autocorrelation, variance and the standard error of the mean may be grossly underestimated. This subsequently affects the accuracy of the results.

3. Presence of autocorrelation invalidates the use of confidence interval estimates, which are very important in the context of simulation. Also, other statistical tests that are based on random sampling may no longer be valid.

We shall henceforth discuss statistical tests for independence or randomness.[2]

Spearman Rank Correlation Test

The Spearman rank correlation test is a measure of association between two variables that are measured in an ordinal scale. This procedure requires that the object being tested (i.e., generated random numbers) be ranked in two ordered series. To illustrate this test, we shall set the following hypothesis:

H_0: The $(N + 1)^{th}$ random number generated by the random number generator is *independent* of the Nth random number generated by the same generator.

H_1: The $(N + 1)^{th}$ random number generated by the random number generator is *dependent* on the Nth random number generated by the same generator.

If H_0 is rejected, then it implies that $(N + 1)^{th}$ random number is, in fact, dependent on the Nth random number. In other words, the "random" numbers generated are serially correlated.

---

[2]If there is no autocorrelation, the data is said to be independent or randomly distributed.

In order to use this test we need two variables, say x and y. If we consider the random numbers produced in Chapter 5 by the Fibonacci and additive congruential methods again, we have only one set of data. Suppose we refer to that data set as X. For each X, we lag the data by a period to obtain Y. Table 6.2 is, therefore, a result of the lagging of X by a period to obtain Y. Notice that as a result of the lag, the total number of observations is reduced by a period since we are not able to obtain Y for the last value of X generated. So, we shall delete the last case which is $X = 92$ in this example. The ranks for X and Y variables are respectively determined. A correction factor is used when ties occur.

Suppose we take X for example, and we rank the random numbers in an ascending order starting with the value of 1. These ranks are given in brackets. Observe, for example, that there are two cases of $X = 2$, $X = 10$, and $X = 68$. They are respectively assigned successive ranks. For example, ranks 1 and 2 are assigned to the two cases of $X = 2$ observed. Since this represents a tie, the average of their ranks is used to denote the rank for $X = 2$.

Once the ranks have been determined, the difference (d_i) between each pair of rank is determined. Suppose that X_i^r and Y_i^r represent the respective ranks for the X_i and Y_i variables, then

$$d_i = X_i^r - Y_i^r \quad where \ i = 1,2, \ldots N \tag{6.1}$$

and N is the number of paired objects. Notice that the magnitude of d_i explains the association between X_i^r and Y_i^r. If $d_i = 0$, it implies that the association between X_i^r and Y_i^r is perfect. On the other hand, when d_i is large, it shows lack of association between X_i and Y_i. The effect of the direction of change is neutralized by taking the square of d_i. Thus Σd_i^2 gives the total magnitude.

Suppose $x = X_r - \bar{X}_r$ and $y = Y_r - \bar{Y}_r$, where $\bar{X}_r$ and $\bar{Y}_r$ are the average ranks on the X and Y variables respectively. Kendall [2] introduced the correlation coefficient as

$$r = \frac{\Sigma xy}{\sqrt{\Sigma x^2 \Sigma y^2}} \tag{6.2}$$

Since X_r and Y_r represent the ranks assigned to the N random numbers, we can easily see that

$$\Sigma X_r = \frac{N(N + 1)}{2} \tag{6.3}$$

since ΣX_r is the sum of consecutive integers as the ranks are assigned as 1, $2, \ldots , N$.

Also, $\Sigma X_r^2 = 1^2 + 2^2 + 3^2 + \ldots + N^2$. We can, therefore, summarize this as:

$$\Sigma X_r^2 = \frac{N(N + 1)(2N + 1)}{6} \tag{6.4}$$

Table 6.2

Rank Assignments to the Random Numbers Generation by Fibonacci and Additive Congruential Methods

X	Y	X^r rank	Y^r rank	d_i	d_i^2
2 (1)	2 (1)	1.5	1.0	0.5	0.25
2 (2)	4 (2)	1.5	2.0	-0.5	0.25
4 (3)	6 (3)	3.0	3.0	0.0	0.00
6 (4)	10 (4)	4.0	4.5	-0.5	0.25
10 (5)	16 (6)	5.5	6.0	-0.5	0.25
16 (7)	26 (8)	7.0	8.0	-1.0	1.00
26 (9)	42 (10)	9.0	10.0	-1.0	1.00
42 (11)	68 (14)	11.0	14.5	-3.5	12.25
68 (15)	10 (5)	15.5	4.5	11	121.00
10 (6)	78 (17)	5.5	17.0	-11.5	132.25
78 (18)	88 (18)	18.0	18.0	0.0	0.00
88 (19)	66 (13)	19.0	13.0	6.0	36.00
66 (14)	54 (11)	14.0	11.0	3.0	9.00
54 (12)	20 (7)	12.0	7.0	5.0	25.00
20 (8)	74 (16)	8.0	16.0	-8.0	64.00
74 (17)	94 (20)	17.0	20.0	-3.0	9.00
94 (20)	68 (15)	20.0	14.5	5.5	30.25
68 (16)	62 (12)	15.5	12.0	3.5	12.25
62 (13)	30 (9)	13.0	9.0	4.0	16.00
30 (10)	92 (19)	10.0	19.0	-9.0	81.00
				Total Σd_i^2	=551.00

Observe also that since $\Sigma x^2 = \Sigma(x_r - \bar{x})^2$, by expansion and substitution of equation 6.4, we can express Σx^2 as

$$\Sigma x^2 = \frac{N(N + 1)(2N + 1)}{6} - \frac{N(N + 1)^2}{4} = \frac{N^3 - N}{12} \qquad (6.5)$$

Similarly,

$$\Sigma y^2 = \frac{N^3 - N}{12}$$

Notice also that since $d = x - y$, and $d^2 = (x - y)^2$, then, $\Sigma d^2 = \Sigma x^2 + \Sigma y^2 - 2\Sigma xy$. Observe the presence of Σxy in equation 6.2. If we also replace r with r_s in that equation to show that the N values are ranked, we shall, by substitution, obtain

$$\Sigma d^2 = \Sigma x^2 + \Sigma y^2 - 2r_s \sqrt{\Sigma x^2 \Sigma y^2} \tag{6.6}$$

Further substitutions in terms of N will yield

$$r_s = 1 - \frac{6 \sum_{i=1}^{N} di^2}{N^3 - N} \tag{6.7}$$

Equation 6.7 is generally known as the *Spearman Rank Correlation*.

When there are tied values, equation 6.7 will still be applicable provided that the proportion of tied values is small. For large numbers of ties, a correction factor has to be applied since $\Sigma x^2 < (N^3 - N)/12$ for such cases. If T is used to denote the correction factor, then

$$T = \frac{t^3 - t}{12} \tag{6.8}$$

where t is the number of tied observations at any given rank. By consideration of tied observations, we can express Σx^2 as

$$\Sigma x^2 = \frac{N^3 - N}{12} - \Sigma T \tag{6.9}$$

So, with equation 6.7 adjusted for ties, we obtain that

$$r_s = \frac{\Sigma x^2 + \Sigma y^2 - \Sigma d^2}{2\sqrt{\Sigma x^2 \Sigma y^2}} \tag{6.10}$$

where

$$\Sigma x^2 = \frac{N^3 - N}{12} - \Sigma Tx \tag{6.11}$$

and

$$\Sigma y^2 = \frac{N^3 - N}{12} - \Sigma T_y \tag{6.12}$$

We illustrated the use of these models in Table 6.2. Suppose we assume that there is no tie or that the number of tied values is very few; we shall then find the Spearman Rank Correlation using equation 6.7. In Table 6.2, we observe that $\Sigma d_i^2 = 551$ and also that $N = 20$. So,

$$r_s = 1 - \frac{6(551)}{20^3 - 20} = 0.5857$$

However, notice that there are some tied ranks in both X and Y. For example, in X we have two ties when $X = 2$; two ties when $X = 10$; and two ties when $X = 68$. We can now use equation 6.8 to compute T_x. So,

$$T_x = \frac{2^3 - 2}{12} = 0.5$$

But there are three cases with two ties each. So, $\Sigma T_x = 0.5 + 0.5 + 0.5 = 1.50$. For Y, we observe that there are two ties when $Y = 10$, and also two ties when $Y = 68$. Similarly, we obtain

$$T_y = \frac{2^3 - 2}{12} = 0.5$$

and since there are only two cases, $\Sigma T_y = 0.5 + 0.5 = 1.00$. Σx^2 and Σy^2 can now be computed using equations 6.11 and 6.12, respectively. Thus,

$$\Sigma x^2 = \frac{20^3 - 20}{12} - 1.5 = 663.5$$

and

$$\Sigma y^2 = \frac{20^3 - 20}{12} - 1 = 664$$

The r_s is now obtained from equation 6.10 as,

$$r_s = \frac{663.5 + 664 - 551}{2\sqrt{(663.5)(664)}} = \frac{776.5}{1,327.50}$$

$$r_s = 0.5849$$

Notice that the r_s obtained with consideration of ties is very close to the case where ties are not considered because the number of tied values is very small.

Now that we have the r_s values, we may want to test if X and Y are associated in the population from which they were sampled. We shall, therefore, formulate a null hypothesis on the premise that X and Y are *not* associated. In other words, we are stating that $r_s = 0$ and that any observed value of $r_s \neq 0$ is due to chance. We shall formally state the hypothesis as

$H_0: r_s = 0$
$H_1: r_s \neq 0$

This hypothesis is tested using the Spearman rank table in the Appendix. Notice, for example, that the critical value of r when $N = 20$ at a level of significance of 0.05 is 0.4451. Since the obtained $r_s = 0.5849$ is in the rejection region, we shall reject H_0. If H_0 is rejected, then H_1 must be accepted. We can, therefore, state that X and Y are indeed associated. Thus, this set of random numbers generated by the Fibonacci and additive congruential methods can be said to be serially correlated, or X and Y are dependent. We can then conclude that this random number generator did not satisfy one of the important measures of the goodness-of-fit of random number generators.

We could have also used the *student t-test* as the test statistic for this problem. The t-test is stated as

$$t = r_s \sqrt{\frac{N - 2}{1 - r_s^2}} \tag{6.13}$$

This model is useful when testing is done with small samples (i.e., $N < 30$). Notice also that the degrees of freedom associated with this t-test is $N - 2$. Using our data, we obtain that

$$t = 0.5849 \sqrt{\frac{20 - 2}{1 - .5849^2}} = 3.059$$

From the t-table presented in the Appendix, it is observed that if the level of significance is .05, then $t_{.025,118} = 2.101$. Since the computed t-value of 3.059 is greater than the obtained t-value of 2.101, our decision is to reject H_0.

When N is large (i.e., $N \geq 30$), the *z-test* statistic should be used. This is given as

$$z = r_s \sqrt{N - 1} \tag{6.14}$$

Runs Test

The *runs test*, often referred to as "*the one-sample runs test*," is a test of randomness when observations can be dichotomized as either a success or failure. In other words, there will be only two possible outcomes. We shall illustrate this test with an example.

Example 6.1. A coin is tossed twenty-five times, and the following sequence of outcomes is observed:

$$\frac{HH}{1} \frac{T}{2} \frac{H}{3} \frac{T}{4} \frac{HHH}{5} \frac{TTT}{6} \frac{H}{7} \frac{TT}{8} \frac{HH}{9} \frac{TT}{10} \frac{H}{11} \frac{TT}{12} \frac{H}{13} \frac{TT}{14} \frac{H}{15}$$

We want to test if these outcomes are independent or, rather, randomly distributed.

It is observed here that in each toss, only an H (head) or a T (tail) can appear. We also notice that in the first two tosses, the outcomes were H then followed by a T. We, therefore, define a *run* as the sequence of identical outcomes before a different outcome is observed. So, the first set of outcomes HH will represent a run. To visualize this, we have numbered the runs under the sequence of outcomes, and we have a total of fifteen runs. We shall introduce a few definitions to enable us to test for statistical independence.

Let

n_1 = The number of elements of type H.

n_2 = The number of elements of type T.

r = The total number of runs.

We can then obtain both the mean and the standard deviation of runs as

$$E(r) = \frac{2n_1 n_2}{n_1 + n_2} + 1 \tag{6.15}$$

$$\sigma_r = \frac{\sqrt{2n_1 n_2 (2n_1 n_2 - n_1 - n_2)}}{(n_1 + n_2)^2 (n_1 + n_2 - 1)} \tag{6.16}$$

The normal distribution approximation is used when n_1, $n_2 > 10$. Thus, the test statistic can be presented as

$$z = \frac{r - E(r)}{\sigma_r} \tag{6.17}$$

There also exists a table of critical values of r [4]. However, since we expect to use n_1, n_2, > 10, we can safely approximate the normal distribution.

Going back to example 6.1, we obtain

$$E(r) = \frac{2(12)(13)}{12 + 13} + 1 = 13.48$$

and

$$\sigma_r = \sqrt{\frac{2(12)(13)[2(12)(13) - 12 - 13]}{(12 + 13)^2 (12 + 13 - 1)}} = 2.44$$

If we set the level of significance as 0.05, we construct the critical region with $z = \pm 1.96$. Observe that $z = 0.62$ falls within the "do not reject" region. Therefore, we conclude that the sequence of H and T is random.

Runs Up and Down Test

This test of randomness is used when the observations cannot be easily dichotomized. For example, the random numbers produced fall within a large continuum of values. Thus, we do not have two mutually exclusive outcomes. We can, therefore, use the sign convention (+ *and* −) to identify the ascending and descending orders of the random numbers. The total number of runs can be derived by counting the number of +'s and −'s. $E(r)$ and σ_r are obtained as

$$E(r) = \frac{(2n - 1)}{3} \tag{6.18}$$

and

$$\sigma_r = \sqrt{\frac{16n - 29}{90}} \tag{6.19}$$

Again, r is approximately normally distributed for large n values [3]. We shall consider only cases where r is normally distributed.

Example 6.2. We can use the runs up and down test to test the randomness of the sequence of random numbers generated by the Fibonacci and additive congruential methods. We shall list that sequence and assign the + and − to identify the runs.

The + is assigned to the generated numbers 4, 6, 10, 16, . . . 68 to show the sequential increase from 2. After the number 68 is generated, the next random number generated is 10 (which is a descent). So, the − sign is assigned. From 10, the generator is on the ascending path again leading to the + for 78 and 88.

$$2\ 2\ \underset{+}{\underline{4}}\ \underset{+}{\underline{6}}\ \underset{+}{\underline{10}}\ \underset{+}{\underline{16}}\ \underset{+}{\underline{26}}\ \underset{+}{\underline{42}}\ \underset{-}{\underline{68}}\ \underset{+}{\underline{10}}\ \underset{+}{\underline{78}}\ \underset{-}{\underline{88}}\ \underset{-}{\underline{66}}\ \underset{-}{\underline{54}}\ \underset{+}{\underline{20}}\ \underset{+}{\underline{74}}\ \underset{-}{\underline{94}}\ \underline{6}$$

Notice also that tie values will not lead to breaks in the run because neither of them represents an ascent or descent. A set of successive signs is considered as a run. So we observe only six runs. The pluses show the runs up as the sequence takes increasing numbers and the minuses show runs down as the sequence takes decreasing numbers. Using equations 6.18 and 6.19, we obtain $E(r) = 13$ and $\sigma_r = 1.798$. Notice that $n = 20$. Therefore, using equation 6.17, we obtain

$$z = \frac{6 - 13}{1.798} = 3.893$$

If we use a level of significance of 0.05, we shall reject the null hypothesis that these numbers form a random sequence. Notice that $z = 3.893 > 1.96$.

REFERENCES

1. Chatterjee, S., and B. Price. *Regression Analysis by Example*. New York: Wiley, 1977.
2. Kendall, M. G. *Rank Correlation Methods*. London: Griffin, 1948.
3. Lindgren, B. E. *Statistical Theory*, 3rd ed. New York: Macmillan Publishing Company, 1976.
4. Swed, F. S., and C. Eisenhart. "Tables for Testing Randomness of Grouping in a Sequence of Alternatives." *Ann. Math. Statist.* 14 (1943): 83–86.

Chapter 7

MODELING OF BASIC QUEUING SYSTEMS

Queuing or waiting line systems are good examples of the application and use of simulation. Queuing systems are also easier to conceptualize because virtually all real-life systems involve some queuing. In this chapter, we shall present some of the basic queuing models as well as their assumptions. The analytical models obtained in this chapter will be useful in subsequent chapters in showing how simulation can be effectively applied.

Consider a cinema that operates with a single ticket seller. Customers wait in a single line in the order in which they arrive to buy the ticket. After the ticket purchase, the customer leaves the line. From existing historical data on this operation, it has been determined that the statistical distribution of interarrival and service times is negative exponentially distributed. In other words, the rates of arrival and service can be described using the Poisson distribution. Also, there is no limit on the number of customers that could enter to purchase these tickets.

From the description of these problems, certain statements about it emerge. First, the problem can be referred to using what is known as the *Kendall's notation—M/M/1*. This implies that this system has negative exponential interarrival and service times. The 1 refers to a single server. It is apparent from the problem statements that the queue discipline is first come, first served (FCFS) or first in, first out (FIFO). In order to derive a single analytical solution to this problem, we shall differentiate this queue system from the more complex variations of the presented problem.

First, there will be *no balking*. Thus, all arriving customers must join the queue irrespective of the queue length or its make up. It is not uncommon to experience balking in real life. People are at times impatient and may not be willing to join the queue when the waiting time is perceived to be excessively high.

Second, *jockeying* is not allowed. Jockeying refers to the switching of lines. In supermarkets where multiple channels are often maintained, customers are often switching to lanes that tend to have shorter waits.

Third, *reneging* is not allowed. That is to say that once a customer has joined the line, he/she must remain in that queue until services are rendered.

Needless to say, these assumptions may limit the applicability of any resulting model. Yet, they are necessary in order to develop a tractable analytical queuing model. It is also imperative to assume that this system operates under a steady-state condition. This latter assumption simplifies the model because the system's operation is not time dependent.

In queuing systems, there are specific performance measures that are of importance in order to effectively manage and control the queues. These performance measures are

L: Expected number of customers in the system.

Lq: Expected number of customers in queue (excluding the customer being served).

W: Expected waiting time in the system.

W_q: Expected waiting time in queue (excluding the customer being served).

ρ: Average utilization factor.

P_n: Probability of n customers in the system at any random point in time.

We shall illustrate a simple approach to derive these performance measures in Figure 7.1. The birth and death process confirms the notion that whatever enters the system must also leave. If we consider the system as starting at an empty state or a state with 0 customer, an arrival triggers a change in the status of the system from state 0 to state 1. An additional arrival while in state 1 will upgrade the system to state 2. Since there are uncertainties involved with the occurrence of these events, we shall associate each state with probabilities of being in those states. Also, a departure after service decrements the state of the system. For

Figure 7.1
Input-Output Diagram for an M/M/1 System

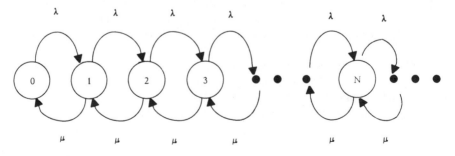

example, if the system is at state 2 and a departure occurs, the state of the system changes to state 1.

We shall introduce the following additional notations to enable us to model this system:

λ: Rate of arrival.

u: Rate of service.

P_n: Probability of n customers in the system.

Using these notations, rate-in rate-out equations can be expressed for each of the states as shown in Table 7.1, which shows that the rate into a system is also equal to the rate out of the system. Also, there is no limit on the number of customers that can enter the system.

Table 7.1
Rate-In Rate-Out Equations

State	Rate in	Rate out
0	uP_1	λP_0
1	$uP_2 + \lambda P_0$	$(\lambda+u)P_1$
2	$uP_3 + \lambda P_1$	$(\lambda+u)P_2$
•	•	•
•	•	•
•	•	•
n-1	$uP_n + \lambda P_{n-2}$	$(\lambda+u)P_{n-1}$
n	$uP_{n+1} + \lambda P_{n-1}$	$(\lambda+u)P_n$

If we consider each particular state of the system starting from state 0, we can express the P_n in terms of λ, u, and P_0 as

$$P_1 = \left(\frac{\lambda}{u}\right) P_0 \tag{7.1}$$

$$P_2 = \left(\frac{\lambda}{u}\right)^2 P_0 \tag{7.2}$$

$$P_3 = \left(\frac{\lambda}{u}\right)^3 P_0 \tag{7.3}$$

By intuition, we can then express P_n as

$$P_n = \left(\frac{\lambda}{u}\right)^n P_0 \tag{7.4}$$

However, equations 7.1 to 7.4 contain P_0, which at this point is an unknown. In order to solve it, we shall employ one of the probability axioms that

$$\sum_{n=0}^{\infty} P_i = 1$$

Thus,

$$P_0 + P_1 + P_2 + \ldots + P_n + P_{n+1} + \ldots = 1 \tag{7.5}$$

By substitution, we obtain that

$$P_0 \left[1 + \left(\frac{\lambda}{u}\right) + \left(\frac{\lambda}{u}\right)^2 + \left(\frac{\lambda}{u}\right)^3 + \cdots + \left(\frac{\lambda}{u}\right)^n + \cdots \right] = 1 \tag{7.6}$$

Notice that this summation forms a geometric series. Thus,

$$P_0 \left[\frac{1}{1 - \dfrac{\lambda}{u}} \right] = 1 \tag{7.7}$$

and

$$P_0 = 1 - \frac{\lambda}{u} \tag{7.8}$$

P_0 is the probability that the system is empty. Equivalently, it represents the idle time of the server since, ideally, it implies that there is no one in the system seeking service. P_0 is, therefore, a measure of the proportion of time the system is idle. Likewise, the server utilization factor is obtained as its complement or

$$\rho = \frac{\lambda}{u} \tag{7.9}$$

Since P_0 is now solvable, P_n can be determined as

$$P_n = \left(\frac{\lambda}{u}\right)^n \left(1 - \frac{\lambda}{u}\right) \tag{7.10}$$

To simplify notation, we shall substitute ρ for λ/u at times. We can now determine L using the definition of expected values. Thus,

$$L = \sum_{n=0}^{\infty} nP_n = \sum_{n=0}^{\infty} n\rho^n(1 - \rho) \tag{7.11}$$

Now, we shall introduce some basic calculus concepts. We can express L by taking the constants outside the summation so,

$$L = (1 - p) \sum_{n=0}^{\infty} np^n \qquad (7.12)$$

Observe, now, that $d/dp \, p^n = np^{n-1}$. So, if we multiply $(1 - p)$ by p, we can use the derivative of p^n to substitute for np^n in the summation. That is,

$$L = (1 - p)p \sum_{n=0}^{\infty} \frac{\partial}{\partial p} p^n \qquad (7.13)$$

$$= (1 - p)p \sum_{n=0}^{\infty} \frac{\partial}{\partial p} p^n \qquad (7.14)$$

Again, the summation $\sum_{n=0}^{\infty} p^n$ forms a geometric series and is equal to $1/1 - p$. So,

$$L = (1 - p)p \frac{\partial}{\partial p} \left(\frac{1}{1 - p} \right) \qquad (7.15)$$

By taking this derivative

$$L = \frac{(1 - p)p}{(1 - p)^2} = \frac{p}{1 - p} \qquad (7.16)$$

Alternatively,

$$L = \frac{\lambda}{u - \lambda}; \qquad \text{where } u > \lambda \qquad (7.17)$$

The condition is that $u > \lambda$ must be satisfied for $M/M/1$ to protect the system from exploding. If $\lambda > u$, service will be overwhelmed by the large arrivals and will be incapable of efficiently delivering the desired service.

The other measure of performance is L_q, which is a measure of the expected number of customers in line. Notice, however, the difference between L and Lq is that in L all customers in the system are considered, while with L_q only those in queue are considered. Since we have a single server, the customer in service is excluded in determining L_q. Using the definition of expected values, we shall define L_q as

$$L_q = \sum_{n=1}^{\infty} (n - 1)P_n \qquad (7.18)$$

$$= \sum_{n=1}^{\infty} nP_n - \sum_{n=1}^{\infty} P_n \tag{7.19}$$

Observe from equation 7.19 that $\sum_{n=1}^{\infty} nP_n = L$ although the limit starts from $n = 1$. However, when $n = 0$, $0.P_0 = 0$. Also, $\sum_{n=1}^{\infty} P_n = 1 - P_0$. So

$$Lq = L - (1 - P_0) \tag{7.20}$$

$$= \frac{p}{1 - p} - p \tag{7.21}$$

$$\frac{p^2}{1 - p} = \frac{\lambda^2}{u(u - \lambda)} \tag{7.22}$$

In order to determine W and W_q, we shall use a popular formula known as the *Little's formula*. This formula defines

$$W = \frac{L}{\lambda} \tag{7.23}$$

and

$$Wq = \frac{L_q}{\lambda} \tag{7.24}$$

Thus,

$$W = \frac{1}{u - \lambda} \tag{7.25}$$

and

$$Wq = \frac{\lambda}{u(u - \lambda)} \tag{7.26}$$

Notice also that by definition

$$W = Wq + \frac{1}{u} \tag{7.27}$$

While L and Lq are unitless since they measure items, products, or people, W and Wq are expressed in units of time.

Suppose that in the example presented earlier, the rate of arrival is 3 customers/hr, the rate of service is 4 customers/hr, and all other assumptions for the model are satisfied, we can easily apply the derived formulas to compute the measures of performance for this system.

Notice that all the formulas presented depend only on λ and u provided that the assumptions of the model are met.

From equation 7.9, we obtain that $p = \frac{3}{4} = 0.75$. This means that the server will be busy on the average for 75% of the time. Thus, the server's proportion of idle time is 25%. Equation 7.10 can be used to compute the probabilities of n customers in the system at any random point in time. Obviously, $P_0 = 0.25$. Using equation 7.10,

$$P_1 = (\tfrac{3}{4})(1 - \tfrac{3}{4}) = \tfrac{3}{16}$$

The expected number of customers in the system and in queue are obtained using equations 7.16 and 7.22 respectively

$$L = \frac{p}{1-p} = \frac{0.75}{0.25} = 3$$

$$Lq = \frac{p^2}{1-p} = \frac{(0.75)^2}{0.25} = 2.25$$

Finally, W and Wq are easily obtained using the Little's formula. Thus, with equations 7.25 and 7.26, we obtain

$$W = \frac{1}{4-3} = 1 \ hr$$

and

$$Wq = \frac{3}{4(4-3)} = 0.75 \ hr$$

M/M/S

In most real-life queuing systems, there will be more than one server even when a single queue is maintained. A typical example is in the bank where a single queue may be maintained, but the customer is channeled to the next available server. Also, the need often arises to evaluate alternative system designs in terms of economic optimality. This system is analogous to the M/M/1 case except that s, which is the number of servers, is greater than 1. Thus $(n - s)$ customers will be in queue at any given time when $n \geq s$.

Suppose we have an M/M/3 case, Figure 7.1 will be modified slightly as shown in Figure 7.2. Observe that when there is only one customer in the system $n = 1$, only one of the three servers is engaged. When $n = 2$, only two servers

Figure 7.2
Network Diagram for an M/M/3

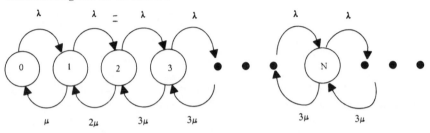

are engaged, and when $n \geq 3$, all three servers are engaged. With the $M/M/S$ configuration, it is possible to evaluate the system by alternating values of s until an optimum s is obtained.

We shall not go through the rigor of developing this procedure although its approach parallels the case presented for the $M/M/1$ case. However, the models follow. Let

$$p = \frac{\lambda}{su} \tag{7.28}$$

Here p refers to the probability of any server being busy. Likewise, the probability of any server being idle is $(1 - p)$. λ/su is known as the traffic intensity or the system service utilization. Observe that $(1 - p)$ is not the same as the proportion of time that at least one server is idle. Rather, that case can be computed as $\sum_{n=0}^{s-1} p_n$. In other words, if we use our example with $s = 3$, then,

$$P \text{ (at least one server is idle)} = P_0 + P_1 + P_2 \tag{7.29}$$

Furthermore, the probability that all the servers are idle will be computed as

$$P_0 = P \text{ (all } s \text{ servers are idle)} = \frac{1}{\left[\sum_{n=0}^{s-1} \frac{\left(\frac{\lambda}{u}\right)^n}{n!}\right] + \frac{\left(\frac{\lambda}{u}\right)^s}{(s-1)!} \frac{u}{su - \lambda}} \tag{7.30}$$

The probability of n customers in the system (P_n) is computed as

$$P_n = \begin{cases} \dfrac{\left(\frac{\lambda}{u}\right)^n}{s! \, s^{n-s}} P_0; & n > s \\[4mm] \dfrac{\left(\frac{\lambda}{u}\right)^n}{n!} P_0; & 1 \leq n \leq s \end{cases} \tag{7.31}$$

The expected number of customers in queue (Lq) is

$$Lq = \frac{\left(\frac{\lambda}{u}\right)^s \lambda u}{(s-1)!\,(su-\lambda)^2} P_0 \qquad (7.32)$$

The expected number of customers in system (L) is

$$L = Lq + \frac{\lambda}{u} \qquad (7.33)$$

The expected waiting time in queue (Wq) is

$$Wq = \frac{Lq}{\lambda} \qquad (7.34)$$

The expected waiting time in system

$$W = Wq + \frac{1}{u} \qquad (7.35)$$

and the probability that an arriving customer will have to wait for service is $(P\omega)$

$$P_\omega = \frac{1}{s!}\left(\frac{\lambda}{u}\right)^s \frac{su}{su-\lambda} P_0 \qquad (7.36)$$

We shall also illustrate the use of these formulas by assuming a multiple channel system with three servers; $\lambda = 3/hr$, and $u = 4/hr$. Also, $\lambda < su$ otherwise the service rate will be incapable of servicing all arrivals. Starting with equation 7.28 we obtain

$$p = \frac{3}{3(4)} = 0.25$$

Thus, the probability of any server being busy is 0.25. In other words, there is a 0.75 probability that any particular server is idle. The probability that at least one server is idle is $\sum_{n=0}^{\infty} P_n = P_0 + P_1 + P_2$. From equation 7.31, we can compute P_n for $n = 0,1,2$. Notice that the second equation in that bracket is used when $n = 1, 2,$ or 3. First, we determine P_0 using equation 7.30 as

$$P_0 = \frac{1}{\left[\displaystyle\sum_{n=0}^{2} \frac{\left(\frac{3}{4}\right)^n}{n!}\right] + \frac{\left(\frac{3}{4}\right)^3}{2!}\,\frac{4}{3(4)-3}}$$

$$\sum_{n=0}^{2} \frac{\left(\frac{3}{4}\right)^n}{n!} = \frac{\left(\frac{3}{4}\right)^0}{0!} + \frac{\left(\frac{3}{4}\right)^1}{1!} + \frac{\left(\frac{3}{4}\right)^2}{2!} = 1 + \frac{3}{4} + \frac{9}{32} = \frac{65}{32}$$

So,

$$P_0 = \frac{1}{\frac{65}{32} + \frac{3}{32}} = \frac{1}{\frac{68}{32}} = \frac{32}{68} = \frac{8}{17}$$

From equation 7.31,

$$P_1 = \frac{\left(\frac{3}{4}\right)}{1} \left(\frac{8}{17}\right) = \frac{6}{17}$$

$$P_2 = \frac{\left(\frac{3}{4}\right)^2}{2} \left(\frac{8}{17}\right) = \frac{9}{68}$$

Thus,

$$P \ (at \ least \ one \ server \ is \ idle) = P_0 + P_1 + P_2 = \frac{8}{17} + \frac{6}{17} + \frac{9}{68} = \frac{65}{68}$$

Using equation 7.32, Lq is obtained as

$$Lq = \frac{\left(\frac{3}{4}\right)^3 3.4}{(3-1) \ ! \ (3.4 - 3)^2} = \frac{1}{32}$$

L is computed from equation 7.33 as

$$L = \frac{1}{32} + \frac{3}{4} = \frac{25}{32}$$

and Wq and W are obtained from equations 7.34 and 7.35 respectively as

$$Wq = \frac{\frac{1}{32}}{3} = \frac{1}{96} \ hr$$

$$W = \frac{1}{96} + \frac{1}{4} = \frac{25}{96} \ hr$$

Finally, the probability that an arriving customer will have to wait is given as

$$P_\omega = \frac{1}{3!}\left(\frac{3}{4}\right)^3 \frac{3.4}{3.4-3}\left(\frac{8}{17}\right)$$

$$= \frac{1}{6}\left(\frac{27}{64}\right)\frac{12}{9}\left(\frac{8}{17}\right)$$

$$= \frac{3}{68}$$

There is, therefore, a very small chance that an arriving customer will have to wait.

Chapter 8

STEADY STATE OUTPUT ANALYSIS

INTRODUCTION

Before we can begin to analyze the outputs of a simulation model, we must first distinguish two types of discrete-event systems, namely terminating and nonterminating systems. This distinction is necessary since the method of analysis depends on the type of system.

Terminating Systems

A *terminating system* is a system where the occurrence of events is terminated at some point in time. Although such systems may be reoccurring, each start of the system begins afresh. In simulating such systems the initial conditions established will influence the measures of performance. Some examples of terminating systems follow.

Example 8.1. A bank opens its doors by 9:00 AM and closes for customers by 3:00 PM. This process is repeated every day for the five-day working week. Thus, the bank's business terminates daily but reoccurs day-by-day. Also, notice that the actual time in operation differs because the customers that enter the bank between 9:00 AM and 3:00 PM must be completely served. In other words, the ending time of the last event in the bank is a variable. If we use t_e to denote the time of occurrence of a particular event, then the simulated time required to bring the bank to an empty state at the close of each business day, as in this case, is at least 6 hours. The system in this case starts at time 0. The simulated time is specified at the beginning of the simulation. This system ends when the last customer has left the bank. This time is a random variable in the interval $(0, t_e)$ where t_e is the time the last customer was completely served and left the bank.

There are several ways we can study this system. For example, we may be interested in studying the bank operation for the different hours of the day and/or the different days of the week. Obviously, some time periods are quite congested and may need more staffing than the slack periods. There may also be an interest in the bank's overall performance during the entire period it was in operation— that is, the time until the departure of the last customer in a given day.

Example 8.2. A registrar's office at a major university is open from 8:00 AM to 6:00 PM during the registration period and closes its window at 6:00 PM or when the last student in service before 6:00 PM is served. Here, the interest may be in knowing how many students were registered during this period and also the queue length at 6:00 PM.

Example 8.3. A car parking lot opens during the business hours from 6:30 AM to 6:00 PM with a capacity of 200 cars. Here, there are two terminating conditions—the time and the capacity of the parking lot. For example, cars that are not picked up by the closing time will be locked in the garage. Also, when a car arrives and the capacity of the parking lot has been reached, the arriving car is denied entry into the parking lot. However, as cars leave the parking lot, new cars are allowed in. Thus, the capacity of the parking lot during the hours of operation is a random variable. Also, notice that the initial state of the system may not always be 0 since uncollected cars are locked in. However, this system terminates since no more cars are allowed in by 6:00 PM.

Nonterminating Systems

A *nonterminating* system is a system where the occurrence of events is not limited. The reoccurring of events is indefinite. Some examples of nonterminating systems follow.

Example 8.4. Consider an interstate highway that maintains a continuous flow of traffic (note that traffic that moves through the highway is a discrete event). The interest may be in knowing the volume of traffic at specific days of the week. Notice that this system is nonterminating because the highway is open at all times of the day.

Example 8.5. A 24-hour supermarket is a nonterminating system. Interest may be in determining the staffing levels for the different times of the day. Obviously, there will be fewer shoppers at midnight so fewer counters should be open.

Example 8.6. The emergency and critical care units of hospitals are, in most cases, open 24 hours with workers being rotated throughout the day. Thus, such systems are nonterminating.

Example 8.7. Many of the major and/or international airports operate on a 24-hour basis and aircraft arrive and take off at different times of the day. Evidently, the traffic intensity varies for the different days and the different times. Nevertheless, the system is nonterminating.

Example 8.8. Consider a city mass transit system that provides bus services to its several communities. A fixed number of buses are required to be in operation at each given time and are backed up by some standby buses. This operation operates continuously even though there may be variations in the number of buses running at any particular time of the day. This system is nonterminating. Emphasis may be on the availability of buses and the utilization of the mass transit system at any point in time.

In discussing nonterminating systems, we concentrate on their typical mode of operation. Although there are instances where some of these agencies may temporarily close (i.e., holidays, renovation, construction, etc.), they are generally nonterminating.

STEADY STATE VERSUS TRANSIENT BEHAVIOR

A steady state in simulation is reached when the performance measure of interest is time invariant. In other words, the performance measure is no longer a function of time and would be the expected outcome as the length of the simulation approaches infinity. Generally, good estimates of the performance measures are obtained when the length of a simulation run is large enough. There are cost trade-offs that are associated with lengthy simulation runs. However, the length of the simulation run must be long enough to avoid the influence of the initial conditions of the system on the performance measures. For example, if the bank's operation for an 8-hour day is studied, it is conceivable that the number of arrivals at time 0 (opening of the bank) may not accurately reflect the arrival of the first customer. Thus, the effect of this initial condition has to be diminished in order to achieve a steady state performance.

In some systems, it may not be necessary to achieve a steady state. If we consider a highway toll gate that is open continuously, the interest may be in determining the traffic intensity at each hour to determine the number of toll gates that should be open at any particular time. Steady state simulation is, therefore, used to study the *typical* behavior of a system. When the performance measures are expected to vary over time as in the toll gate example, the interest will be on the *transient* behavior of the system.

In analyzing discrete-event systems, we shall first determine if the system is terminating or nonterminating. Subsequently a decision is made on the nature of output that is of interest to the modeler (i.e., steady state or transient). We shall illustrate a steady state example below.

Example 8.9. Consider an express checkout line at a supermarket for customers with ten items or less. There is only one express counter and the customers line up in a single line to receive service. The checkout line is opened at 9:00 AM and closes by 5:00 PM (a total of 8 hours). We are interested in determining the average waiting time of customers in this line. Assume that the conditions for the express line satisfy the assumptions for the $M/M/1$ system. The service time is determined as 15 minutes and the interarrival time is 20 minutes.

We shall start this analysis by first stating that this supermarket is classified as a terminating system because the express lane must close by 5:00 PM. Steady state results may also not be appropriate in modeling this system since the performance measures are bound to change over time. We shall, however, present the result for the transient and steady state behavior.

Figure 8.1 is the flow diagram for this problem, and it shows the sequence of events that commence with the arrival of a customer at the express lane. As shown in this diagram, the customer queues for service on arrival. The queuing discipline is the first in first out (FIFO) or the first come first served (FCFS). When the checkout clerk is idle, the first in line advances to receive service. Once in for service, that customer is discounted from the queue. The checkout clerk is now considered busy since only one customer is served at a time. At the completion of service, the checkout clerk is released by the customer, and the next customer can advance to the checkout counter. This process continues for all the arriving customers. The served customer leaves the express lane. This system terminates when the operational time is reached, say 8 hours. However, in real application, the system terminates when the operational time has been reached and/or the last customer already in queue is served.

The waiting line systems discussed in Chapter 7 are applicable to this problem if we assume that both the interarrival times and the service time follow the negative exponential distribution and also that a steady state behavior is observed. Suppose that assumptions are made here, and also that the rate of arrival and service rates are 3/hr and 4/hr respectively, we can easily apply the M/M/1 models presented in Chapter 7 to compute the system's performance measures. Application of those models will yield that the server utilization factor is $p = 0.75$, the expected number of customers in the system is $L = 3$, the expected number of customers in queue is $Lq = 2.25$; average waiting time in the system is $W = 60\ minutes$, and the expected waiting time in queue is $Wq = 45\ minutes$. However, in deriving the M/M/1 models, we made the assumption of a steady state behavior by the system. This assumption is satisfied when the system operates at its peak.

We shall solve this same problem using simulation to see how the results of the transient and steady state cases will differ remarkably and also to compare the queuing model (M/M/1) to the simulation result obtained under similar conditions.

TRANSIENT BEHAVIOR VERSUS STEADY STATE BEHAVIOR

If the particular system discussed above is modeled via simulation, the results obtained for the major performance measures over the 8-hour work day are presented in Table 8.1. GPSS/H is used for the coding of this problem. These results are based on the average realizations of the performance measures over one hundred replications. These replications refer to the rerunning of the simulation model with different random number seeds. Due to the variability in simulation outputs, interval estimates of these performance measures are preferred to the point estimates.

Figure 8.1
Express Lane Checkout

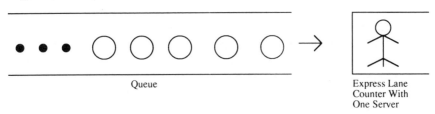

| Queue | Express Lane Counter With One Server |

As observed from these results, the performance measures change dramatically as the simulation run length (time) is changed. For example, after the model has run for 1 hour, the server utilization factor is observed to be 0.42 and $Lq = 0.27$ is realized. Notice, however, as the simulation run time is increased say to 2 hours or 3 hours, different values are observed for the performance measures even after the average of one hundred replications is taken. Furthermore, these values tend to differ remarkably. For example, Lq goes from 0.27 for 1 hour to 0.6 for 2 hours of simulation run length and then to 0.72 for 3 hours. Similar jumps are observed for W and Wq. Thus, this system is exhibiting a transient behavior. Also, notice that for the 8 hours of simulation time presented here, the system is still transient and has not yet achieved its peak. Emphatically, if this system is an 8-hour operation, it is impossible to achieve a steady state behavior.

Table 8.1
Performance Measures for M/M/1 with Shorter Simulation Runs

Time (hr)	FR P	Service time (secs.) (1/u)	L_q	W (secs.)	W_q (secs.)
1	0.42 (0.049)	668.32 (601.08)	0.27 (0.50)	390.86 (479.69)	222.76 (330.17)
2	0.56 (0.05)	856.67 (380.45)	0.60 (0.78)	926.73 (806.92)	584.48 (603.92)
3	0.59 (0.049)	880.15 (312.08)	0.72 (0.87)	1206.95 (858.85)	781.22 (805.06)
4	0.63 (0.048)	904.50 (318.36)	0.89 (0.98)	1354.05 (966.63)	931.44 (904.59)
5	0.63 (0.048)	910.2 (263.66)	1.02 (1.22)	1587 (1109.61)	1092.17 (1034.23)
6	0.65 (0.048)	926.63 (261.79)	1.16 (1.41)	1742.07 (1323.2)	1244.05 (1271.51)
7	0.66 (0.047)	923.95 (263.21)	1.31 (1.45)	1986.33 (1517.1)	1458.21 (1426.12)
8	0.67 (0.047)	912.74 (212.79)	1.38 (1.53)	2081.91 (1530.67)	1556.14 (1495.56)

If we contrast this result to the analytical results obtained using the models of Chapter 7, we observe wide errors if one is used as an approximation to the other. For example, the steady state model of M/M/1 gives $p = 0.75$, $Lq = 2.25$, $W = 60$ minutes, and $Wq = 45$ minutes. However, the simulation results obtained after 8 hours of run yield $p = 0.67$, $Lq = 1.38$, $W = 34.7$ minutes, and $Wq = 25.94$ minutes. Table 8.1 presents some of the results. Observe that the simulation model tends to underestimate the analytical model. The percentage errors are also quite high. It will, therefore, be erroneous to use the estimates obtained for the performance measures for this problem after 8 hours to estimate a steady state behavior. You may recall that a major assumption of the analytical model is that of steady state behavior. The particular system studied here is unable to reach a steady state behavior after 8 hours of simulation run. Thus, the simulation results presented earlier represent transient behavior.

As the run length of the simulation approaches infinity, the measures of performance attain more stable values, and lesser variations are obtained as the length of the simulation is increased.

Achieving steady state behavior is not always an easy task and may be costly. Additional simulation results to example 8.1 are introduced to show steady state behavior. Table 8.2 shows the results from further simulation runs. For the measures of performance studied in this problem, p is relatively more stable after 60 hours of simulation. However, at this point, relative "instability" is observed in other measures of performance. In fact, steady state behavior is observed for all the measures of performance when the length of the simulation is 1440 hours or more. Notice that the results obtained when length of the simulation is 1440 hours and 4000 hours are very close. Figure 8.2 also shows a graph of W obtained from 40 hours to 4000 hours of simulation. Observe the trend in this graph as the length of the simulation is increased. This graph shows that W approaches a horizontal asymptote when the length of the simulation is 1440 hours or more. Due to cost and efficiency considerations, we shall then use the simulation time of 1440 hours for more experimentation of this system.

Table 8.3 shows the comparisons of the analytical model to the steady state observations. Notice that these results are very close. In fact, when the simulation time is either 3000 hours or 4000 hours, the results obtained are exactly the same as for the analytical model. Another important observation from the results presented in Tables 8.1 and 8.2 is that the standard deviation given in brackets in those tables will generally tend to decrease as the length of the simulation is increased. This is expected as there is less fluctuation between the results observed during the steady state than during the transient state. Also, notice that the standard error of the mean approaches zero as the sample size increases to infinity. So with each replication the measures of performance generated will be closer. When the simulation run length is short, enough queue is not built up before the simulation is terminated. Consequently, estimates observed for the measures of performance tend to be biased towards the low values. In fact, they often represent the initial state of the system rather than a system operating at its peak. If the simulation is not run long enough, this initial state of the system will

Table 8.2
Performance Measures for M/M/1 with Longer Simulation Runs

Timer	$\rho = \dfrac{\lambda}{u}$	$\dfrac{1}{u}$	Lq	W (hr)	Wq (hr)
40 hr	0.73	0.25	1.91	0.83	0.63
			1.40	0.48	0.43
60 hr	0.74	0.25	2.02	0.88	0.67
			1.46	0.51	0.47
80 hr	0.74	0.25	2.01	0.89	0.67
			1.03	0.36	0.33
120 hr	0.74	0.25	2.07	0.92	0.69
			0.81	0.30	0.26
240 hr	0.75	0.25	2.10	0.93	0.70
			0.60	0.20	0.19
480 hr	0.75	0.25	2.16	0.96	0.72
			0.49	0.18	0.16
960 hr	0.75	0.25	2.19	0.98	0.73
			0.36	0.13	0.12
1440 hr	0.75	0.25	2.27	1.01	0.76
			0.32	0.12	0.10
2000 hr	0.75	0.25	2.27	1.01	0.76
			0.28	0.10	0.09
3000 hr	0.75	0.25	2.25	1.00	0.75
			0.23	0.09	0.07
4000 hr	0.75	0.25	2.25	1.00	0.75
			0.20	0.08	0.06

Table 8.3
Performance Measures for Steady State Output and Analytical Model*

Analytical Model		Simulation Model	Absolute % Error
P	0.75	0.75	0
L_q	2.25	2.27	0.89
W	60	61	1.67
W_q	45	45.6	1.33

*Simulation Time = 1440 hr

Figure 8.2
Steady State Analysis of Waiting Time

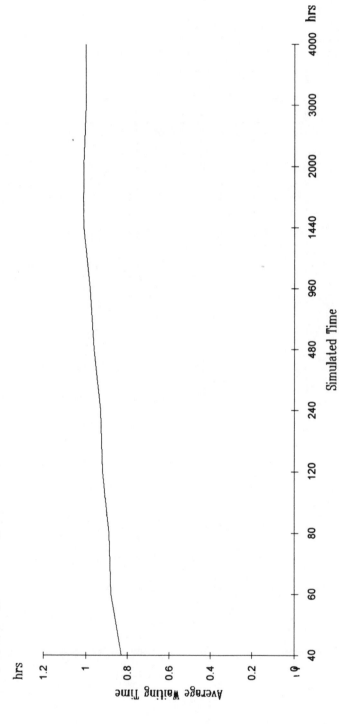

bias the estimates obtained for the measures of performance. The longer the simulation is run, however, the more time for the system to achieve its peak and the results obtained will be more realistic.

ANALYSES OF SIMULATION OUTPUTS

Simulation outputs are subject to random variations. It would, therefore, be meaningless to use a fixed point to estimate a particular measure of performance without any notion of the variance in such outputs. In reporting simulation results it is, therefore, preferable to use interval rather than point estimates. The use of interval estimates requires that some statistical assumptions be made, however. If these assumptions are not satisfied, incorrect conclusions may be drawn about the behavior of the process being modeled. These assumptions follow:

1. The observations are statistically independent. This assumption implies that the outcome of a particular observation does not influence the outcome of any other observation. A simple example of statistical independence can be derived from an experiment that involves the tossing of a fair coin. In each toss, the outcome will either be a head or a tail. The occurrence of a head or a tail in a particular toss does not influence the occurrence in subsequent toss of the fair coin. Thus, we can say that each toss is independent.
2. Steady state outcomes are observed.
3. Samples are drawn from a normal distribution. Statistical tests for normal distribution were presented in Chapter 6. This assumption is also satisfied when the number of observations is large (at least thirty). This follows from the central limit theorem. We shall use example 8.9 to illustrate how simulation outputs can be analyzed for a terminating system.

Terminating System

In example 8.9, a basic queuing system was analyzed and both the transient and steady state results were obtained for the performance measures. It was shown in Table 8.1 that steady-state performance is not attainable within the 8 hours the express checkout line operates in a day. It was also observed that our results for the performance measures are given in terms of mean and standard deviation. Indeed, these are important statistical properties that are quite often used to represent simulation results. Since simulation outputs are subject to random variations, standard deviations can convey useful information on the variability of the performance measure when different random number seeds are generated. In order to estimate the true mean (u) and variance (σ^2), we need to ensure that the statistical properties of both the mean and variance are satisfied by our estimators. These properties include the following:

$E(\bar{x})$ $= u$ for all i. Therefore, $E(x) = u$

$E(S^2) = \sigma^2$

These basic properties imply that $\bar{x}$ and s^2 are *unbiased estimators* of u and σ^2, respectively. Notice that an unbiased estimator may not provide useful individual estimates. Rather, the estimate may be correct on the average. The deviations of the individual estimates from the population value may be noticeably large in some cases. Observe also that $\bar{x}$ is the sample mean, which can be represented as

$$\bar{X} = \frac{\sum\limits_{i=1}^{n} X_i}{n} \tag{8.1}$$

It is required that the $X_i s$ be independent and also, that $E(X_i) = u$ for all of the observations in order for $E(s^2) = \sigma^2$. The condition of independence is not required for the mean.

Method of Replication

The method of replication is commonly used to estimate the performance measures for terminating systems. This method often ensures that the observations are independent and have a common expected mean. Independent replications of the simulation experiment is conducted by either changing the random number seeds or collecting statistics at specific points during the simulation or after certain events have taken place. In example 8.9 this is accomplished by changing the random number seeds. We shall present the method used in Tables 8.1 and 8.2 here.

Notice that the use of different random numbers ensures statistical independence for the replications. Observe also that even though a timer was used to control the length of simulation run, different numbers of customers went through the system at each replication of the experiment. Therefore, for each simulation run length presented the average of performance measure for the number of customers that went through the system is taken over the number of replications. For example, suppose that m customers went through each replication and there are n replications. If the performance measure is W (average waiting time), and Y_i is the waiting time in the system for customer i, then

$$\hat{W} = \frac{1}{m} \sum\limits_{i=1}^{m} Y_i \tag{8.2}$$

Also, each replication of the experiment is started at the same initial condition. For the M/M/1 problem described here, it is required that the system be empty in each replication of the experiment. $\hat{W}$ is an estimator of the average waiting time in the system (W). For each of the jth replication, the $\hat{W}_j s$ obtained are independent and identically distributed random variables. Thus, $W = E(\bar{W})$. Based on this definition, the results presented in Tables 8.1 and 8.2 are obtained. As we already observed, the results in Table 8.1 are not steady state outcomes. For

M/M/1 it is necessary that we achieve a steady state. Notice that a steady state is achieved when the simulation run length was set at 1440 hours. With these results established, the confidence intervals can be constructed for the performance measures. Suppose we continue with the results presented in Table 8.2 where we observed that the average waiting time for one hundred replications is 1.01 hour with a standard deviation of 0.01 hour. Then,

$$\bar{W} = \frac{1}{n} \sum_{j=1}^{n} W_j \tag{8.3}$$

and

$$S_W^2 = \sum_{j=1}^{n} (W_j - \bar{W})^2/(n - 1) \tag{8.4}$$

where n is the number of replications. The $(1 - \alpha)$ 100% confidence interval is, therefore, constructed as

$$\bar{W} \pm t_{\alpha/2}, (n - 1) \frac{S_W}{\sqrt{n}} \tag{8.5}$$

For the example already presented, we obtain

$$1.01 \pm t_{.025}, (99) \frac{0.12}{\sqrt{100}} = 1.01 \pm 1.96 \frac{(0.12)}{10} = 1.01 \pm .0235$$

$$0.9865 \leq W \leq 1.0335$$

Here, we are assuming a 95% confidence level and also that the independent and identically distributed observations are approximately normally distributed. This confidence interval could be referred to as an approximate 95% confidence interval because the assumption of normal random variables is rarely satisfied in practice. Caution should also be exercised in interpreting confidence intervals. The 95% confidence interval already established does not imply that we are confident that 95% of the customers will wait between 0.9865 and 1.0335 hours. Rather, if this process is repeated an infinite number of times and one hundred replications are drawn from that population 95% of the time, we should observe an average waiting time between 0.9865 and 1.0335 hours. In other words, 95% of the $\bar{W}$ values of replications of size 100 would lie in the range of 0.9865 and 1.0335 hours if repeated samples were drawn from this population.

It is often desirable to determine the number of independent runs or replications to achieve some desired precision in our estimate of the performance measure. For example, how large should n be?

Suppose we define E as the maximum error of the sample estimate from the population parameter, then

$$E = Z \cdot \frac{\sigma}{\sqrt{n}} \tag{8.6}$$

where Z is the standard z-score for a normal distribution. Therefore, n can be obtained as

$$n = \frac{Z^2 \cdot \sigma^2}{E^2} = \left[\frac{z\sigma}{E} \right]^2 \tag{8.7}$$

If the maximum error E is set at 1.0 minute and the confidence level is set at 95%, and σ^2 is estimated using the sample variance, the required number of replications to achieve this degree of precision would be

$$n = \frac{[1.96(0.12)]^2}{0.01667} = 198.35 \cong 199$$

In order to achieve this degree of precision, we would need 199 replications of the simulation experiment. Clearly, more simulation runs will be required as the maximum error of the estimate from the population parameter is reduced.

For proportions like the average server utilization (ρ) we can establish the confidence interval and also determine n. For such cases we will have

$$\hat{p} \pm z\sqrt{\hat{p}(1 - \hat{p})/n} \tag{8.8}$$

as the $(1 - \alpha)$ 100% confidence interval. The number of replications n is determined as

$$n = \frac{z^2\hat{p}(1 - \hat{p})}{E^2} \tag{8.9}$$

Using equations 8.8 and 8.9 and our steady state results, we obtain the confidence interval for ρ and the n when E is 0.05 as follows:

$$0.75 \pm 1.96\sqrt{0.75(0.25)/100} = 0.75 \pm 0.085$$

So,

$$0.665 \leq \rho \leq 0.835$$

and

$$n = \frac{1.96^2(0.75)(0.25)}{(0.05)^2} = 288.12 \cong 289$$

Notice that $\hat{p}$ is a sample proportion used to estimate ρ.

Chapter 9

CLASSICAL FACTORIAL DESIGNS AND REGRESSION METAMODELS

INTRODUCTION

There is an avalanche of literature on the application of statistical designs in computer simulation, and many of these papers have focused on how to develop regression metamodels [9–11]. A succinct definition of the term *regression metamodel* was provided in Friedman and Pressman [5]. Although this trend of thought is very promising because it expands the power and the usage of simulation, especially in solving complex problems, some important questions regarding how to effectively apply these models have not been discussed.

Regression metamodels often employ statistical designs, such as the one-factor-at-a-time, full or fractional factorial designs, when determining the input values of the independent variables. With the one-factor-at-a-time method, one factor is varied at a time while the other factors are held constant [1]. Clearly, the one-factor-at-a-time design is inefficient since it requires massive data collection and is, therefore, time consuming and wasteful. The full factorial design, though very efficient, may suffer the same fate as the one-factor-at-a-time design, however, if the number of independent variables is large. Consider for example, an experiment with ten variables studied only at two levels. Thus, a total of 2^{10} simulation trials must be conducted in order to completely study all the input variables. This also does not consider the fact that a single design point will consist of a substantial number of replications of the simulation run. Thus when large numbers of factors are considered for experimentation the full factorial design becomes impossible.

Fractional factorial designs may, on the other hand, overcome this problem. For example, a 2^{10-6}_{III} design may be applicable to this problem. If such is the case, the number of simulation runs will be reduced from 1024 for the factorial design to 16 runs for this particular case. Observe, however, that this fractional factorial design is of resolution III. With this design, the main effects will confound with the two-factor interactions. The resolution of an experiment gives us an idea about which factors we should be able to establish clearly. Since the main effects are *confounded* with the two-factor interactions, it becomes difficult to clearly separate out the significant factors. Furthermore, in most experiments, we are concerned with the estimation of both the main and the two-factor interaction effects. Due to the resolution of this experiment, the experimenter has to worry about the alias structure of the factors or the confounding pattern that may be present in the experiment. In fact, the only resolution that will avoid this confounding pattern when only the main effects and the two-factor interactions are of interest will be resolution V. In order to use this resolution, $2_V^{10-3} = 128$ simulation runs will be required. Although this is still a significant reduction in the number of runs, it is still large when one considers the fact that only linear effects can be estimated with two-level designs. Although there are procedures to deal with this problem, it is not easily done [1]. Thus, the use of fractional factorial design is delicate and very risky, especially to the nonstatistician. Obviously, most simulation modelers are practitioners and not statisticians.

Many of the regression metamodels consider the input variables only at two levels. When this is done, only linear effects can be estimated. In other words, higher order effects are not estimable with such designs. Some of the designs have also resorted to the 3^k designs (k is the number of input factors) when it is absolutely necessary to study linear and quadratic effects. The problem is further compounded, however, when either factorial or fractional factorial designs are used and k is large. An interesting approach for overcoming this problem is the use of a group screening design. However, in order to effectively use this design approach, its axiomatic conditions have to be satisfied [3].

Finally, the research in this area has not yet provided systematic guidance on how regression metamodels can be developed when both linear and nonlinear effects are of interest to the designer.

These problems are addressed in the following chapters, where we also present a sequential and a systematic approach to develop a regression metamodel.

Classical Factorial Designs

There are two major approaches to the design of experiments—the classical and Taguchi. The classical approach can be further classified into three groups: (1) one-factor-at-a-time designs, (2) full factorial designs, and (3) fractional factorial design. The classical designs are discussed in this chapter while the Taguchi designs are going to be addressed in the next chapter.

ONE-FACTOR-AT-A-TIME DESIGNS VERSUS (FRACTIONAL) FACTORIAL DESIGNS

If we are dealing with factors that are expressed in integral range and if each factor k has a range expressed as $a_i \leq k_i \leq b_i$ where $i = 1, 2, \ldots, n$, then in the one-factor-at-a-time design the total number of runs required is Πv_i where $v_i = b_i - a_i + 1$ for any i. Conversely, a full factorial design with two levels will require a total of 2^k runs, while for any given level L a total of L^k will be required. In both the one-factor-at-a-time and the full factorial designs, we have enough information to estimate both main effects and interaction effects without worrying about the confounding patterns.

When fractional designs are introduced, say L^{k-p} designs, we significantly reduce the number of runs required. At the same time, we are working with fewer degrees of freedom and are unable to estimate some of the higher order effects. Attention also has to be paid to the resolution of the experiment. With this design, data collection is considerably less. Therefore, for any L^{k-p} design, a total of $((k - p)/k)100\%$ is achieved over the full factorial design.

For example, a full factorial design with four factors each at two levels will require a total of $2^4 = 16$ simulation runs. With a 2^{k-1} factorial experimental design, this reduces to $2^3 = 8$ simulation runs. Thus, a 50% reduction in the number of simulation runs is realized. Due to the reduction in experimental costs and the fact that satisfactory solutions are obtainable, we strongly recommend the use of fractional factorial designs.

FULL FACTORIAL DESIGNS

In the initial stage of many experiments, a large number of factors may have to be tested simultaneously. In such experiments, a large number of runs will be required in order to consider all the possible combinations of the different levels specified for the controllable factors (i.e., a full factorial design). For example, when an experiment consists of only ten factors, each at two levels, the number of factor combinations is 2^{10}. Thus, a total of 1024 design points will be required for the experiment. Furthermore, if the designs were replicated ten times in order to achieve the desired level of precision in the estimate, then we would have to make 10,240 separate simulation runs.

Box et al. [1] indicate that these designs (i.e., full factorial designs at two levels) are of importance for a number of reasons: (1) they can indicate major trends and so determine a promising direction for further experimentation, (2) they form the basis for two-level fractional factorial designs, (3) these designs and the corresponding fractional designs may be used as building blocks so that the degree of complexity of the finally constructed design can match the sophistication of the problem, and (4) the interpretation of the result is easy.

Dey [4] also points out that full factorial design experiments are too expensive and impracticable in most situations. It is, therefore, not necessary to carry out such large experiments especially when the interest is to estimate only lower order effects. Under this situation, higher order effects are assumed insignificant. The economy of space and material in such situations could be achieved by considering only a fraction of a factorial design (i.e., a fractional factorial design). By using a fractional factorial design, however, we lose some information that may otherwise be available if a factorial design is used.

Kelton [7] noted that by carrying out a fractional rather than a full factorial design we give up the ability to estimate higher-order interactions and receive in return a more modest requirement in terms of the number of runs. Therefore, how to select an appropriate fractional factorial design by which useful information can be obtained with a reasonable degree of precision from less than a full factorial experiment design is an important issue.

FRACTIONAL FACTORIAL DESIGNS

The experimental design is started by presuming that there are k factors that may possibly be of importance in determining the system's outputs. Again, if each factor has L possible levels, then the total experimental runs (or simulation runs) needed is L^k. In order to reduce the number of simulation runs, screening designs such as two-level full factorial or fractional factorial designs are often used. The two levels may represent the "low" and the "high" values of the independent variables. The selection of two-level full or fractional factorial designs depends on the metamodel form. If the interest is in examining the main effects and all the possible higher-order interactions of k factors, then 2^k factorial design is necessary to carry out the experiment. This design is referred to as a 2^k factorial design because all the possible combinations of the two levels of each factor are considered in the experiment. Otherwise, only a fraction of 2^k combinations is needed. When fractional factorial designs are used, it is necessary to pay attention to the resolution of the design. By knowing the resolution of the design, we are able to identify the alias structure of the experiment or the confounding pattern of the design.

To reiterate, the reduction in the number of design points with the use of fractional designs reduces our ability to estimate some higher-order interaction effects. Thus, there is a trade-off in using this design. Nevertheless, its advantages are overwhelming since we are seldom concerned with more than two-factor interactions. A summary of some useful fractional designs and their corresponding resolutions is given by Box et al. [1].

Notice that the 2^k factorial design can only be helpful in estimating an individual variable's linear effects. Although the assumption of linear effects is advantageous because of its simplicity, nonlinear effects may present smaller variances. In order to examine the nonlinear effects of quantitative factors, more than two-level designs are needed. For example, with a three-level factorial design, it is possible to estimate both linear and quadratic effects.

Table 9.1
Comparison of Experimental Designs

Design Type *	No. Runs	Estimate interactions	Resolution	Functional Relations
2^{k-1}	8	Some higher order inter- actions are estimatable	Need to know the resolution of the design	linear
2^k	16	All	Not necessary	linear
3^{k-1}	27	Some higher order inter- actions are estimatable	Need to know the resolution of the design	linear & quadratic
one-at- a-time	40	All	Not necessary	All possible relationships

*$k = 4$

Real life perspective on how to conduct experiments: "There has been a group of statisticians working on incredibly interesting theories on how to conduct experiments," says Soren Bisgaard, associate director of the Center for Quality & Productivity Improvement at the University of Wisconsin. In the traditional approach, an engineer builds a series of prototypes, each differing from the next in a crucial way, such as the shape of the valves on an auto engine. But there are so many key factors that no designer can test more than a fraction of the possible combinations. Enter statistics. Building on ideas of British scientist R. A. Fisher in the 1920s, statisticians such as Wisconsin's George E. P. Box have devised methods to identify the few combinations that are likely to lead to the best design.

A general comparison of these design types is presented in Table 9.1. For example, if $k = 4$, the one-at-a-time requires a total of forty simulation runs while the 3^{k-1} design requires a total of twenty-seven runs. The use of the 3^{k-1} design helps in normalizing the size of the values of the independent variables by including their mid-values.

AN ILLUSTRATION

Problem Definition

In a maintenance float network (Figure 9.1), N independent and identical machines are required to be in operation simultaneously. When a failure occurs, the number of operating units is reduced to $N - 1$. If there are any standby units,

Figure 9.1
Maintenance Float System

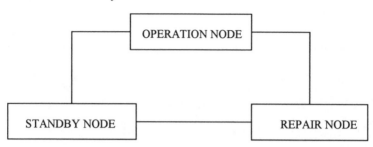

The notations used in this chapter are presented below:

N   =   the number of machines initially in operation or required to be in operation
              at all times.

MTBF =   mean time between failure or the expected interarrival time of a failed unit
              for repair.

MTTR =   mean time to repair.

EU   =   the average equipment utilization. This gives the proportion of N units in
              an operational status.

CV   =   coefficient of variation for the failure distribution expressed as the ratio of
              standard deviation to its mean.

S   =   the number of independent and identical repairpersons or servers.

F   =   the maintenance float required to support the N machines that are in
              operation or standby units.

the failed unit is replaced to restore the number of operating units to *N*. The failed
unit goes in for repair and is returned to a standby status if the total number of
operating units at the time of completion of repair is up to *N*. Otherwise, it is sent
into operation. It is assumed that the failed unit is completely rejuvenated after
repair.

The following example presents a model to predict the average equipment
utilization (EU) of a maintenance float system. An important operations management decision is to determine the optimum combination of repairpersons and
standby units needed to maintain on the average *N* units of independent and
identical machines in operation. The need to maintain standby units and repairpersons is caused by uncertainties associated with equipment failures. Failure
inevitably leads to high operational costs due to the operating system's inability
to satisfy the management's set service level. However, the performance of the
operating system can be substantially improved by providing standby units
and/or repairpersons as protection against failure. Thus, developing an efficient
maintenance float policy will aid in minimizing the cost of lost production.
Maintenance policies have wide implications to both manufacturing and service

sectors. In both sectors, there is a need to achieve high equipment availability in order to improve productivity and the quality of services provided to customers.

The Simulation Model

Since maintenance float systems with gamma failure distribution are too complex to be modeled using the analytical approach, simulation modeling is necessary in order to understand the behavior of such systems. In our case, once a valid simulation is established then the experimentation can be carried out. In this example, a steady state simulation model using the general purpose systems simulator (GPSS) language was implemented on an IBM/360 series mainframe. Statistical tests were conducted to assure that serial correlation effects were not present and that steady state results were achieved [15]. The minimum run length used was 124,800 time units. In some cases when parameter values were changed, the run length was extended to achieve steady state behavior. The assumption of normality in the EU values realized from simulation was confirmed by a Lilliefors' goodness-of-fit test.

Chrissis and Grecan [2] presented a method to validate a simulation model for a closed queuing network of this form, and their approach was followed in this example. Since no exact mathematical models exist for the maintenance float problem when the failure distribution is gamma, we were able to validate the simulation model only for the case of the exponential failure distribution ($CV = 1$).

The Metamodel Form

The major task in this section is to estimate the functional relationships between the response variable (EU) and the independent variables (F, S, N, MTTR, MTBF).

Kleijnen [8] discussed the use of metamodels. Essentially, this is based on the use of an ordinary least square (OLS) algorithm to compute the parameters of a regression model. The input data are usually obtained through simulation experiments. One metamodel, presented here, starts by assuming a simple additive regression model such as:

$$Y = \beta_0 + \sum_{i=1}^{K} \beta_i X_i + e \qquad (9.1)$$

where Y is the system response; β_0 is the grand mean; β_i is the coefficients of the factor i; and X_i denotes the ith input factor. From this basic relationship, an appropriate experimental design matrix can be selected. If this model is not suitable, there may be a need to revise the metamodel form. For example, other models may be postulated and their significance tested until the best estimate of EU is obtained. The model of equation 9.1 assumes that only main effects are of interest to the experimenter. In other words, interactions between the different independent variables are ignored or assumed to be negligible. These interaction effects are, therefore, added to the error term.

However, due to the lack of prior knowledge on which main effects or higher-order interactions are important, it is desirable that all the possible two-factor interactions be considered when postulating a metamodel. Our confinement to only two-factor interactions stems from the fact that it is difficult to give practical interpretation to the significance of interaction factors that are more than two [1,6]. We further assume that the simulation model yields a system performance Y equal to the additive effectives of the inputs X_i, $i = 1, \ldots, k$. Thus the following metamodel form is proposed

$$Y = \beta_0 + \sum_{i=1}^{K} \beta_i X_i + \sum_{i \in S} \sum_{j \in S} \beta_{ij} X_i X_j + e \qquad (9.2)$$

where S is a subset of $\{(i,j),\ i < j,\ j = 2, \ldots, n,\ i,j \in positive\ integers\}$, β_{ij} denotes the coefficient of the interaction between the factor i and j.

In the initial stage of the experiment, we recommend the experimenter to anticipate all the possible two-factor interactions. The cost to the experimenter is more runs, however, the experimenter can benefit from gaining some knowledge and by gathering useful evidence.

In the maintenance float problem presented here, the EU is the response variable, and it has to be controlled by the operations managers in order to improve the performance of the maintenance system.

Here, we assume that the failure distribution follows Erlang-2—a special case of the gamma distribution. The Erlang-2 is an example of an increasing failure rate distribution. The metamodel form of equation 9.2 is assumed since we are interested in two-factor interactions in the design. Thus, we postulate a more complex relationship, and those factors found insignificant can be dropped.

Experimental Design and Test

A 2_V^{k-1} factorial design is used in this experiment (Table 9.2). With resolution V, the main effects confound with four-factor interactions while two-factor interactions confound with three-factor interactions. Since we are not interested in both the three- and four-factor interactions, we do not bother with these confounding patterns. We are, therefore, able to estimate both the main effects and the two-factor interactions.

After the simulation outputs are realized (Table 9.3), the ANOVA test is used to analyze the data and determine which of the factors are significant and whether or not any interacted. The ANOVA test is a more direct approach than the use of a stability test, and its results are more definitive and less tedious. With only a single replicate in our simulation study, it is not possible to compute an estimate

Table 9.2
Formal 2_V^{5-1} Fractional Factorial Design

Run	1	2	3	4	5
1	-	-	-	-	+
2	+	-	-	-	-
3	-	+	-	-	-
4	+	+	-	-	+
5	-	-	+	-	-
6	+	-	+	-	+
7	-	+	+	-	+
8	+	+	+	-	-
9	-	-	-	+	-
10	+	-	-	+	+
11	-	+	-	+	+
12	+	+	-	+	-
13	-	-	+	+	+
14	+	-	+	+	-
15	-	+	+	+	-
16	+	+	+	+	+

Source: Box et al. (1978), p. 387.

Table 9.3
The Systematic Assignment of the Levels to the Five Factors and the Simulation Results

Run	F	N	MTBF	MTTR	S	EU
1	1	5	40	8	5	.944
2	5	5	40	8	1	.899
3	1	15	40	8	1	.355
4	5	15	40	8	5	.986
5	1	5	80	8	1	.946
6	5	5	80	8	5	.999
7	1	15	80	8	5	.958
8	5	15	80	8	1	.708
9	1	5	40	20	1	.395
10	5	5	40	20	5	.986
11	1	15	40	20	5	.616
12	5	15	40	20	1	.137
13	1	5	80	20	5	.918
14	5	5	80	20	1	.770
15	1	15	80	20	1	.274
16	5	15	80	20	5	.957

of experimental error [14]. We shall point out that the single replicate used in the experimental design represents the average realizations of EU from the simulation output. Here, we combine higher-order interactions that are negligible to estimate the experimental error. The degrees of freedom of the pooled error are about half of the total degrees of freedom.

Since the sum of square (S.S.) of F*N, F*MTBF, F*MTTR, F*S, N*MTBF, N*MTTR, and MTBF*MTTR are quite low, we pooled them together to estimate the experimental error. The ANOVA table (Table 9.4) shows that N, MTTR, and S are significant at $\alpha = 0.001$, while F, MTBF, N*S, and R*S are significant at $\alpha = 0.01$. By using these main effects and two-factor interactions found significant in the regression model, we obtain the following:

$$EU = 1.0612 + 0.0324*F + 0.0038*MTBF - 0.0326*MTTR -$$
$$0.0526*S - 0.0459*N + 0.00754*S*N + 0.0048*MTTR*S \qquad (9.3)$$

However, notice from Table 9.5 that although S is presented in equation 9.3, it is not statistically significant. Since S is a major decision variable, we may explore the possibility of using transformation to generate a better regression model. Another approach would be to reduce the experimental range of the input variables in order to obtain a significant S. Alternatively, we may drop the main effect of S from equation 9.3 and estimate it from its two-factor interactions as they are shown to be statistically significant. Of all these strategies, it is easiest to

Table 9.4
ANOVA of All Factors

Factor	S.S	D.F.	M.S.	F
F	0.067081	1	0.067801	12.68**
N	0.217622	1	0.217622	41.13***
MTBF	0.091809	1	0.091809	17.35**
MTTR	0.189660	1	0.189660	35.84***
S	0.518400	1	0.518400	97.97***
F*N	0.001122#	1	-	-
F*B	0.008100#	1	-	-
F*R	0.004160#	1	-	-
F*S	0.000169#	1	-	-
N*B	0.000970#	1	-	-
N*R	0.005766#	1	-	-
N*S	0.090902	1	0.090902	17.18**
B*R	0.008010#	1	-	-
B*S	0.023409	1	0.023409	5.82
R*S	0.053130	1	0.053130	10.04**

Pool error: 0.0370400; M.S. of error: 0.0052914; $F_{1.7.0.95} = 5.59$; $F_{1.7.0.99} = 12.25$; $F_{1.7.0.999} = 29.25$.

Table 9.5
Regression Model (without transformation)

Source	M.S.	F	Significant level
Regression	0.175515	23.23	0.0001
Error	0.007556		
$R^2 = 0.953106$			

Estimated parameter	Coefficient	t	Significant level
Intercept	1.06122917	7.26	0.0001
F	0.03237500	2.98	0.0176
MTBF	0.00378750	3.49	0.0083
MTTR	-0.03255208	-4.99	0.0011
S	-0.05260417	-1.50	0.1725
N	-0.04593750	-5.86	0.0004
S*N	0.00753750	3.47	0.0085
MTTR*S	0.00480208	2.65	0.0292

carry out the transformation of variables. Since the functional relationship between EU and the independent variables N, F, S, MTTR, and MTBF are unknown, trial and error was followed to determine the best fit regression model, and a series of transformations was tried. One of these involved the natural logarithmic transformation of each of the independent variables. This transformation seemed to yield a best fit model with all the input variables statistically significant in explaining EU. In fact, this result, which is presented in Table 9.6, is similar to the results obtained in Table 9.5. For example, r^2 is the same at 0.953, and the regression is also statistically significant at (F-ratio = 23.23, p = 0.0001). However, they are dissimilar in the sense that all the variables are statistically significant when this transformation is made. Thus, the regression metamodel for EU with the Erlang-2 failure distribution is expressed as

$$EU = 1.412 + 0.08*Ln(F) + 0.004*MTBF - 0.028*MTTR -$$
$$0.312Ln(S) - 0.35*Ln(N) + 0.17*Ln(S)*Ln(N) + 0.012*MTTR*Ln(S) \qquad (9.4)$$

These models provide new tools to operations managers for identifying the combination of repairpersons (S) and standby units (F) needed to achieve a set service level. EU is of major consideration in this example since the cost of lost production is considered to be exorbitantly high. EU values can also be applied in a cost structure to determine the optimum standby units (F^*) and the optimum number of repairpersons (S^*).

Table 9.6
Regression Model (with transformation)

Source	M.S.	F	Significant level
Regression	0.175515	23.23	0.0001
Error	0.007556		
$R^2 = 0.953106$			

Estimated parameter	Coefficient	t	Significant level
Intercept	1.41154983	8.86	0.0001
LF	0.08046287	2.98	0.0176
MTBF	0.00378750	3.49	0.0083
MTTR	-0.02775000	-5.42	0.0006
Log(S)	-0.31151011	-2.47	0.0390
Log(N)	-0.34953186	-6.25	0.0002
Log(S)*Log(N)	0.17051737	3.47	0.0085
MTTR*Log(S)	0.01193481	2.65	0.0292

SUMMARY

The importance of fractional factorial designs in reducing the number of simulation runs has been illustrated in this chapter. We also demonstrated how a regression metamodel can be developed for a maintenance float problem. It was shown that satisfactory predictions for EU can be obtained through the use of regression metamodels. In general, we can state some of the advantages of the proposed approach as follows: (1) the number of simulation runs required to generate a good explanatory model is significantly reduced through experimental design, (2) it offers a simple and easy to use model, and (3) most important, it enables us to model a complex operations management problem without restrictive assumptions. Notice that existing analytical models deal mostly with exponential failure distributions and the other cases, such as Weibull and the gamma, are often modeled only through simulation. Even for the exponential case, existing models are often complex and difficult to use.

The approach presented in this chapter has wider implications. Apart from offering a simple way to model the maintenance float problem for the more complex failure distributions and equipment replacement rules, this approach can be extended to other complex modeling areas of operations management. Current methods often require either the introduction of limiting assumptions in order to generate an analytical model or the use of extensive computer simulation runs. With the use of fractional factorial designs in developing regression metamodels such assumptions can be relaxed.

REFERENCES

1. Box, G.E.P., W. G. Hunter, and J. S. Hunter. *Statistics for Experimenters.* New York: Wiley, 1978.
2. Chrissis, J. W., and A. S. Grecan. "Multi-echelon System Design via Simulation." *Simulation* 47 (1986): 240–243.
3. Cochran, J. K., and J. Chang. "Optimization of Multivariate Simulation Output Models Using a Group Screening Method." *Computers and Industrial Engineering* 18 (1) (1990): 95–103.
4. Dey, A. *Orthogonal Fractional Factorial Designs.* New York: Wiley, 1985.
5. Friedman, L. W., and I. Pressman. "The Metamodel in Simulation Analysis: Can It Be Trusted?" *Journal of Operational Research Society* 39 (10) (1988): 939–948.
6. Hicks, C. R. *Fundamental Concepts in the Design of Experiments,* 2nd ed. New York: Holt, Rinehart and Winston, 1973.
7. Kelton, W. D. "Statistical Design and Analysis." *Proceedings of the 1986 Winter Simulation Conference,* 1986, 45–51.
8. Kleijnen, J.P.C. *Statistical Tools for Simulation Practitioners.* New York: Marcel Dekker, 1987.
9. Kleijnen, J.P.C., and C. R. Strandridge. "Experimental Design and Regression Analysis in Simulation: An FMS Case Study." *European Journal of Operational Research* 33 (1988): 257–261.
10. Lin, C. "Output Analysis of an Automated Flow Line—Taguchi Experimental Design and Regression Metamodel." *Southeastern Simulation Conference,* 1989, 169–174.
11. Madu, C. N. "Simulation in Manufacturing: A Regression Metamodel Approach." *Computers and Industrial Engineering* 18 (3) (1990): 381–389.
12. Madu, C. N. "Determination of Maintenance Floats Using Buzen's Algorithm." *International Journal of Production Research* 26 (1988a): 1385–1394.
13. Madu, C. N. "A Closed Queuing Maintenance Network with Two Repair Centers." *Journal of the Operational Research Society* 39 (10) (1988b): 959–967.
14. Montgomery, D. C. *Design and Analysis of Experiments.* New York: Wiley, 1984.
15. Solomon, S. L. *Simulation of Waiting-Line Systems.* Englewood Cliffs, NJ: Prentice-Hall, 1983.

Chapter 10

TAGUCHI DESIGNS

INTRODUCTION

Taguchi designs are primarily used in quality control problems for off-line process control. Generally, two orthogonal arrays (i.e., design matrices) are needed. The first array specifies the experimental conditions for the controllable factors, while the second array represents the conditions for the uncontrollable factors. Consequently, an experiment is conducted based on the combination of these two arrays. Byrne and Taguchi [2] discussed a design layout of this form, however, such design layouts are often not suitable in simulation. This is because in most simulation studies, only controllable factors are considered. Since we are dealing only with those independent variables that are controllable, we use a one-array design. This is also often referred to as an inner array Taguchi method. The Taguchi design can be useful in the experimental design of computer simulation.

HISTORICAL BACKGROUND AND USE IN SIMULATION

Apart from those classical experimental design techniques we discussed in Chapter 9, Genichi Taguchi had proposed experimental design tables (i.e., orthogonal array) that are supplemented by the use of linear graphs and triangular interaction tables. His procedures were primarily developed for practitioners to deal with quality control problems [15]. These procedures were initially applied in Japan's manufacturing system. The main purpose of Taguchi designs is to identify the setting of product and process parameters that will reduce performance variation. Many Japanese, European, and US companies have experienced success with Taguchi's strategy for off-line quality control [5,18]. Because Taguchi's method is easy to use, his approach has gained wide applicability in

Japan. It was not until the mid-1980s, however, that the United States became aware of Taguchi's approach [14].

Pignatiello [13] distinguishes two different aspects of the Taguchi method: the Taguchi strategy and the Taguchi tactics. The former is the conceptual framework for planning a product or process design experiment, while the latter is a collection of specific methods and techniques, such as the Taguchi design and signal-to-noise ratios suggested by Taguchi [19].

There are two major characteristics of the Taguchi design: (1) the experimental design and (2) the process to find the optimum level of each controllable factor. In the Taguchi experimental design, main effects and almost all the possible combinations of the two-factor interactions of controllable factors can be considered in the design of an experiment. In the process to find the optimum level of each controllable factor, the effects of each controllable factor and their two factors interactions can be tested by the use of ANOVA as suggested by Taguchi and Wu [17]. Thus, the optimum combination levels and their contributions can be found.

Taguchi experimental design's approach is very efficient because: (1) the statistical techniques are very simple, (2) the number of experiments can be reduced, (3) the significant controllable factors can easily be identified, and (4) it is easy to find the optimum design of a system for decision makers.

Because of these advantages, Taguchi's experimental designs have found widespread applications in both Japan and Taiwan. For instance, Taguchi and Wu [17] reported that in 1976, 2700 experiments conducted in Japan used orthogonal tables. In 1966, Professor Yu-In Wu, one of the authors of the English version of Taguchi's method [17], introduced Taguchi methodology to Taiwan. Since then, this method has gained wide acceptance in several industries. For example, mechanical, electrical, chemical, petroleum, sugar, latex, assembly, and manufacturing industries in Taiwan continue to use Taguchi's method. Recent applications of Taguchi's methods in the United States and in Europe are documented in Taguchi and Wu [18].

Corporations such as General Motors, Chrysler, General Electric, Goodyear, Xerox, AT&T, Texas Instruments, and the International Technology Institute (ITI) have been very successful in applying this method in shortening the product development cycle, improving quality, and reducing costs.

INTRODUCTION TO LINEAR GRAPHS

A unique feature of the Taguchi design is the use of linear graphs and triangular tables. Discussions on the use of these linear graphs, triangular tables, and their relationships to orthogonal array tables are presented in Taguchi and Wu [17], Taguchi [19], Ross [14], and Roy [15].

Roy [15] described linear graphs as follows: "Linear graphs are made up of numbers, dots and lines where a dot and its assigned number identifies a factor, a connecting line between two dots indicates interaction and the number assigned to the line indicates the column number in which interaction effects will be compounded."

Fractional factorial designs are not difficult to generate once the experimenter knows the design generators. However, graphical techniques, such as Taguchi's linear graph, can be easily understood and implemented by practitioners as well as researchers having only a limited knowledge of statistics and experimental design.

GENERATION OF THE ORTHOGONAL ARRAY MATRIX AND DATA COLLECTION

Setting Appropriate Levels

It is seldom clear just what values should be used to test for each factor. Therefore, prior knowledge of the system itself is important. For instance, in a two-level factorial design, Kelton [7] suggested to choose the levels to be extreme in some sense, which needs the judgment by someone familiar with the actual system being simulated. Another suggestion is to use prior information from published papers about a similar system to set the appropriate levels.

Design the Experiment According to an Appropriate Orthogonal Array and Linear Graph

As noted by Kelton [6], a carefully designed course of simulation experimentation sets the stage for an appropriate and effective analysis of the output from these simulations. Therefore, a suitable Taguchi design for a specific problem must be chosen with caution. To design these experiments efficiently, we need a set of tables and simple procedures to construct orthogonal designs with minimum effort. Orthogonal arrays and their linear graphs that were developed by Taguchi [18] satisfy this need very well. Based on the number of factors, the levels of interest and the assumptions about higher order effects, an appropriate orthogonal array can be selected. By referring to linear graph, each factor and its interactions can be assigned to the appropriate columns in the orthogonal array.

For example, Taguchi and Wu [17] suggest the use of a L_{16} orthogonal experimental design (or array) to accommodate five factors with two levels. In the orthogonal array, every pair of columns in the array and all combinations of levels occur an equal number of times. Because of this balanced arrangement, one factor does not influence the estimate of the effect of another factor and vice versa [14]. The L_{16} array (see Table 10.1) specifies that sixteen experimental runs be conducted and used in order to find the best combinations of the 2^5 design. As noted by Byrne et al. [2], this can be done since the design is orthogonal, a property that permits the effect of each factor to be separated out. If all the higher-order interactions, such as two-factor interactions, can be neglected, the number of runs needed can be reduced dramatically.

Table 10.1
$L_{16}(2^{15})$ **Orthogonal Array**

	1	2	3	4	5	6	7	8	9	10	11	12	13	14	15
1	1	1	1	1	1	1	1	1	1	1	1	1	1	1	1
2	1	1	1	1	1	1	1	2	2	2	2	2	2	2	2
3	1	1	1	2	2	2	2	1	1	1	1	2	2	2	2
4	1	1	1	2	2	2	2	2	2	2	2	1	1	1	1
5	1	2	2	1	1	2	2	1	1	2	2	1	1	2	2
6	1	2	2	1	1	2	2	2	2	1	1	2	2	1	1
7	1	2	2	2	2	1	1	1	1	2	2	2	2	1	1
8	1	2	2	2	2	1	1	2	2	1	1	1	1	2	2
9	2	1	2	1	2	1	2	1	2	1	2	1	2	1	2
10	2	1	2	1	2	1	2	2	1	2	1	2	1	2	1
11	2	1	2	2	1	2	1	1	2	1	2	2	1	2	1
12	2	1	2	2	1	2	1	2	1	2	1	1	2	1	2
13	2	2	1	1	2	2	1	1	2	2	1	1	2	2	1
14	2	2	1	1	2	2	1	2	1	1	2	2	1	1	2
15	2	2	1	2	1	1	2	1	2	2	1	2	1	1	2
16	2	2	1	2	1	1	2	2	1	1	2	1	2	2	1

Source: Taguchi and Wu (1980).

Make Simulation Runs for Each Experimental Design Point

At each design point, an appropriate replication (i.e., using different random number seeds) should be chosen.

Since simulation results are random events, a single run at any design point would be meaningless. Therefore, appropriate replications should be conducted. The average of the system responses that result from different random number seeds is considered as the output of this particular design point.

Note that the interaction conditions cannot be controlled when conducting an experiment because they are dependent on the main factor levels. Only the analysis is concerned with the interaction columns.

APPLICATION OF ANOVA (ANALYSIS OF VARIANCE)

Evaluate the Main Effects and Two-Factor Interactions by Taguchi Algorithm

After simulation outputs are realized, it will take a simple computer program only a few seconds to analyze the data and determine which of the factors are significant and whether or not any interacted (i.e., construct the associated ANOVA table). ANOVA is a statistical decision tool for detecting any differences in average performance of the groups of items tested. The major purpose of the ANOVA table is to separate the total variation of the observations into accountable sources, such as factors influences and experimental error. To complete the ANOVA calculations, one other component must be considered, the degrees of freedom (d.f.). A d.f. in a statistical sense is associated with each piece of information that is estimated from the data. Another way to think of the idea of d.f. is to allow 1 d.f. for each independent comparison that can be made in the data [14]. For instance, level 1s of factor A compared to level 2s of factor A has 1 d.f. The following steps are taken in order to obtain the ANOVA for $L_{16}(2^{15})$ design.

1. Calculate the sum of simulation results related to level 1 of each factor and record the results in column 1 of the ANOVA table.
2. Calculate the sum of simulation results related to level 2 of each factor and record the results in column 2 of the ANOVA table.
3. Calculate $[(\text{column } 1 - \text{column } 2)^2 / 16]$.
4. Calculate the sum of all error messages. There are two sources of error messages (or experimental error). One possibility is to use unassigned columns in the orthogonal array to represent an estimate of error variation. Another possibility depends on some smaller column effects relative to others. These smaller effects are used as estimates of the error variance [14,17].
5. Determine the d.f. The d.f. for each factor is the number of levels minus one. The d.f. for an interaction is the product of the interacting factor's d.f. [14].
6. Calculate the mean square for each factor.
7. Calculate the F value.

Experimental design is, in general, a learning and sequential process. As noted by Box et al. [1], the preliminary experimental design and result may be used as building blocks for further analysis. Kuei et al. [9] provide two propositions about choosing additional runs for further analysis on realized experimental results from a series of simulation experiments.

Proposition 1. If any independent factor is significant in the ANOVA, it should be considered as an important independent variable in explaining the system's response.

Proposition 2. If any factor is highly significant (e.g., its mean square is too high compared to other factors), then it may be necessary to change this factor's level from two (or three) levels to other, higher levels in the experimental design.

Interpret the Result

The main effect of a factor should be individually interpreted only if there is no evidence that the factor interacts with other factors [1]. When there is evidence of one or more such interaction effects, the interacting factors should be considered jointly. Taguchi and Wu [17] also suggest the following procedure for data analysis and estimation:

1. Calculate the total of system response by the factor and its level.
2. Divide the total by the number of observations for this factor and its level. This is the estimation of the effect of this factor at this level.
3. Calculate the range of error for these values (i.e., the estimations) by the F distribution. The statistic used is

$$\pm \sqrt{(F_{v1,v2},\alpha, *(V_e/n_e))}$$

where, V_e is the value of the error variance used for verification of factors' significance in the ANOVA, n_e is the mean number of observations for one particular factor and its level, and v_1 and v_2 are the degrees of freedom.

Furthermore, graphical presentation used to supplement the ANOVA table is strongly recommended by Taguchi and Wu [17], Box et al. [1], Hicks [4], and Ryan [16].

CONTRAST WITH THE CLASSICAL STATISTICAL DESIGN

Three experimental designs are considered in the following comparison: full factorial design, fractional factorial design, and the Taguchi design.

These three designs can be compared on five dimensions: (1) number of simulation runs required; (2) ease of implementation; (3) flexibility of the design; (4) recognition of confounding pattern; and (5) ease of analysis. These comparisons are presented in Table 10.2.

Number of Simulation Runs Required

Suppose we consider a two-level design in which eight controllable variables have to be studied. In this case, $2^8 = 256$ experimental conditions have to be

Table 10.2
Evaluation of Three Types of Experimental Designs

Dimensions	FD	FFD	TAGUCHI
1) number of simulation runs required	Large	Small	Small
2) ease of implementation	Yes	No	Yes
3) flexibility of the design	High	Low	Medium
4) recognition of confounding pattern	-	Yes	Yes
5) ease of analysis	Yes	Yes	Yes

FD: Full factorial design; FFD: fractional factorial design

tested with a factorial design. Consequently, all the main effects and all the possible interaction effects can be estimated. Since there are eight variables, the number of effects that can be evaluated is estimated as the combination of x distinct objects out of a total of eight distinct objects, or $\binom{8}{x}$, where $x = 1, 2, \ldots, 8$. However, higher-order interactions are seldom of significance and may be disregarded [1]. In fact, full factorial designs often result in redundancies. Box et al. [1] note that fractional factorial designs exploit these redundancies. If we are, therefore, not interested in higher-order interactions such as three-factor interactions or higher, then a design with resolution V may be selected. With the eight variables discussed here, that will imply a $2_V^{8-2} = 64$ design. Taguchi [19] offers a family of orthogonal arrays that can be used to generate fractional factorial plans.

A comparison of the number of runs required by both the Taguchi orthogonal array and a full factorial design is shown in Table 10.3. Table 10.4 presents a comparison of the number of runs required by both the simplest version of Taguchi orthogonal array and a fractional factorial design with different resolutions. The term "resolution" is used in the experimental design literature to express what can be estimated from a particular fractional factorial design. Box et al. [1] give a detailed discussion of this concept. A comparison of the number of runs required by the Taguchi orthogonal arrays, fractional factorial designs, and full factorial designs with resolution V is shown in Table 10.5.

From Tables 10.3, 10.4, and 10.5, it is observed that greater savings on the number of simulation runs are possible with the use of larger orthogonal arrays or fractional factorial designs. A major part of Taguchi's idea is that some interactions can often be safely neglected based on prior knowledge of a particular problem and quick industrial experiment responses. Moreover, one of his explicit

Table 10.3
A Comparison of Number of Runs Needed Between Taguchi Orthogonal Array and a Full Factorial Design (FD)

Number of factors	Number of levels	Orthogonal array	Number of runs needed for a FD
3	2	L_4	8
7	2	L_8	128
11	2	L_{12}	2048
15	2	L_{16}	32768
31	2	L_{32}	$2.1474 * 10^9$
4	3	L_9	81
13	3	L_{27}	1594323

L_n: the n indicates the number of runs needed for a particular orthogonal array.

Table 10.4

A Comparison of Number of Runs Needed Between Taguchi Design and a Fractional Factorial Design (FFD) with Different Resolutions

Number of factors	Number of levels	Orthogonal array	Number of runs needed for a fractional F.D.		
			III	IV	V
3	2	L_4	4	-	-
7	2	L_8	8	16	-
11	2	L_{12}	16	32	128
4	3	L_9	9	27	-

F.D.: factorial design; L_n: the n indicates the number of runs needed for a particular orthogonal array; III: resolution III design; IV: resolution IV design; V: resolution V design.

Table 10.5

A Comparison of Number of Runs Needed for Two-Level Design with Resolution V

Number of factors	Number of levels	Orthogonal array	F.F.D.	F.D.
4	2	L_{16}	-	16
5	2	L_{16}	16	13
6	2	L_{32}	-	64
7	2	L_{64}	-	128
8	2	L_{64}	64	256
9	2	L_{64}	-	512
10	2	-	128	1024
11	2	-	128	2048

L_n: the n indicates the number of runs needed for a particular orthogonal array.

assumptions is that higher-order interactions, such as three-factor interactions, four-factor interactions, and so on, have no significant effect on experiments in manufacturing industries. Therefore, both fractional factorial design and Taguchi design need smaller numbers of runs compared to that of a full factorial design.

Ease of Implementation

A unique feature of the Taguchi method is the use of linear graphs to generate and implement fractional factorial design plans [19]. These linear graphs serve as graphical aids and are easily applied by industrial practitioners and nonstatisticians. In contrast, the construction of classical fractional factorial designs is not easy. For example, the design generators must be known for the different levels and resolutions of the design. A fraction of the full factorial design is then determined by those generators. When dealing with a large number of controllable factors, the construction of fractional factorial designs becomes extremely difficult.

The implementation of a full factorial design is very easy because the total number of design points in need is simply the product of the number of levels for each factor.

Flexibility of the Design

In the classical approach the most widely used design levels are the two- and three-level designs [1,4]. Taguchi [19] and Ross [14] present a way to modify linear graphs in order to extend two- or three-level designs to even four-, eight-, and nine-level designs. By using a "dummy level technique," a seven-level design plan can be generated from an eight-level design plan by simply duplicating one of the eight levels [14]. Moreover, five-level and mixed-factor-level designs and their corresponding linear graphs have been presented in Taguchi [19]. The use of higher level designs makes it possible to consider polynomial effects when first-order effects do not adequately describe the model.

Mixed-factor-level designs, such as L_{18}, L_{36}, and L_{54} and linear graphs, are also available in Taguchi [19]. When all the two-factor interactions can be assumed to be very small, L_{18} can be used when one two-level factor and seven three-level factors are considered in the experiment; L_{36} can be applied when eleven two-level factors and twelve three-level factors are considered in the experiment; L_{54} can be used when one two-level factor and twenty-five three-level factors are realized. In Box et al. [1] or other experimental design textbooks, the most common designs are 2^k, 2^{k-p}, 3^k, and 3^{k-p}.

Generally, Taguchi design is more flexible when compared to classical fractional factorial experimental designs. A full factorial design is also very flexible. Experimenters can apply any level they want for each factor, but the consequence is that a large number of experimental runs will be required.

Recognition of Confounding Pattern

Taguchi also provides confounding information (i.e., alias structures of main effects and higher-order interactions) in an orthogonal array table [16]. Therefore, it is very easy to identify the confounding pattern for any design. In a classical approach, this information has to be generated by the experimenter. Thus, the confounding information that Taguchi provides can help in effectively selecting an appropriate orthogonal array and then generating a suitable fractional factorial design plan.

Applying Taguchi's design methods could be quite risky if experimenters do not realize the confounding pattern of higher-order interactions in their design. For example, the L_{16} orthogonal array is the same as the 2_V^{5-1} fractional factorial design discussed by Box et al. [1]. This is also obvious from the way we arrange factors and two-factor interactions on the orthogonal array's columns. 2_V^{5-1} fractional factorial design is a resolution V experiment. The resolution power indicates the clarity of which individual factors and interactions may be seen (or evaluated) in an experiment [14]. Suppose we have five factors (A, B, C, D, and E), which are assigned to columns (one, two, four, eight, and fifteen, respectively) (see Table 10.1). Two-factor interactions can be assigned to the remaining columns based on the suitable linear graph. This is the most complex version of L_{16} design. One of the design generators of the classical approach for this particular case is $-ABCDE$. Once the design generator is given, the alias structure can easily be obtained by taking the generalized interactions of the relevant effect with each of the components of the design generator. For instance, if the design generator is $I = -ABCDE$ and the alias structure of A is $-BCDE$, which is a generalized interaction of A and $-BCDE$, the alias relationships are as follows:

A = $-BCDE$;   B = $-ACDE$;   C = $-ABDE$;   D = $-ABCE$;   E = $-ABCD$;

AB = $-CDE$;   AC = $-BDE$;   AD = $-BCE$;   AE = $-BCD$;   BC = $-ADE$;

BD = $-ACE$;   BE = $-ACD$;   CD = $-ABE$;   CE = $-ABD$;   DE = $-ABC$

In view of the aliasing of effects among themselves in a Taguchi fractional factorial set up, assumptions regarding the absence of certain effects have to be made to obtain unbiased estimates of other effects. For example, in the example quoted earlier, A can be estimated under the assumption that the four-factor interaction $-BCDE$ is absent and so on. Also, AB can be estimated under the assumption that the three-factor interaction $-CDE$ is zero or very small and so on. If the simplest version of the L_{16} design is used (i.e., 15 two-level factors experiment), all the higher-order interactions are then assumed to be zero or very small.

Two-level and three-level fractional factorial designs were discussed by Box et al. [1] and Montgomery [12], respectively. Box et al. [1] also provided a comprehensive list of design generators for a two-level fractional factorial design with three to eleven factors.

Thus, desired confounding patterns can be realized in both Taguchi design and standard fractional factorial experimental designs. Obviously, knowledge of the underlying confounding pattern plays a crucial role in applying the Taguchi design as well as the classical fractional factorial experimental design.

Ease of Analysis

Both the Taguchi design as well as the classical fractional factorial design are easy to analyze. Taguchi algorithm for constructing the associated ANOVA table can be applied to two-level, three-level, and multiple-level designs. Using a personal computer, it takes just a few seconds to identify the significant factors and/or two-factor interactions and construct the associated ANOVA table. In the simulation experiment, an experimenter may obtain an experimental response without replication at each design point. In this situation, the Taguchi algorithm for constructing the ANOVA table is also applied, and it is very easy to use. The 2^k and 2^{k-p} designs are also easy to analyze [1].

FINAL REMARKS

Notice that Taguchi's philosophy is not entirely different from the classical design methods. In fact, it can be argued that Taguchi publicized the use of classical experimental designs and perhaps made their applications easier for practitioners by introducing linear graphs, triangular interaction tables, and orthogonal array tables that provide information on confoundedness. Lucas [11] notes that Taguchi publicized the use of statistical designs to achieve a robust process. That is to say that if the process is robust, it will be insensitive to variations in uncontrollable variables.

Lucas [11] further evaluated the classical response surface designs and the Taguchi designs on their ability to achieve a robust design. He also identified some of the similarities between classical and Taguchi designs. Lochner [10] posited that "Western statisticians, over the years, have developed some excellent, sophisticated methods which are generally comparable or superior to Taguchi's methods. However, they spoke in general models rather than specific applications, and communicated in the language of mathematics and theoretical statistics rather than applied engineering" (p. 538). He further notes that "Taguchi developed a practical, innovative approach for designing quality into products and manufacturing processes." While Lochner accepted that most Taguchi methods are simple variations of early experimental results by R. A. Fisher, he pointed out that Taguchi presented them in ways that make them easily understandable and applicable.

Gunter [3] commented on the use of experiment designs as follows: "[T]here is controversy among adherents of various approaches to the application of design of experiments, especially between the advocates of the Taguchi methods vs. those of standard methods. Controversy in science is normal and usually healthy. Unfortunately, much of the present debate seems to have degenerated to the level of argument about which soap powder sells better. This is an argument in which I definitely do not want to get involved. . . . I would like to focus on the need to do something, rather than stand around and do nothing while waiting for the smoke to clear" (p. 63).

REFERENCES

1. Box, G.E.P., W. G. Hunter, and J. S. Hunter. *Statistics for Experimenters.* New York: Wiley, 1978.

2. Byrne, D. M., and S. Taguchi. "The Taguchi Approach and Parameter Design." *Quality Progress* (Dec. 1987): 19–26.

3. Gunter, B. "Statistically Designed Experiments: Part 1: Quality Improvement, the Strategy of Experimentation, and the Road to Hell." *Quality Progress* (Dec. 1989): 63–64.

4. Hicks, C. R. *Fundamental Concepts in the Design of Experiments,* 2nd ed. New York: Holt, Rinehart and Winston, 1973.

5. Kacker, R. N. "Taguchi's Quality Philosophy: Analysis and Commentary." *Quality Progress* (1986): 21–29.

6. Kelton, W. D. "Statistical Design and Analysis." *Proceedings of the 1986 Winter Simulation Conference,* 1986, 45–51.

7. Kelton, W. D. "Designing Computer Simulation Experiments." *Proceedings of the 1988 Winter Simulation Conference,* 1988, 15–18.

8. Kleijnen, J.P.C. *Statistical Tools for Simulation Practitioners.* New York: Marcel Dekker, 1987.

9. Kuei, C. H., M. Chanin, and C. Lin. "Taguchi Design and Regression Analysis for Maintenance Float Decision Models." *Proceedings of 1990 Northeast Decision Sciences Institute,* Saratoga Springs, NY, 320–323.

10. Lochner, R. H. "Pros and Cons of Taguchi." *Quality Engineering* 3 (4) (1991): 537–549.

11. Lucas, J. M. "Using Response Surface Methodology to Achieve a Robust Process." *ASQC Quality Conference Transactions.* Milwaukee, WI, 1991, 383–392.

12. Montgomery, D. C. *Design and Analysis of Experiments.* New York: Wiley, 1984.

13. Pignatiello, J. J. "An Overview of the Strategy and Tactics of Taguchi." *IIE Transactions* (1988): 247–254.

14. Ross, P. J. *Taguchi Techniques for Quality Engineering.* New York: McGraw-Hill Book Company, 1988.

15. Roy, R. *A Primer on the Taguchi Method.* New York: Van Nostrand Reinhold, 1990.

16. Ryan, T. P. *Statistical Methods for Quality Improvement.* New York: Wiley, 1989.

17. Taguchi, C., and Y. Wu. *Introduction to Off-line Quality Control.* Nogoya, Japan: Central Japan Quality Control Association, 1980.

18. Taguchi, C., and Y. Wu. *Taguchi Methods—Case Studies from the U.S. and Europe.* Michigan: ASI Press, 1989.

19. Taguchi, C. *System of Experimental Design.* New York: Kraus International Publications, 1987.

Chapter 11

GROUP SCREENING

INTRODUCTION

It is unwise to investigate all the independent factors in an experiment simultaneously when large numbers of variables are involved. Box et al. [1] suggested the use of a sequential approach as an investigation strategy. They indicated that no more than 25% of the experimental effort should be spent in the initial design. Kleijnen [5] also presented a procedure for sequential simulation experimentation. In this procedure, the initial experiment depends on the number of controllable factors that must be studied. If there are very few input factors, a resolution III design that estimates only main effects can be used. Follow-up experiments may be conducted to consider two-factor interactions. This approach was implemented by Kleijnen and Strandridge [6] in modeling a flexible manufacturing system.

If, however, there are many controllable factors to be considered, a group-screening design should be used [4]. It is, however, recommended that, in this case, resolutions IV or higher should be used in order to study interaction effects [4].

A group screening method was first introduced by Watson [15]. With this method, individual factors at two levels are partitioned into groups. By assigning the same level to all members within each group, the groups are then referred to as group-factors. In the initial stage of an experiment, group-factors are evaluated as if they were single factors. In the follow-up experiment, only the individual factors within the significant groups are tested.

GROUPING OF FACTORS

Cochran and Chang [2] pointed out that some prior knowledge of the factors is required in order to group them. They summarize grouping techniques as follows:

1. If the direction of the factor is unknown, put this factor in one group.
2. Put the positive important factors in one group.
3. Put the factors with the same direction and possible effect in one group.
4. Put the factors with the same direction and little effect in one group.

Because the number of group-factors is much smaller than the original number of the controllable factors, we can easily evaluate them. Cochran and Chang [2] suggested the use of full factorial design in order to avoid missing any interaction between factors if there are only three or four groups. However, when there are more than four groups, fractional factorial design can be used since higher-order interactions (e.g., three-factor interactions) are often not important. We must, however, point out that there is a trade-off in using highly fractionated designs. For example, when they are used it becomes difficult to estimate some higher-order interactions.

TEST FOR SIGNIFICANCE OF GROUPS

As discussed previously, the group-screening technique is used to aggregate the independent factors into groups of factors. Each group of factors is referred to as a group-factor. If a group-factor is not significant, it is concluded that all its members are not important. In other words, we should drop all the members of that group from further analysis. If some of the group-factors are significant, then further investigation of those significant group-factors is required.

The present technique thus serves as a good means of screening out significant factors. A considerable amount of time is saved by not focusing specifically on each factor at the initial phase of the experiment. Rather, they are categorized and studied as groups.

As a result, a systematic approach is needed to separate out the effect of each factor. Analysis of variance (ANOVA) tests [7,9] and stability analysis tests [6] are useful in detecting the factors that are statistically significant. Many experimenters prefer to analyze their experiments using a normal probability paper that requires a graphical plot of effects and visual identification of the significant factors. We, however, shall use the ANOVA.

EXPANSION OF THE TESTS

In this stage, all the single factors in the significant group-factors found in the previous stage are disaggregated and their main effects and/or two-factor interaction effects are further investigated in a follow-up experiment.

AN ILLUSTRATION

The procedure for using the group-screening method and Taguchi design is presented in Figure 11.1. First an operation's problem must be defined and a

Figure 11.1
Methodology for the Illustration

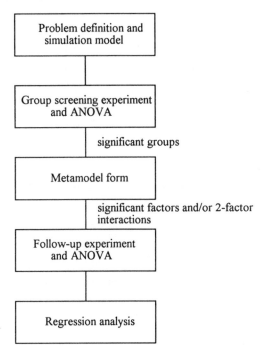

simulation model developed for the given system. Second, an appropriate grouping technique should be chosen. Once this is done, a suitable Taguchi's orthogonal array, which is of resolution IV or higher design, is selected. ANOVA is then carried out on the realized simulation results. Third, an appropriate metamodel structure for significant individual factors is then proposed. Fourth, based on the metamodel structure, Taguchi design is used to generate the experimental design plan. The ANOVA procedure is used to test the significance of the independent variables. Finally, a regression metamodel is developed based on the results of the ANOVA tests.

Problem Definition and Simulation Model

We shall extend the maintenance float problem presented in Chapter 9 to the case where there are two manufacturing cells. Figure 11.2 is used to depict that system [9].

There are three major parts in the simulation model. The first and second parts consist of one manufacturing cell with a supply of standby units, respectively. The third part represents the repair shop. A transaction is used to simulate a major component of a machine while the machines themselves are simulated

Figure 11.2
Two Manufacturing Cells Maintenance Float System

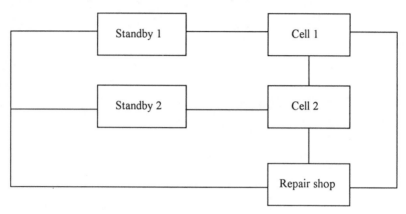

with a storage. When a unit fails, it is replaced by a standby in its own cell if one exists. Meanwhile, the failed unit is sent to the repair shop. When the unit is repaired, it is returned to its own cell's standby node. The repair persons are also simulated with a storage. The failed unit goes into repair after it captures one of the repair persons. This procedure is implemented on general purpose systems simulation (GPSS).

From the problem description, eight individual factors affect this maintenance float system's operation and their assumed levels are enclosed in parentheses next to the definition of variables.

S: The number of repair persons (10 and 15).

$MTTR$: Mean time to repair (5 and 7).

B_1:   Mean time between failure of manufacturing cell 1 (20 and 24).

B_2:   Mean time between failure of manufacturing cell 2 (10 and 12).

F_1:   The number of standby units for manufacturing cell 1 (5 and 10).

F_2:   The number of standby units for the manufacturing cell 2 (5 and 10).

N_1:   The number of machines in the manufacturing cell 1 (15 and 20).

N_2:   The number of machines in the manufacturing cell 2 (10 and 15).

Here we are interested in the relationship between the dependent variables, which are the average equipment utilization (EU) of both cells, and all the independent variables—S, MTTR, B_1, B_2, F_1, F_2, N_1, and N_2.

Because only two levels are considered for each of the independent variables, the system responses are assumed to be approximately linear [3]. Since there are a total of eight independent variables in this problem, a 2_V^{8-2} design will entail conducting sixty-four simulation runs if only two levels are considered. Thus, if ten replications are appropriate for each run, a total of 640 simulation runs will be required. Clearly, even the use of fractional factorial design would result in a large number of simulation runs. Therefore, a group-screening technique is needed in the initial stage of this experiment.

Group Screening Experiment and Test for Significance of Groups

As suggested by Cochran and Chang [2] and also based on the extensive study of these independent variables by Kuei et al. [7], the following group-factors were generated:

1. X_1: N_1 and N_2
2. X_2: F_1 and F_2
3. X_3: B_1 and B_2.
4. X_4: MTTR
5. X_5: S

Using this technique, the independent variables have been reduced from eight to five. Group-factors 1 and 4 are based on rule number 3, and group-factors 2, 3, and 5 are based on rule number 2 as provided in this list.

These five group-factors were further evaluated using the L_{16} orthogonal array. Taguchi [14] and Roy [12] presented a design matrix that has fifteen column assignments to the independent variables consisting of the main effects and the two-factor interaction effects. This column assignment is followed in this example.

The L_{16} orthogonal array provides an efficient orthogonal (balanced) design to accommodate the five group-factors at two levels each. Again, the objective of this design is to find the best combination of the $2^5 = 32$ combinations that exist. This is possible since the orthogonality of the design permits the effect of each factor to be separated out. The group factors considered in the L_{16} array are all controllable and there are no noise (or uncontrollable) factors considered. Thus, we are dealing with an inner array. Clearly, the use of group screening has helped to reduce the number of design points from 256 to 16.

The ANOVA tests for EU1 (i.e., the equipment utilization of first cell) show that X_1, X_4, and X_5 are statistically significant at $\alpha = 0.01$, while X_3, X_4*X_5, and X_1*X_5 are significant at $\alpha = 0.05$. Since the Sum of Square (S.S.) value of the interaction terms X_1*X_2, X_1*X_3, X_2*X_3, X_2*X_4, X_3*X_5, X_3*X_4, X_2*X_5 are relatively small, they are used to estimate the error variance [11]. The pooled error is obtained as 0.001308.

For EU2 (i.e., the equipment utilization of second cell), the ANOVA tests show that X_4 is significant at $\alpha = 0.001$, while X_1 and X_5 are significant at $\alpha = 0.01$. Furthermore, X_2, X_3, X_4*X_5, and X_1*X_5 are significant at $\alpha = 0.05$. Since the S.S. values of the interaction terms X_1*X_2, X_1*X_3, X_2*X_3, X_2*X_4, X_3*X_5, X_3*X_4, and X_2*X_5 are relatively small, they are used as estimates of the error variance. The pooled error is estimated as 0.002538.

These tests confirm that all the group-factors are significant. As a result, further investigation of all the group-factors is required.

Metamodel Form

Metamodel forms for EU1 and EU2 are proposed based on the information derived from the group-screening tests. In other words, all the single factors in the significant group-factors found in the previous stage are disaggregated and their main effects and/or two-factor interaction effects are further investigated in a follow-up experiment. A general predictor model for the two cases follows.

$$EU_i = \beta_0 + \sum_{j=1}^{8} \beta_j x_j + \sum_{j=1}^{7} \sum_{k=j+1}^{8} \beta_{jk} x_j x_k \tag{11.1}$$

where $i = 1, 2$.

Here, EU_i is the system performance measure—average equipment utilization; β_0 is the grand mean; β_j is the coefficients of the factor j; x_j is the value of the jth input factors (i.e., x_1: S; x_2: MTTR; x_3: B_1; x_4: B_2; x_5: F_1; x_6: F_2; x_7: N_1; x_8: N_2); and the coefficient β_{jk} denotes interaction between the factors j and k.

The adequacy of this model is tested in a follow-up experiment.

Follow-up Experiment and Test for Significance of Individual Variables

An L_{32} orthogonal array is used to obtain the experimental design. Again, this orthogonal array matrix is presented in Taguchi [14] and Roy [12]. The column assignments are made as follows: First, assign those factors that are assumed to have interaction effects to the nodes of the linear graph (L_{32}). Since factors N_1, N_2, F_1, F_2, R, and S may have interaction effects, they are assigned accordingly to columns 1, 2, 4, 8, 15, and 16. Once the main effects have been assigned, the assignment for the interaction effects is easily made. Since B_1 and B_2 have no joint effects [7], they are arbitrarily assigned to nodes twenty-two and twenty-five, respectively. These two nodes are among the free nodes of an $L_{32}(2^{31})$ linear graph shown in Table 11.1. The systematic assignment of the levels to the eight factors are presented in Table 11.1 with the corresponding values of EU1 and EU2 obtained after thirty-two simulation runs with ten replications.

The ANOVA tests show (see Table 11.2) that MTTR and S are statistically significant at $\alpha = 0.001$, while N_1, F_1, and MTTR*S are significant at $\alpha = 0.01$. N_2, B_1, and B_2 are also found to be significant at $\alpha = 0.05$. $S*N_1$ is also found to be significant at $\alpha = 0.1$. Since the S.S. values of N_1*N_2, N_1*F_1, N_2*F_1,

Table 11.1
The Systematic Assignment of the Levels to the Eight Factors and the Simulation Results

Run No.	N_1	N_2	F_1	F_2	B_1	B_2	MTTR	S	EU_1	EU_2
1	20	12	10	10	24	12	7	15	.985	.930
2	20	15	10	10	20	10	7	10	.703	.516
3	20	15	10	5	24	10	5	15	.999	.885
4	20	15	10	5	20	12	5	10	.975	.826
5	20	15	5	10	24	12	5	15	.967	.992
6	20	15	5	10	20	10	5	10	.907	.866
7	20	15	5	5	24	10	7	15	.892	.742
8	20	15	5	5	20	12	7	10	.805	.642
9	20	10	10	10	24	12	5	15	.999	.999
10	20	10	10	10	20	10	5	10	.993	.977
11	20	10	10	5	24	10	7	15	.984	.842
12	20	10	10	5	20	12	7	10	.947	.772
13	20	10	5	10	24	12	7	15	.946	.991
14	20	10	5	10	20	10	7	10	.708	.764
15	20	10	5	5	24	10	5	15	.983	.943
16	20	10	5	5	20	12	5	10	.950	.942
17	15	15	10	10	24	10	5	15	.999	.984
18	15	15	10	10	20	12	5	10	.990	.946
19	15	15	10	5	24	12	7	15	.998	.836
20	15	15	10	5	20	10	7	10	.893	.534
21	15	15	5	10	20	10	7	15	.920	.885
22	15	15	5	10	24	12	7	10	.832	.761
23	15	15	5	5	20	12	5	15	.985	.927
24	15	15	5	5	24	10	5	10	.977	.835
25	15	10	10	10	20	10	7	15	.995	.973
26	15	10	10	10	24	12	7	10	.977	.926
27	15	10	10	5	20	12	5	15	.999	.968
28	15	10	10	5	24	10	5	10	.999	.926
29	15	10	5	10	24	10	5	15	.993	.998
30	15	10	5	10	20	12	5	10	.976	.996
31	15	10	5	5	24	12	7	15	.973	.911
32	15	10	5	5	20	10	7	10	.875	.752

Table 11.2
The ANOVA Table for the EU1

Factor	S.S.	D.F.	F
N_1	0.012720	1	8.89**
N_2	0.006903	1	4.83*
F_1	0.017391	1	12.16**
MTTR	0.049455	1	34.57***
S	0.038503	1	26.92***
$S*N_1$	0.005618	1	3.93
B_1	0.007875	1	5.51*
B_2	0.007320	1	5.12*
MTTR*S	0.198000	1	13.84**

$*F_{1,22,0.95} = 4.3$.
$**F_{1,22,0.99} = 7.95$.
$***F_{1,22,0.999} = 14.38$.
S.S. of error $= \Sigma e_i + N1*N2 + N1*F1 + N2*F1 + MTTR*F2 + F2 + N1*F2 + N2*F2 + F1*MTTR + F1*F2 + N2*MTTR + N1*MTTR + S*N2 + S*F1 + B1*N1 + F2*S + N2*B2 = 0.03146$; D.F. of error $= 22$; Pooled error $=$ S.S. of error/D.F. of error $= 0.00143$.

$MTTR*F_2$, F_2, N_1*F_2, N_2*F_2, F_1*MTTR, F_1*F_2, N_2*MTTR, N_1*MTTR, $S*N_2$, $S*F_1$, B_1*N_1, F_2*S, and N_2*B_2 are relatively small, they are used to estimate the error variance. The other source of the error variance is estimated from the unassigned columns of 19, 21, 26, 28, 29, and 30 from the L_{32} linear graph [11,14]. The pooled error is, therefore, 0.00143.

These tests yield an alternative metamodel that can be expressed as

$$EU1 = \beta_0 + \beta_1 N_1 + \beta_2 N_2 + \beta_3 F_1 + \beta_4 MTTR + \beta_5 S + \beta_6 B_1$$
$$+ \beta_7 B_2 + \beta_{15} N_1 S + \beta_{45} SMTTR \qquad (11.2)$$

A similar ANOVA procedure is followed for EU2 (see Table 11.3). The results show that N_2, F_2, MTTR, S, B_2 and R*S are significant at $\alpha = 0.001$, while N_2*MTTR and $S*N_2$ are significant at $\alpha = 0.01$. In addition, B_1 is significant at $\alpha = 0.05$. Again, since the S.S. value of N_1, N_1*N_2, F_1, N_1*F_1, N_2*F_1, $MTTR*F_2$, N_1*F_2, N_2*F_2, F_1*MTTR, F_1*F_2, N_1*MTTR, $S*N_1$, $S*F_1$, B_1*N_1, F_2*S, and N_2*B_2 were very small, they are used in conjunction with those for the unassigned columns to estimate the error variance. The obtained pooled error estimate is 0.001355.

Also, an alternative metamodel for EU2 is proposed:

$$EU2 = \beta_0 + \beta_1 N_2 + \beta_2 F_2 + \beta_3 MTTR + \beta_4 S + \beta_5 B_1 + \beta_6 B_2$$
$$+ \beta_{13} N_2 MTTR + \beta_{14} N_2 S + \beta_{34} SMTTR \qquad (11.3)$$

Table 11.3
The ANOVA Table for the EU2

Factor	SSE	D.F.	F
N_2	0.077322	1	57.05***
F_2	0.046588	1	34.37***
N_2*MTTR	0.011137	1	8.22**
MTTR	0.155821	1	114.96***
S	0.104082	1	76.79***
S_2*N_2	0.014663	1	10.82**
B_1	0.010476	1	7.73*
B_2	0.027789	1	20.50***
MTTR*S	0.035178	1	25.95***

*$F_{1.22.0.95}$ = 4.3.
**$F_{1.22.0.99}$ = 7.95.
***$F_{1.22.0.999}$ = 14.38.
S.S. of error = Σe_i + N1 + N1*N2 + F1 + N1*F1 + N2*F1 + MTTR*F2 + N1*F2 + N2*F2 + F1*MTTR + F1*F2 + N1*MTTR + S*N1 + S*F1 + B1*N1 + F2*S + N2*B2 = 0.02981; D.F. of error = 22; Pooled error = S.S. of error/D.F. of error = 0.001355.

Regression Analysis

Regression analysis is further used to test the two proposed metamodels. The data obtained from the follow-up experiment (see Table 11.1) is implemented into this statistical module. The regression metamodel derived for EU1 can be stated as:

$$EU1 = 1.562 - 0.008*N_1 - 0.006N_2 + 0.009*F_1 - 0.161*MTTR$$
$$-0.045*S + 0.008*B_1 + 0.015*B_2 + 0.01*MTTR*S \qquad (11.4)$$

It is further observed that EU1 is significantly related to the input factors proposed in equation 11.2 ($R^2 = 0.8113$, $p = 0.0001$) (see Table 11.4).

$$EU_2 = 2.140 - 0.062N_2 + 0.015F_2 - 0.235MTTR - 0.099S$$
$$+ 0.009B_1 + 0.029B_2 + 0.013MTTR*S + 0.003N_2*S \qquad (11.5)$$

The regression analysis for equation (11.5) is presented in Table 11.5. An analysis of residuals is further conducted to test the aptness of the regression metamodel [10].

The residual plot shows that there are no systematic patterns. Also notice that by using the group-screening technique and the Taguchi design in the two stages of this experiment, a total of sixteen simulation runs were required in the first

Table 11.4
Analysis of Variance for EU1

Source	Mean square	F	Significance level
Regression	0.15987830	12.36	0.0001
error	0.03718380		
$R^2 = 0.811305$			

Estimated parameter	coefficient	t	Significance level
Intercept	1.5619630	6.11	0.0001
N_1	-0.0081984	-2.88	0.0084
N_2	-0.0059586	-2.05	0.0517
F_1	0.0091015	3.20	0.0040
MTTR	-0.1614530	-4.45	0.0002
S	-0.0447078	-2.58	0.0166
B_1	0.0075644	2.13	0.0444
B_2	0.0145664	2.05	0.0522
MTTR*S	0.0097265	3.42	0.0024

There is also a significant relationship between EU2 and all the input factors proposed in the equation (11.3) except for the N_2*MTTR. The R^2 is 0.92 and p is 0.00001.

Table 11.5
Analysis of Variance for EU2

Source	Mean square	F	Significance level
Regression	0.05899031	33.13	0.0001
error	0.00178073		
$R^2 = 0.920144$			

Estimated parameter	Coefficient	t	Significance level
Intercept	2.1398437	6.65	0.0001
N_2	-0.0624750	-4.11	0.0004
F_2	0.0152625	5.11	0.0001
MTTR	-0.2355625	-6.19	0.0001
S	-0.0995750	-4.24	0.0003
B_1	0.0090469	2.43	0.0235
B_2	0.0294687	3.95	0.0006
MTTR*S	0.0132625	4.44	0.0002
N_2*S	0.0034250	2.87	0.0087

stage and thirty-two simulation runs were required in the second stage. Thus, a total of forty-eight rather than sixty-four simulation runs were conducted. Also, notice that a full factorial design would have required a total of 256 simulation runs.

EU1 is not equal to EU2 since the load intensity at cells 1 and 2 of Figure 11.2 are different. Also, the pool of standby units, mean time between failure and the size of N differ for these two cells even though they have a common service center. The regression metamodel obtained through this approach can be applied in a cost structure.

SUMMARY

This chapter illustrates an application of a group-screening technique to a multiechelon maintenance float system with eight independent variables. Since it is often difficult to obtain an easy to use analytical model for such problems, it becomes necessary to use simulation models. There are problems, however, with the use of simulation. One is the fact that it is difficult to generalize simulation results. Second, it is difficult to determine the appropriate levels for each of the independent variables. The model proposed depends on the decision maker's knowledge of the possible ranges of the independent variables. Experimental design techniques are then used to determine the required number of simulation runs; the L^k design and, in most cases, the 2^k design are the most popular. As discussed previously, a prohibitive number of simulation runs would still be required. Even when fractional designs are followed, we encounter the problem of confounding patterns. Furthermore, they may still require a large number of simulation runs. A group-screening design is presented and applied in generating the design plan for the multiechelon maintenance float problem. In this case, factors that share common attributes are grouped into the same class, and these classes now replace the original number of independent variables in the simulation experiment. Fractional factorial designs can then be applied in order to reduce the number of required simulation runs. This approach, in effect, reduces the number of simulation runs by grouping factors into classes that have common characteristics. On this basis, simulation becomes attractive in solving complex problems.

REFERENCES

1. Box, G.E.P., W. G. Hunter, and J. S. Hunter. *Statistics for Experiments*. New York: Wiley, 1978.
2. Cochran, J. K., and J. Chang. "Optimization of Multivariate Simulation Output Models Using a Group Screening Method." *Computers and Industrial Engineering* 18 (1) (1990): 95–103.
3. Hicks, C. R. *Fundamental Concepts in the Design of Experiments*, 2nd ed. New York: Holt, Rinehart and Winston, 1973.

4. Kleijnen, J.P.C. "Screening Designs for Poly-factor Experimentation." *Technometrics* 17 (4) (1975): 487–493.

5. Kleijnen, J.P.C. *Statistical Tools for Simulation Practitioners.* New York: Marcel Dekker, 1987.

6. Kleijnen, J.P.C., and C. R. Strandridge. "Experimental Design and Regression Analysis in Simulation: An FMS Case Study." *European Journal of Operational Research* 33 (1988): 257–261.

7. Kuei, C. H., M. Chanin, and E. Lin. "Taguchi Design and Regression Analysis for Maintenance Float Decision Models." *Proceedings of 1990 Northeast Decision Sciences Institute,* Saratoga Springs, NY, 1990, 320–323.

8. Madu, C. N., and M. N. Chanin. "A Regression Metamodel of a Maintenance Float Problem with Erlang-2 Failure Distribution." *International Journal of Production Research* 30 (4) (1992): 871–885.

9. Madu, C. N., and C. H. Kuei. "Group Screening and Taguchi Design in the Optimization of Multi-echelon Maintenance Float Simulation Metamodels." *Computers and Operations Research* 19 (2) (1992): 95–105.

10. Neter, J., W. Wasserman, and M. H. Kutner. *Applied Linear Statistical Models.* Homewood, IL: Irwin, 1985.

11. Ross, P. J. *Taguchi Techniques for Quality Engineering.* New York: McGraw-Hill, 1988.

12. Roy, R. *A Primer on the Taguchi Method.* New York: Van Nostrand Reinhold, 1990.

13. Ryan, T. P. *Statistical Methods for Quality Improvement.* New York: Wiley, 1989.

14. Taguchi, C. *System of Experimental Design.* New York: Kraus International Publications, 1987.

15. Watson, G. S. "A Study of the Group Screening Method." *Technometrics* 3 (3) (1961): 371–388.

Chapter 12

POLYNOMIAL DECOMPOSITION

INTRODUCTION

This chapter combines polynomial regression method and three-level Taguchi design to examine the nonlinear effects of certain quantitative variables that influence the primary response variable of a complex production system. A polynomial decomposition method is used to determine the significant factors [8].

SEQUENTIAL APPROACH IN SIMULATION EXPERIMENT

Box et al. [2] noted that the best time to design an experiment is after it is completed. Clearly, more information is available by the time the experiment is completed. It is inconceivable, however, to conduct an experiment when all the required information has become available.

In simulation studies, we are often confronted with a large number of independent variables whose influence on the dependent variable may be unknown or not easily determined. The dilemma faced by the experimenter is how to obtain crucial information with a limited number of simulation runs before a full-blown experiment may be carried out. This is necessary because it is very expensive to conduct simulation experiments, especially when the experimenter is unaware of the relationships between the dependent and the set of independent variables.

Kleijnen [6] recommended the use of fewer observations in the early stages of the experiment and then increasing the number of observations as the need arises. Anderson and Mclean [1] discussed a more formal approach by using two-level designs in the early stage of the experiment and, consequently, introducing more levels of the significant input variables. Delahey and Emirinia [3] recommended the use of fractional factorial designs at the beginning stage of an experiment to explore the relationship between the dependent and independent variables. More complex designs may then be introduced for detailed analysis. Mason et al. [1] also discussed a special class of fractional factorial designs known as the Plackett-Burman designs. However, these designs are of resolution III and are, therefore, only able to clearly estimate main effects if all other effects are assumed to be negligent.

Lochner and Matar [9] caution against the use of three- or more level factorial designs in initial experimentation. Such designs often require a considerable amount of experimental trials, may have confounding relationships that are difficult to identify, and do not include easily understood interaction effects.

CONSIDERATION OF LINEAR VARIABLES

Thus, we initiate a simulation experiment by assuming that the Y, which is the major factor of interest or the dependent variable, is linear over the range of the controllable factors being considered. Only two levels of each of these input factors were, therefore, considered in developing the experimental plan. If we further assume that these input factors may interact, then the following mathematical model may be proposed:

$$Y = \beta_0 + \sum_{i=1}^{K} \beta_i x_i + \sum_{i<j}^{K} \sum_{j=2} \beta_{ij} x_i x_j + e, \qquad i = 1, \ldots, n \qquad (12.1)$$

where Y is the value of system performance (i.e., EU in our example); x_i is the value of the ith input factors; β_0 is the grand mean; β_i is the coefficients of the factor i; β_{ij} denotes the coefficient of interaction between factors i and j; and e is the error term (i.e., the experimental error). In general, this model allows us to study the linear main effects and the two-factor interactions of the independent variables.

Based on the proposed mathematical model, an appropriate full factorial or fractional factorial design could be selected. Simulation outputs were then generated according to the experimental design plan. The appropriate design for this particular experiment is the L_{16} fractional factorial design [14]. This choice is made in order to estimate the main effects of the independent variables and their two-factor interaction effects with as little data as possible. Also, note that the assumption of the linear main effects is consistent with this design since only two levels of each of the independent variables are considered.

CONSIDERATION OF NONLINEAR EFFECTS

In order to examine the nonlinear effects of quantitative factors and their interactions, more than two-level designs are needed. Since cubic and other higher-order effects are often difficult to interpret [12], we are concerned only with quadratic effects. Usually, a three-level factorial design is used at the follow-up stage and only those factors with significant linear effects at the initial stage are decomposed in order to study the significance of their quadratic terms. In order to estimate both linear and quadratic effects with three-level designs, it is required that all the independent variables be quantitatively defined and that their levels be equally spaced [12]. As a result, the mid-values of these variables are used to establish one of the three levels while their extreme values are used to represent the other two levels.

Again, if we maintain the definition of terms as in equation (12.1), a new model results from this polynomial consideration. This model is stated as equation (12.2). However, in this model, the independent variables may have linear and quadratic main and two-factor interaction effects.

$$
Y = \beta_0 + \sum_{i=1}^{K} \beta_i x_i + \sum_{i=1}^{K} \beta_i x_i^2 + \sum_{i<j} \sum_{j=2}^{K} \beta_{ij} x_i x_j
$$

$$
+ \sum_{i<j} \sum_{j=2}^{K} \beta_{ij} x_i x_j^2 + \sum_{i<j} \sum_{j=2}^{K} \beta_{ij} x_i^2 x_j
$$

$$
+ \sum_{i<j} \sum_{j=2}^{K} \beta_{ij} x_i^2 x_j^2 + e \tag{12.2}
$$

Based on this mathematical model, an L_{81} orthogonal array is used [14]. Again, the choice of an L_{81} design is a function of the number of effects we intend to estimate. For example, we should be able to estimate the main effects (linear and quadratic) of all the independent variables and also the mixture of linear and quadratic interaction effects between these variables. We should also select the design that is capable of estimating these terms with the least number of simulation runs. Input factors are then assigned to the appropriate columns on the L_{81} orthogonal array due to the corresponding linear graph.

ANOVA APPROACH TO POLYNOMIAL DECOMPOSITION

The ANOVA (analysis of variance) procedure is used to compute the Sum of Squares (S.S.) of the input factors and interaction terms. Since each factor is set at three levels, the linear and quadratic responses for the significant factors can be estimated.

Once the S.S. of main effect or interaction effects are decomposed into polynomial effects, the smaller insignificant polynomial effects are pooled in order to estimate the error term. The F-ratio test is then used to determine if any of the hypotheses presented in equation (12.2) is statistically significant.

AN ILLUSTRATION

In the following example, the polynomial regression method is used in conjunction with the Taguchi design to model the average equipment utilization (EU) for a maintenance float system.

Problem Definition

Consider a manufacturing or a service facility where a fixed number of machines is used to provide goods and services to customers. Due to demand fluctuations, the required number of machines varies between five and fifteen units. Also, it has been determined from experience that between one and five repairpersons will be required to maintain and repair the machines. Similarly, the mean time to repair has been estimated to vary from 4 to 10 hours; the mean time between failures varies from 20 to 40 hours; and the number of standby units varies from 1 to 5 units. Management is interested in determining a satisfactory number of standby units and repairpersons to satisfy a prespecified service level. Furthermore, management is concerned with the high cost of machine downtime and intends to minimize this cost by implementing optimum levels of standby units and repairpersons for any given value of the independent variables within the specified ranges. This mode of operation was presented in Figure 9.1.

In order to address these issues, we resort to simulation. But first we shall define the major variables of this problem; in parentheses the three levels of these variables in the design are shown.

N: Number of machines initially in operation (5, 10, 15).

S: Number of repairpersons (1, 3, 5).

R: Mean time to repair (MTTR) (4, 7, 10).

F: Number of standby machines (1, 3, 5).

B: Mean time between failure (MTBF) (20, 30, 40).

EU: Average equipment utilization.

Prior Knowledge

Kuei et al. [7] examined the effects of several controllable factors, such as the number of machines initially in operation (N), the number of repairpersons (S), the mean time to repair (R), and the number of standby machines (F) on the maintenance float system response—average EU. They considered two extreme levels and found that N, S, R, F, N*S, N*R, and S*R have significant effects on EU.

However, their study assumed that the EU response surface is linear over the range of the controllable factors. Thus, only two levels of each of these factors were used in developing the metamodel for EU. In such cases, the 2^k factorial or the fractional factorial designs can be helpful in estimating linear effects [4,10]. Although the assumption of linear effects is advantageous because of its simplicity, quadratic effects may present smaller prediction bias. Polynomial approximations (metamodels) are nonlinear in the independent variables but linear in the regression parameters. Thus, linear regression analysis applies.

In order to examine the quadratic effects of quantitative factors, designs with more than two levels are needed. With a three-level factor design it is possible to estimate both first-order linear and quadratic effects.

Simulation Model and Research Hypotheses

GPSS/H is used to code the simulation model, which was subsequently implemented on a personal computer. The simulation model has only one major segment, namely the machine breakdown, repair, and return process. We use the storage block in GPSS/H to represent an operating facility with N identical machines, and the repair shop with S repairpersons. The transactions generated for the model represent the number of machines. Since standby units or floats are considered, they are simply added to N. In this example, it is assumed that repair and failure times follow the exponential distribution. A steady-state realization of EU was obtained when the simulation clock was set to 124,800 hours. The average of thirty replications of EUs is used in the study for a design point.

Eight hypotheses emerge as we consider the respective main and interaction effects of the independent variables on the only dependent variable—EU. These hypotheses are stated in the null form in Table 12.1. The failure to reject a specific null hypothesis will indicate that the corresponding main effect or interaction term is not significant in determining EU.

In order to test the significance of these hypotheses, each of the independent variables is considered at three levels. This enables us to study the polynomial (i.e., quadratic) effects of the independent variables. The values assigned to the three levels, as already stated, are equally spaced. The use of equally spaced levels makes it easier to solve linear and quadratic regression problems. This also follows from the use of orthogonal polynomials where the equispaced levels are

Table 12.1
Test for Main and Interaction Effects on EU

H_1: N has no impact on the EU.
H_2: S has no impact on the EU.
H_3: R has no impact on the EU.
H_4: F has no impact on the EU.
H_5: B has no impact on the EU.
H_6: N*S has no impact on the EU.
H_7: N*R has no impact on the EU.
H_8: S*R has no impact on the EU.

---

coded such that the sum of the coefficients is zero. For the three levels used here, the coefficients of the orthogonal polynomial are $-1, 0, 1$ and $1, -2, 1$ for linear and quadratic polynomials, respectively. Unequally spaced levels would also permit the estimation of quadratic effects. For example, in central composite designs, the five unequally spaced levels are symmetric around the center. The coefficients of the orthogonal polynomial for that case would be $2, -1, -2, -1, 2$ for a quadratic polynomial.

Orthogonal Array and Linear Graph

Table 12.2 shows an $L_{27}(3^{13})$ orthogonal array design, which is capable of examining thirteen three-level factors in twenty-seven runs or examining three to

Table 12.2
$L_{27}(3^{13})$ Orthogonal Array

Col. #	1	2	3	4	5	6	7	8	9	10	11	12	13
Run #													
1	1	1	1	1	1	1	1	1	1	1	1	1	1
2	1	1	1	1	2	2	2	2	2	2	2	2	2
3	1	1	1	1	3	3	3	3	3	3	3	3	3
4	1	2	2	2	1	1	1	2	2	2	3	3	3
5	1	2	2	2	2	2	2	3	3	3	1	1	1
6	1	2	2	2	3	3	3	1	1	1	2	2	2
7	1	3	3	3	1	1	1	3	3	3	2	2	2
8	1	3	3	3	2	2	2	1	1	1	3	3	3
9	1	3	3	3	3	3	3	2	2	2	1	1	1
10	2	1	2	3	1	2	3	1	2	3	1	2	3
11	2	1	2	3	2	3	1	2	3	1	2	3	1
12	2	1	2	3	3	1	2	3	1	2	3	1	2
13	2	2	3	1	1	2	3	2	3	1	3	1	2
14	2	2	3	1	2	3	1	3	1	2	1	2	3
15	2	2	3	1	3	1	2	1	2	3	2	3	1
16	2	3	1	2	1	2	3	3	1	2	2	3	1
17	2	3	1	2	2	3	1	1	2	3	3	1	2
18	2	3	1	2	3	1	2	2	3	1	1	2	3
19	3	1	3	2	1	3	2	1	3	2	1	3	2
20	3	1	3	2	2	1	3	2	1	3	2	1	3
21	3	1	3	2	3	2	1	3	2	1	3	2	1
22	3	2	1	3	1	3	2	2	1	3	3	2	1
23	3	2	1	3	2	1	3	3	2	1	1	3	2
24	3	2	1	3	3	2	1	1	3	2	2	1	3
25	3	3	2	1	1	3	2	3	2	1	2	1	3
26	3	3	2	1	2	1	3	1	3	2	3	2	1
27	3	3	2	1	3	2	1	2	1	3	1	3	2

"1" represents a low value for a factor, "2" represents an intermediate value, and "3" represents a high value.
Source: Taguchi (1987).

Figure 12.1
Use of L_{27} Linear Graph for Column Assignments

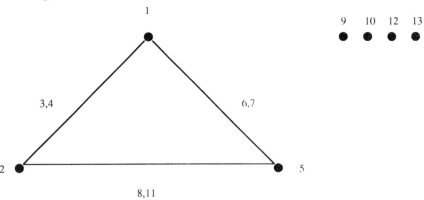

seven factors and some of their interactions. Clearly, there is a considerable reduction in the number of simulation runs when orthogonal array designs of this form are used. With this design it is possible to study the main and two-factor interaction effects on EU.

This particular case is presented in the linear graph of Figure 12.1 adopted from Taguchi and Wu [13]. This linear graph serves as a graphic aid in generating the experimental design.

With this graph, three factors, N, S, and R, may be assigned to columns 1, 2, and 5 of the orthogonal array table, respectively. Their interaction effects may be evaluated from the ANOVA procedure. For example, N*S is represented by columns 3 and 4, N*R is represented by columns 6 and 7, and S*R is represented by columns 8 and 11. In addition, four more three-level factors (assuming no interactions) may be assigned to columns 9, 10, 12, and 13, respectively. These columns are also represented with dark dots in Figure 12.1.

This procedure is implemented in the present example as follows: Based on the results of Kuei et al. [7] it is assumed that N, S, and R may have interaction effects on the EU. They are, therefore, assigned first. N, S, and R are assigned to the nodes in $L_{27}(3^{13})$ linear graph that represent columns 1, 2, and 5 of the orthogonal array table respectively (Table 12.2). The interaction of N and S is represented by 3 and 4 in the linear graph; the interaction of N and R is represented by 6 and 7; and the interaction of S and R is represented by 8 and 11. In a three-level Taguchi design, each factor has two degrees of freedom. The interaction between two factors has $2 \times 2 = 4$ degrees of freedom. So, two columns are needed to represent a single interaction effect under such cases. The linear graph of Figure 12.1 shows the interaction effects with two columns [13]. The remaining factors, F and B (assuming no interactions), may be arbitrarily assigned to the remaining nodes 9, 10, 12, and 13 in the linear graph. F and B were, therefore, assigned to nodes 10 and 13, respectively.

Table 12.3
Experimental Design

Column number	Factor
1	N
2	S
3	N*S
4	N*S
5	R
6	N*R
7	N*R
8	S*R
9	Error
10	F
11	S*R
12	Error
13	B

Unassigned columns may be used to represent the estimate of error variation [12]. As a result, nodes 9 and 12 represent the estimates of error variation. Table 12.3 presents the complete column assignments for this study.

ANOVA and Polynomial Decomposition

Based on the designs presented in Tables 12.2 and 12.3, the steady state simulation outputs for EU are obtained from the simulation model and are presented in Table 12.4.

The ANOVA procedure is used to compute the S.S. values of the main effects and interaction terms. It is observed that the S.S. for N*R and S*R are quite low (see Table 12.5). They are, therefore, used to better estimate the error variance [13]. This process of combining nonsignificant effects to estimate error variance is referred to as "pooling" [12]. The pooled error is, therefore, calculated as follows:

1. Calculate the S.S. of the error term as follows:

S.S. of error = S.S. of N*R + S.S. of S*R + S.S. of error = 0.034889

2. Calculate the corresponding degrees of freedom (d.f.) as follows:

d.f. of error = d.f. of N*R + d.f. of S*R + d.f. of error = 4 + 4 + 4 = 12

3. Calculate the pooled error as follows:

Pooled error = S.S. of error/d.f. of error = 0.034889/12 = 0.002907

Table 12.4
Experimental Design and the Simulation Results

Run Number	N	S	R	F	B	EU
1	5	1	4	1	20	.779
2	5	1	7	3	30	.777
3	5	1	10	5	40	.765
4	5	3	4	3	40	.999
5	5	3	7	5	20	.985
6	5	3	10	1	30	.860
7	5	5	4	5	30	.999
8	5	5	7	1	40	.949
9	5	5	10	3	20	.936
10	10	1	4	5	40	.894
11	10	1	7	1	20	.286
12	10	1	10	3	30	.300
13	10	3	4	1	30	.941
14	10	3	7	3	40	.971
15	10	3	10	5	20	.597
16	10	5	4	3	20	.979
17	10	5	7	5	30	.993
18	10	5	10	1	40	.872
19	15	1	4	3	30	.500
20	15	1	7	5	40	.381
21	15	1	10	1	20	.134
22	15	3	4	5	20	.897
23	15	3	7	1	30	.758
24	15	3	10	3	40	.762
25	15	5	4	1	40	.956
26	15	5	7	3	20	.819
27	15	5	10	5	30	.876

This pooled error is used to compute the F-ratios (mean square of treatment/mean square error) presented in Table 12.5 for all the independent variables. At this point, we test the significance of both the main and interaction effects based on the size of their sum of squares. This is actually a form of screening that enables us to focus on the few highly significant factors. In developing the regression metamodel, however, it may be necessary to see if the less significant factors that were pooled to obtain the error term contribute significantly in explaining EU. Kleijnen [6] and Ross [12] note that this pooling strategy increases the risk of the Type I error. However, a follow-up experiment may be conducted in order to reduce this risk.

The ANOVA results for EU (see Table 12.5) show that N, S, and R are statistically significant at $\alpha = 0.01$, while F, B, and N*S are significant at $\alpha = 0.05$. Thus, all the null hypotheses presented in Table 12.1 with the exception of H_7 and H_8 should be rejected.

Since each factor is set at three levels, the quadratic effects of the significant

Table 12.5
ANOVA for EU

Source of Variation	Sum of Squares	Degrees of Freedom	Mean Square	F
N	0.218988	2	0.109494	37.66***
S	0.807418	2	0.403709	138.85***
R	0.189511	2	0.094755	32.59***
F	0.040914	2	0.020457	7.04**
B	0.071864	2	0.035932	12.36**
N*S	0.117217	4	0.029304	10.08**
N*R	0.059793	4	0.014948	
S*R	0.063980	4	0.015995	
Error	0.015785	4	0.003964	

$*F_{2,12,0.95} = 3.89$; $**F_{2,12,0.99} = 6.93$; $***F_{2,12,0.999} = 12.97$.

factors can also be estimated. Based on the results obtained from Table 12.5, the next set of hypotheses concerns the test for linear and quadratic effects. Their interaction terms are also tested for significance. These hypotheses are presented in Table 12.6.

It is possible to decompose the main effect in Table 12.5 into linear and quadratic effects [4,10,12]. This is accomplished as follows: Let A represent a main effect, then the sum of squares of its linear and quadratic effects is

S.S. of linear effect of A_i $= (-1*A_1 + (0)*A_2 + 1*A_3)/w*n$,
S.S. of quadratic effect of factor $A_i = (1*A_1 + (-2)*A_2 + 1*A_3)/w*n$

Table 12.6
Test for Linear and Quadratic Effects on EU

H_9: N has no linear impact on the EU.
H_{10}: N has no quadratic impact on the EU.
H_{11}: S has no linear impact on the EU.
H_{12}: S has no quadratic impact on the EU.
H_{13}: R has no linear impact on the EU.
H_{14}: R has no quadratic impact on the EU.
H_{15}: F has no linear impact on the EU.
H_{16}: F has no quadratic impact on the EU.
H_{17}: B has no linear impact on the EU.
H_{18}: B has no quadratic impact on the EU.
H_{19}: N*S has no linear impact on the EU.
H_{20}: N*S has no quadratic impact on the EU.

where A_i is the sum of all the EU values at level i ($i = 1, 2,$ and 3); n is the number of EU values at level i (n is equal to the number of samples at a level), and w is the coefficient that is appropriate for a particular polynomial effect. For example, in a three-level factorial design, $w = 2$ for linear effects and $w = 6$ for quadratic effects [12]. The coefficients $-1, 0,$ and $+1$ are used to denote the low, intermediate, and high levels of factor A when measuring its linear effects. Conversely, the coefficients $+1, -2,$ and $+1$ are used to measure the quadratic effects of factor A. Thus, the S.S. of factor A in Table 12.5 comprises both its S.S. of linear effects and its S.S. of quadratic effects. Each of the S.S. has a d.f. of 1.

Application of these procedures leads to the ANOVA in Table 12.7, which is the polynomial decomposition of N, S, R, F, and B. The S.S. of each factor is also represented by the combined S.S. of its linear and quadratic effects, as the comparison of Tables 12.5 and 12.7 shows. This procedure, however, is only useful in decomposing main effects. The procedure to decompose the interaction effects, such as N*S, is presented in the Supplement at the end of this chapter.

As noted by Logothetis and Wynn [10], in practice it is sufficient to focus only

Table 12.7
ANOVA for the Quadratic Effects of EU

Source of Variation	Sum of Squares	Degrees of Freedom	Mean Square	F
N	0.218988	2	0.109494	37.66**
(Linear)	(0.214949)	1	(0.214949)	(73.93***)
(Quadratic)	(0.004038)	1	(0.004038)	(1.39)
S	0.807418	2	0.403709	138.85***
(Linear)	(0.705672)	1	(0.705672)	(242.71***)
(Quadratic)	(0.101745)	1	(0.101745)	(34.99***)
R	0.189511	2	0.094755	32.59***
(Linear)	(0.188702)	1	(0.188702)	(64.90***)
(Quadratic)	(0.000808)	1	(0.000808)	(0.28)
F	0.040914	2	0.020457	7.04**
(Linear)	(0.040422)	1	(0.040422)	(13.90**)
(Quadratic)	(0.000492)	1	(0.000492)	(0.17)
B	0.071864	2	0.035932	12.36**
(Linear)	(0.071820)	1	(0.071820)	(24.70***)
(Quadratic)	(0.000044)	1	(0.000044)	(0.02)
N*S	0.117217	4	0.029304	10.08**
(N_L*S_L)	(0.095765)	1	(0.095765)	(32.94***)
(N_Q*S_L)	(0.007744)	1	(0.007744)	(2.66)
(N_L*S_Q)	(0.013702)	1	(0.013702)	(4.50)
(N_Q*S_Q)	(0.000635)	1	(0.000635)	(0.22)

$*F_{1,12,0.95} = 4.75; **F_{1,12,0.99} = 9.33; ***F_{1,12,0.999} = 18.64.$

on the interaction components A_L*B_L, A_L*B_Q, and A_Q*B_L, when A and B are multilevel quantitative factors. Indeed, these interactions provide good estimates when multilevel factors are involved. Oftentimes, interaction terms, such as A_Q*B_Q and A_L*B_Q, may be negligible and difficult to interpret.

Experimental Results and Regression Metamodel

Once the S.S. of main effect or interaction effects are decomposed into quadratic effects, the F-ratio test is used to determine if any of the hypotheses presented in Table 12.6 is statistically significant [12]. The results of these tests are presented in Table 12.7. So it is observed from this table that H_9, H_{11}, H_{12}, H_{13}, H_{15}, H_{17}, and H_{19} should all be rejected. Apparently, only S has a significant quadratic effect on EU. Furthermore, only the interaction effects of N and S are significant on EU. All the main effects also have significant linear effects on EU. Consequently, the smaller insignificant polynomial effects can be pooled in order to estimate the error term [12]. These include the quadratic effects of N, R, F, and B, and N_L*S_Q, N_Q*S_L, and N_Q*S_Q.

A regression metamodel is developed by concentrating initially on the significant factors as screened out in the ANOVA and the polynomial decomposition subsection. The explanatory model for EU is obtained as

$$EU = 0.7383 - 0.0487N + 0.205S - 0.0341R + 0.0237F$$
$$+ 0.0063B - 0.0326S^2 + 0.0089N*S \qquad (12.3)$$

All the factors included in this model are statistically significant in explaining EU ($p < 0.001$). However, N and R seem to contribute mostly to the variability in EU within the specified ranges of the independent variables. An r^2 (regression coefficient) of 0.8949 and a standard error estimate of 0.0936 were also observed. This shows that about 89.49% of the total variation in EU is explained by N, S, R, F, B, S^2, and N*S. There were no systematic patterns exhibited by the residuals.

The next attempt was to see if the standard error of estimate can be further reduced by reintroducing those factors that were screened out and pooled to obtain the mean square error. Thus, the following interaction terms were introduced: N*R and S*R. The result showed that N*R is indeed statistically insignificant whereas S*R is significant in explaining EU. Furthermore, the standard error of estimate was reduced from 0.0936 to 0.0826 as a result of the inclusion of the interaction between S and R in the model; r^2 also increased from 0.8949 to 0.9225. This time N, S, R, F, B, S^2, N*S, and S*R account for about 92.25% of the total variation in EU. Detailed results show that N and R again contribute mostly to explaining the variability in EU within the specified ranges of the independent variables. Their partial r^2s increased from 0.5939 and 0.5308 to 0.6647 and 0.5545, respectively. In addition, S^2 and N*S also have high partial r^2 values of 0.4531 and 0.4384, respectively.

Based on the significant improvements observed on introducing S*R into the model, we present the best fit model for EU as

$$EU = 0.9494 - 0.0487N + 0.1346S - 0.0643R + 0.0237F + 0.0063B$$
$$- 0.0326S^2 + 0.0089N*S + 0.0101S*R \qquad (12.4)$$

SUMMARY

In this chapter, Taguchi's experimental design technique was used to determine the input values of the controllable variables in a maintenance float system. Each of these factors was considered at three levels thus enabling us to assess quadratic effects.

Unlike the previous chapters that concentrated primarily on measuring first-order effects, we showed how both linear and quadratic effects could be considered in order to obtain a regression metamodel. Furthermore, the interaction effects associated with both linear and quadratic effects were estimated. A polynomial decomposition method was used. Although the emphasis was on three-level factorial designs, the example we considered benefits from earlier results on two-level designs. The two-level designs provided a form of screening tests by identifying the significant controllable factors. Further decomposition of these factors into three levels made it possible to study quadratic effects.

REFERENCES

1. Anderson, V. L., and R. A. Mclean. *Design of Experiments*. New York: Marcel Dekker, 1974.
2. Box, G.E.P., W. G. Hunter, and J. S. Hunter. *Statistics for Experiments*. New York: Wiley, 1978.
3. Delahey, W., and E. Vaccari. *Dynamic Models and Discrete Event Simulation*. New York: Marcel Dekker, 1989.
4. Hick, C. R. *Fundamental Concepts in the Design of Experiments*. New York: Holt, Rinehart and Winston, 1982.
5. Kleijnen, J.P.C. "Screening Designs for Poly-factor Experimentation." *Technometrics* 17 (4) (1975): 487–493.
6. Kleijnen, J.P.C. *Statistical Tools for Simulation Practitioners*. New York: Marcel Dekker, 1987.
7. Kuei, C. H., M. N. Chanin, and C. Lin. "Taguchi Design and Regression Analysis for Maintenance Float Decision Models." *1990 Northeast DSI Proceedings*, 320–323.
8. Kuei, C. H., and C. N. Madu. "Polynomial Metamodeling and Taguchi Designs in Simulation with Application to the Maintenance Float System." *European Journal of Operation Research* (forthcoming).
9. Lochner, R. H., and J. E. Mater. *Designing for Quality—An Introduction to the Best of Taguchi and Western Methods of Statistical Experimental Design*. Milwaukee, WI: ASQC Quality Press.

10. Logothetis, N., and H. P. Wynn. *Quality Through Design—Experimental Design, Off-line Quality Control and Taguchi's Contributions.* Oxford: Clarendon Press, 1989.
11. Mason, R. L., R. F. Gunst, and J. L. Hess. *Statistical Design and Analysis of Experiment.* New York: Wiley, 1989.
12. Ross, P. J. *Taguchi Techniques for Quality Engineering.* New York: McGraw-Hill Book Company, 1988.
13. Taguchi, C., and Y. Wu. *Introduction to Off-line Quality Control.* Nogoya, Japan: Central Japan Quality Control Association, 1980.
14. Taguchi, C. *System of Experimental Design.* New York: Kraus International Publications, 1987.

Supplement: Procedures for the Use of ANOVA
in Polynomial Modeling

1. Identify the corresponding EU values based on level i in column 1 (i.e., factor N) and level j in column 2 (i.e., factor S). For example, when $i = 1$ and $j = 1$, we obtain the following from Table 12.4:

Run No.	N	S	(EU)
1	5	1	.779
2	5	1	.777
3	5	1	.765

2. Calculate the sum of EUs for cell N_iS_j.

Example: $(i = 1, j = 1)$

$N_iS_j = .779 + .777 + .765 = 2.321$

3. Fill out all the cells for every combination of factor N and S.

	S1	S2	S3
N1	2.321	2.844	2.885
N2	1.480	2.509	2.844
N3	1.015	2.417	2.651

4. Calculate the S.S. of N_L*S_L and N_Q*S_L. The L and Q subscripts represent linear and quadratic, respectively.

   In calculating the sum of squares (S.S.) of the controllable factors, the coefficients $L1 = -1$, $L2 = 0$, and $L3 = 1$ represent the orthogonal coefficients corresponding to the linear effects for the three levels of any of the controllable factors. Also, $Q1 = 1$, $Q2 = 2$, and $Q3 = 1$ are the orthogonal coefficients corresponding to the quadratic effects for the same three-level factor.

   a. Calculate the following contrasts for each level of N:

   $S_L(Ni) = (L1)*(NiS1) + (L2)*(NiS2) + (L3)*(NiS3)$, where $i = 1, 2,$ and 3.

   Example:

   $S_L(N1) = (-1)*(2.321) + (0)*(2.844) + (1)*(2.885) = 0.564$
   $S_L(N2) = (-1)*(1.480) + (0)*(2.509) + (1)*(2.844) = 1.364$
   $S_L(N3) = (-1)*(1.015) + (0)*(2.417) + (1)*(2.651) = 1.636$

   b. Calculate the S.S. of N_L*S_L:

   $[(L1)*(S_L(N1)) + (L2)*(S_L(N2)) + (L3)*(S_L(N3))]^2/(m*L*L)$.

   m is the number of observations in each cell NiSj (i.e., $m = 3$ in our case).

   $L = (L1)^2 + (L2)^2 + (L3)^2$, and $Q = (Q1)^2 + (Q2)^2 + (Q3)^2$

Example:

$$[(-1)*(0.564) + (0)*(1.364) + (1)*(1.636)]^2/3*(2)*(2) = 0.095765$$

c. Calculate the S.S. of N_Q*S_L:

$$[(Q1)*(S_L(N1)) + (Q2)*(S_L(N2)) + (Q3)*(S_L(N3))]^2/(m*L*Q).$$

Example:

$$[(+1)*(0.564) + (-2)*(1.364) + (+1)*(1.636)]^2/3*(6)*(2) = 0.007744$$

5. Calculate the S.S. of N_L*S_Q and N_Q*S_Q:
   a. Calculate the following contracts for each level of N:

   $S_Q(Ni) = (Q1)*(NiS1) + (Q2)*(NiS2) + (Q3)*(NiS3)$
   $i = 1, 2,$ and 3.

   Example:

   $S_Q(N1) = (1)*(2.321) + (-2)*(2.844) + (1)*(2.885) = -0.482$
   $S_Q(N2) = (1)*(1.480) + (-2)*(2.509) + (1)*(2.844) = -0.694$
   $S_Q(N3) = (1)*(1.015) + (-2)*(2.417) + (1)*(2.651) = -1.168$

   b. Calculate the S.S. of N_L*S_Q:

   $$[(L1)*(S_L(N1)) + (L2)*(S_L(N2)) + (L3)*(S_L(N3))]^2/(m*L*Q).$$

   Example:

   $$[(-1)*(-0.482) + (0)*(-0.694) + (1)*(-1.168)]^2/3*(2)*(6) = 0.013072$$

   c. Calculate the S.S. of N_Q*S_Q:

   $$[(Q1)*(S_L(N1)) + (Q2)*(S_L(N2)) + (Q3)*(S_L(N3))]^2/(m*Q*Q).$$

   Example:

   $$[(1)*(-0.482) + (-2)*(-0.694) + (1)*(-1.168)]^2/3*(6)*(6) = 0.000635$$

6. Verify the results:
   The S.S. of $N*S$ should be equal to the combined S.S. of N_L*S_L, N_Q*S_L, N_L*S_Q, and N_Q*S_Q.

Example:

S.S. of $N*S$ = the S.S. of N_L*S_L + the S.S. of N_Q*S_L + the S.S. of N_L*S_Q + the S.S. of N_Q*S_Q
$0.117217 = 0.095765 + 0.007744 + 0.013072 + 0.000635$

APPENDIX

Kolmogorov-Smirnoff Critical Values

Degrees of Freedom (N)	One-Sample Test* $D_{0.10}$	$D_{0.05}$	$D_{0.01}$
1	0.950	0.975	0.995
2	0.776	0.842	0.929
3	0.642	0.708	0.828
4	0.564	0.624	0.733
5	0.510	0.565	0.669
6	0.470	0.521	0.618
7	0.438	0.486	0.577
8	0.411	0.457	0.543
9	0.388	0.432	0.514
10	0.368	0.410	0.490
11	0.352	0.391	0.468
12	0.338	0.375	0.450
13	0.325	0.361	0.433
14	0.314	0.349	0.418
15	0.304	0.338	0.404
16	0.295	0.328	0.392
17	0.286	0.318	0.381
18	0.278	0.309	0.371
19	0.272	0.301	0.363
20	0.264	0.294	0.356
25	0.24	0.27	0.32

(continued)

Kolmogorov-Smirnoff Critical Values (Continued)

Degrees of Freedom (N)	One-Sample Test*		
	$D_{0.10}$	$D_{0.05}$	$D_{0.01}$
30	0.22	0.24	0.29
35	0.21	0.23	0.27
Over 35	$\dfrac{1.22}{\sqrt{N}}$	$\dfrac{1.36}{\sqrt{N}}$	$\dfrac{1.63}{\sqrt{N}}$

*Used for testing goodness of fit of a sample to a theoretical distribution where N = sample size.

From Robert E. Shannon, *Systems Simulation: The Art and Science,* © 1975, p. 380. Reprinted by permission of Prentice-Hall, Englewood Cliffs, NJ.

Percentile Values (χp^2) for the Chi-Square Distribution, with ν Degrees of Freedom (Shaded Area $= p$)

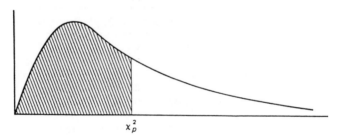

$$\chi_p^2$$

ν	$\chi_{0.995}^2$	$\chi_{0.99}^2$	$\chi_{0.975}^2$	$\chi_{0.95}^2$	$\chi_{0.90}^2$
1	7.88	6.63	5.02	3.84	2.71
2	10.60	9.21	7.38	5.99	4.61
3	12.84	11.34	9.35	7.81	6.25
4	14.96	13.28	11.14	9.49	7.78
5	16.7	15.1	12.8	11.1	9.2
6	18.5	16.8	14.4	12.6	10.6
7	20.3	18.5	16.0	14.1	12.0
8	22.0	20.1	17.5	15.5	13.4
9	23.6	21.7	19.0	16.9	14.7
10	25.2	23.2	20.5	18.3	16.0
11	26.8	24.7	21.9	19.7	17.3
12	28.3	26.2	23.3	21.0	18.5
13	29.8	27.7	24.7	22.4	19.8
14	31.3	29.1	26.1	23.7	21.1
15	32.8	30.6	27.5	25.0	22.3
16	34.3	32.0	28.8	26.3	23.5
17	35.7	33.4	30.2	27.6	24.8
18	37.2	34.8	31.5	28.9	26.0

Percentile Values ($\chi\rho^2$) for the Chi-Square Distribution (Continued)

ν	$\chi^2_{0.995}$	$\chi^2_{0.99}$	$\chi^2_{0.975}$	$\chi^2_{0.95}$	$\chi^2_{0.90}$
19	38.6	36.2	32.9	30.1	27.2
20	40.0	37.6	34.2	31.4	28.4
21	41.4	38.9	35.5	32.7	29.6
22	42.8	40.3	36.8	33.9	30.8
23	44.2	41.6	38.1	35.2	32.0
24	45.6	43.0	39.4	36.4	33.2
25	49.6	44.3	40.6	37.7	34.4
26	48.3	45.6	41.9	38.9	35.6
27	49.6	47.0	43.2	40.1	36.7
28	51.0	48.3	44.5	41.3	37.9
29	52.3	49.6	45.7	42.6	39.1
30	53.7	50.9	47.0	43.8	40.3
40	66.8	63.7	59.3	55.8	51.8
50	79.5	76.2	71.4	67.5	63.2
60	92.0	88.4	83.3	79.1	74.4
70	104.2	100.4	95.0	90.5	85.5
80	116.3	112.3	106.6	101.9	96.6
90	128.3	124.1	118.1	113.1	107.6
100	140.2	135.8	129.6	124.3	118.5

From Robert E. Shannon, *Systems Simulation: The Art and Science,* © 1975, p. 372. Reprinted by permission of Prentice-Hall, Englewood Cliffs, NJ.

F Distribution

v_2 \ v_1	1	2	3	4	5	6	7	8	9	10	11	12	14	16	20	24	30	40	50	75	100	200	500	∞
1	161 / 4,052	200 / 4,999	216 / 5,403	225 / 5,625	230 / 5,764	234 / 5,859	237 / 5,928	239 / 5,981	241 / 6,022	242 / 6,056	243 / 6,082	244 / 6,106	245 / 6,142	246 / 6,169	248 / 6,208	249 / 6,234	250 / 6,261	251 / 6,286	252 / 6,302	253 / 6,323	253 / 6,334	254 / 6,352	254 / 6,361	254 / 6,366
2	18.51 / 98.49	19.00 / 99.00	19.16 / 99.17	19.25 / 99.25	19.30 / 99.30	19.33 / 99.33	19.36 / 99.36	19.37 / 99.37	19.38 / 99.39	19.39 / 99.40	19.40 / 99.41	19.41 / 99.42	19.42 / 99.43	19.43 / 99.44	19.44 / 99.45	19.45 / 99.46	19.46 / 99.47	19.47 / 99.48	19.47 / 98.48	19.48 / 99.49	19.49 / 99.49	19.49 / 99.49	19.50 / 99.50	19.50 / 99.50
3	10.13 / 34.12	9.55 / 30.82	9.28 / 29.46	9.12 / 28.71	9.01 / 28.24	8.94 / 27.91	8.88 / 27.67	8.84 / 27.49	8.81 / 27.34	8.78 / 27.23	8.76 / 27.13	8.74 / 27.05	8.71 / 26.92	8.69 / 26.83	8.66 / 26.69	8.64 / 26.60	8.62 / 26.50	8.60 / 26.41	8.58 / 26.35	8.57 / 26.27	8.56 / 26.23	8.54 / 26.18	8.54 / 26.14	8.53 / 26.12
4	7.71 / 21.20	6.94 / 18.00	6.59 / 16.69	6.39 / 15.98	6.26 / 15.52	6.16 / 15.21	6.09 / 14.98	6.04 / 14.80	6.00 / 14.66	5.96 / 14.54	5.93 / 14.45	5.91 / 14.37	5.87 / 14.24	5.84 / 14.15	5.80 / 14.02	5.77 / 13.93	5.74 / 13.83	5.71 / 13.74	5.70 / 13.69	5.68 / 13.61	5.66 / 13.57	5.65 / 13.52	5.64 / 13.48	5.63 / 13.46
5	6.61 / 16.26	5.79 / 13.27	5.41 / 12.06	5.19 / 11.39	5.05 / 10.97	4.95 / 10.67	4.88 / 10.45	4.82 / 10.29	4.78 / 10.15	4.74 / 10.05	4.70 / 9.96	4.68 / 9.89	4.64 / 9.77	4.60 / 9.68	4.56 / 9.55	4.53 / 9.47	4.50 / 9.38	4.46 / 9.29	4.44 / 9.24	4.42 / 9.17	4.40 / 9.13	4.38 / 9.07	4.37 / 9.04	4.36 / 9.02
6	5.99 / 13.74	5.14 / 10.92	4.76 / 9.78	4.53 / 9.15	4.39 / 8.75	4.28 / 8.47	4.21 / 8.26	4.15 / 8.10	4.10 / 7.98	4.06 / 7.87	4.03 / 7.79	4.00 / 7.72	3.96 / 7.60	3.92 / 7.52	3.87 / 7.39	3.84 / 7.31	3.81 / 7.23	3.77 / 7.14	3.75 / 7.09	3.72 / 7.02	3.71 / 6.99	3.69 / 6.94	3.68 / 6.90	3.67 / 6.88
7	5.59 / 12.25	4.74 / 9.55	4.35 / 8.45	4.12 / 7.85	3.97 / 7.46	3.87 / 7.19	3.79 / 7.00	3.73 / 6.84	3.68 / 6.71	3.63 / 6.62	3.60 / 6.54	3.57 / 6.47	3.52 / 6.35	3.49 / 6.27	3.44 / 6.15	3.41 / 6.07	3.38 / 5.98	3.34 / 5.90	3.32 / 5.85	3.29 / 5.78	3.28 / 5.75	3.25 / 5.70	3.24 / 5.67	3.23 / 5.65
8	5.32 / 11.26	4.46 / 8.65	4.07 / 7.59	3.84 / 7.01	3.69 / 6.63	3.58 / 6.37	3.50 / 6.19	3.44 / 6.03	3.39 / 5.91	3.34 / 5.82	3.31 / 5.74	3.28 / 5.67	3.23 / 5.56	3.20 / 5.48	3.15 / 5.36	3.12 / 5.28	3.08 / 5.20	3.05 / 5.11	3.03 / 5.06	3.00 / 5.00	2.98 / 4.96	2.96 / 4.91	2.94 / 4.88	2.93 / 4.86
9	5.12 / 10.56	4.26 / 8.02	3.86 / 6.99	3.63 / 6.42	3.48 / 6.06	3.37 / 5.80	3.29 / 5.62	3.23 / 5.47	3.18 / 5.35	3.13 / 5.26	3.10 / 5.18	3.07 / 5.11	3.02 / 5.00	2.98 / 4.92	2.93 / 4.80	2.90 / 4.73	2.86 / 4.64	2.82 / 4.56	2.80 / 4.51	2.77 / 4.45	2.76 / 4.41	2.73 / 4.36	2.72 / 4.33	2.71 / 4.31
10	4.96 / 10.04	4.10 / 7.56	3.71 / 6.55	3.48 / 5.99	3.33 / 5.64	3.22 / 5.39	3.14 / 5.21	3.07 / 5.06	3.02 / 4.95	2.97 / 4.85	2.94 / 4.78	2.91 / 4.71	2.86 / 4.60	2.82 / 4.52	2.77 / 4.41	2.74 / 4.33	2.70 / 4.25	2.67 / 4.17	2.64 / 4.12	2.61 / 4.05	2.59 / 4.01	2.56 / 3.96	2.55 / 3.93	2.54 / 3.91
11	4.84 / 9.65	3.98 / 7.20	3.59 / 6.22	3.36 / 5.67	3.20 / 5.32	3.09 / 5.07	3.01 / 4.88	2.95 / 4.74	2.90 / 4.63	2.86 / 4.54	2.82 / 4.46	2.79 / 4.40	2.74 / 4.29	2.70 / 4.21	2.65 / 4.10	2.61 / 4.02	2.57 / 3.94	2.53 / 3.86	2.50 / 3.80	2.47 / 3.74	2.45 / 3.70	2.42 / 3.66	2.41 / 3.62	2.40 / 3.60
12	4.75 / 9.33	3.88 / 6.93	3.49 / 5.95	3.26 / 5.41	3.11 / 5.06	3.00 / 4.82	2.92 / 4.65	2.85 / 4.50	2.80 / 4.39	2.76 / 4.30	2.72 / 4.22	2.69 / 4.16	2.64 / 4.05	2.60 / 3.98	2.54 / 3.86	2.50 / 3.78	2.46 / 3.70	2.42 / 3.61	2.40 / 3.56	2.36 / 3.49	2.35 / 3.46	2.32 / 3.41	2.31 / 3.38	2.30 / 3.36

v_2 \ v_1	1	2	3	4	5	6	7	8	9	10	11	12	14	16	20	24	30	40	50	75	100	200	500	∞
13	4.67 9.07	3.80 6.70	3.41 5.74	3.18 5.20	3.02 4.86	2.92 4.62	2.84 4.44	2.77 4.30	2.72 4.19	2.67 4.10	2.63 4.02	2.60 3.96	2.55 3.85	2.51 3.78	2.46 3.67	2.42 3.59	2.38 3.51	2.34 3.42	2.32 3.37	2.28 3.30	2.26 3.27	2.24 3.21	2.22 3.18	2.21 3.16
14	4.60 8.86	3.74 6.51	3.34 5.56	3.11 5.03	2.96 4.69	2.85 4.46	2.77 4.28	2.70 4.14	2.65 4.03	2.60 3.94	2.56 3.86	2.53 3.80	2.48 3.70	2.44 3.62	2.39 3.51	2.35 3.43	2.31 3.34	2.27 3.26	2.24 3.21	2.21 3.14	2.19 3.11	2.16 3.06	2.14 3.02	2.13 3.00
15	4.54 8.68	3.68 6.36	3.29 5.42	3.06 4.89	2.90 4.56	2.79 4.32	2.70 4.14	2.64 4.00	2.59 3.89	2.55 3.80	2.51 3.73	2.48 3.67	2.43 3.56	2.39 3.48	2.33 3.36	2.29 3.29	2.25 3.20	2.21 3.12	2.18 3.07	2.15 3.00	2.12 2.97	2.10 2.92	2.08 2.89	2.07 2.87
16	4.49 8.53	3.63 6.23	3.24 5.29	3.01 4.77	2.85 4.44	2.74 4.20	2.66 4.03	2.59 3.89	2.54 3.78	2.49 3.69	2.45 3.61	2.42 3.55	2.37 3.45	2.33 3.37	2.28 3.25	2.24 3.18	2.20 3.10	2.16 3.01	2.13 2.96	2.09 2.98	2.07 2.86	2.04 2.80	2.02 2.77	2.01 2.75
17	4.45 8.40	3.59 6.11	3.20 5.18	2.96 4.67	2.81 4.34	2.70 4.10	2.62 3.93	2.55 3.79	2.50 3.68	2.45 3.59	2.41 3.52	2.38 3.45	2.33 3.35	2.29 3.27	2.23 3.16	2.19 3.08	2.15 3.00	2.11 2.92	2.08 2.86	2.04 2.79	2.02 2.76	1.99 2.70	1.97 2.67	1.96 2.65
18	4.41 8.28	3.55 6.01	3.16 5.09	2.93 4.58	2.77 4.25	2.66 4.01	2.58 3.85	2.51 3.71	2.46 3.60	2.41 3.51	2.37 3.44	2.34 3.37	2.29 3.27	2.25 3.19	2.19 3.07	2.15 3.00	2.11 2.91	2.07 2.83	2.04 2.78	2.00 2.71	1.98 2.68	1.95 2.62	1.93 2.59	1.92 2.57
19	4.38 8.18	3.52 5.93	3.13 5.01	2.90 4.50	2.74 4.17	2.63 3.94	2.55 3.77	2.48 3.63	2.43 3.52	2.38 3.43	2.34 3.36	2.31 3.30	2.26 3.19	2.21 3.12	2.15 3.00	2.11 2.92	2.07 2.84	2.02 2.76	2.00 2.70	1.96 2.63	1.94 2.60	1.91 2.54	1.90 2.51	1.88 2.49
20	4.35 8.10	3.49 5.85	3.10 4.94	2.87 4.43	2.71 4.10	2.60 3.87	2.52 3.71	2.45 3.56	2.40 3.45	2.35 3.37	2.31 3.30	2.28 3.23	2.23 3.13	2.18 3.05	2.12 2.94	2.08 2.86	2.04 2.77	1.99 2.69	1.96 2.63	1.92 2.56	1.90 2.53	1.87 2.47	1.85 2.44	1.84 2.42
21	4.32 8.02	3.47 5.78	3.07 4.87	2.84 4.37	2.68 4.04	2.57 3.81	2.49 3.65	2.42 3.51	2.37 3.40	2.32 3.31	2.28 3.24	2.25 3.17	2.20 3.07	2.15 2.99	2.09 2.88	2.05 2.80	2.00 2.72	1.96 2.63	1.93 2.58	1.89 2.51	1.87 2.47	1.84 2.42	1.82 2.38	1.81 2.36
22	4.30 7.94	3.44 5.72	3.05 4.82	2.82 4.31	2.66 3.99	2.55 3.76	2.47 3.59	2.40 3.45	2.35 3.35	2.30 3.26	2.26 3.18	2.23 3.12	2.18 3.02	2.13 2.94	2.07 2.83	2.03 2.75	1.98 2.67	1.93 2.58	1.91 2.53	1.87 2.46	1.84 2.42	1.81 2.37	1.80 2.33	1.78 2.31
23	4.28 7.88	3.42 5.66	3.03 4.76	2.80 4.26	2.64 3.94	2.53 3.71	2.45 3.54	2.38 3.41	2.32 3.30	2.28 3.21	2.24 3.14	2.20 3.07	2.14 2.97	2.10 2.89	2.04 2.78	2.00 2.70	1.96 2.62	1.91 2.53	1.88 2.48	1.84 2.41	1.82 2.37	1.79 2.32	1.77 2.28	1.76 2.26
24	4.26 7.82	3.40 5.61	3.01 4.72	2.78 4.22	2.62 3.90	2.51 3.67	2.43 3.50	2.36 3.36	2.30 3.25	2.26 3.17	2.22 3.09	2.18 3.03	2.13 2.93	2.09 2.85	2.02 2.74	1.98 2.66	1.94 2.58	1.89 2.49	1.86 2.44	1.82 2.36	1.80 2.33	1.76 2.27	1.74 2.23	1.73 2.21
25	4.24 7.77	3.38 5.57	2.99 4.68	2.76 4.18	2.60 3.86	2.49 3.63	2.41 3.46	2.34 3.32	2.28 3.21	2.24 3.13	2.20 3.05	2.16 2.99	2.11 2.89	2.06 2.81	2.00 2.70	1.96 2.62	1.92 2.54	1.87 2.45	1.84 2.40	1.80 2.32	1.77 2.29	1.74 2.23	1.72 2.19	1.71 2.17
26	4.22 7.72	3.37 5.53	2.98 4.64	2.74 4.14	2.59 3.82	2.47 3.59	2.39 3.42	2.32 3.29	2.27 3.17	2.22 3.09	2.18 3.02	2.15 2.96	2.10 2.86	2.05 2.77	1.99 2.66	1.95 2.58	1.90 2.50	1.85 2.41	1.82 2.36	1.78 2.28	1.76 2.25	1.72 2.19	1.70 2.15	1.69 2.13

Continued

n_2 \ n_1	1	2	3	4	5	6	7	8	9	10	11	12	14	16	20	24	30	40	50	75	100	200	500	∞
27	4.21 / 7.68	3.35 / 5.49	2.96 / 4.60	2.73 / 4.11	2.57 / 3.79	2.46 / 3.56	2.37 / 3.39	2.30 / 3.26	2.25 / 3.14	2.20 / 3.06	2.16 / 2.98	2.13 / 2.93	2.08 / 2.83	2.03 / 2.74	1.97 / 2.63	1.93 / 2.55	1.88 / 2.47	1.84 / 2.38	1.80 / 2.33	1.76 / 2.25	1.74 / 2.21	1.71 / 2.16	1.68 / 2.12	1.67 / 2.10
28	4.20 / 7.64	3.34 / 5.45	2.95 / 4.57	2.71 / 4.07	2.56 / 3.76	2.44 / 3.53	2.36 / 3.36	2.29 / 3.23	2.24 / 3.11	2.19 / 3.03	2.15 / 2.95	2.12 / 2.90	2.06 / 2.80	2.02 / 2.71	1.96 / 2.60	1.91 / 2.52	1.87 / 2.44	1.81 / 2.35	1.78 / 2.30	1.75 / 2.22	1.72 / 2.18	1.69 / 2.13	1.67 / 2.09	1.65 / 2.06
29	4.18 / 7.60	3.33 / 5.42	2.93 / 4.54	2.70 / 4.04	2.54 / 3.73	2.43 / 3.50	2.35 / 3.33	2.28 / 3.20	2.22 / 3.08	2.18 / 3.00	2.14 / 2.92	2.10 / 2.87	2.05 / 2.77	2.00 / 2.68	1.94 / 2.57	1.90 / 2.49	1.85 / 2.41	1.80 / 2.32	1.77 / 2.27	1.73 / 2.19	1.71 / 2.15	1.68 / 2.10	1.65 / 2.06	1.64 / 2.03
30	4.17 / 7.56	3.32 / 5.39	2.92 / 4.51	2.69 / 4.02	2.53 / 3.70	2.42 / 3.47	2.34 / 3.30	2.27 / 3.17	2.21 / 3.06	2.16 / 2.98	2.12 / 2.90	2.09 / 2.84	2.04 / 2.74	1.99 / 2.66	1.93 / 2.55	1.89 / 2.47	1.84 / 2.38	1.79 / 2.29	1.76 / 2.24	1.72 / 2.16	1.69 / 2.13	1.66 / 2.07	1.64 / 2.03	1.62 / 2.01
32	4.15 / 7.50	3.30 / 5.34	2.90 / 4.46	2.67 / 3.97	2.51 / 3.66	2.40 / 3.42	2.32 / 3.25	2.25 / 3.12	2.19 / 3.01	2.14 / 2.94	2.10 / 2.86	2.07 / 2.80	2.02 / 2.70	1.97 / 2.62	1.91 / 2.51	1.86 / 2.42	1.82 / 2.34	1.76 / 2.25	1.74 / 2.20	1.69 / 2.12	1.67 / 2.08	1.64 / 2.02	1.61 / 1.98	1.59 / 1.96
34	4.13 / 7.44	3.28 / 5.29	2.88 / 4.42	2.65 / 3.93	2.49 / 3.61	2.38 / 3.38	2.30 / 3.21	2.23 / 3.08	2.17 / 2.97	2.12 / 2.89	2.08 / 2.82	2.05 / 2.76	2.00 / 2.66	1.95 / 2.58	1.89 / 2.47	1.84 / 2.38	1.80 / 2.30	1.74 / 2.21	1.71 / 2.15	1.67 / 2.08	1.64 / 2.04	1.61 / 1.98	1.59 / 1.94	1.57 / 1.91
36	4.11 / 7.39	3.26 / 5.25	2.86 / 4.38	2.63 / 3.89	2.48 / 3.58	2.36 / 3.35	2.28 / 3.18	2.21 / 3.04	2.15 / 2.94	2.10 / 2.86	2.06 / 2.78	2.03 / 2.72	1.98 / 2.62	1.93 / 2.54	1.87 / 2.43	1.82 / 2.35	1.78 / 2.26	1.72 / 2.17	1.69 / 2.12	1.65 / 2.04	1.62 / 2.00	1.59 / 1.94	1.56 / 1.90	1.55 / 1.87
38	4.10 / 7.35	3.25 / 5.21	2.85 / 4.34	2.62 / 3.86	2.46 / 3.54	2.35 / 3.32	2.26 / 3.15	2.19 / 3.02	2.14 / 2.91	2.09 / 2.82	2.05 / 2.75	2.02 / 2.69	1.96 / 2.59	1.92 / 2.51	1.85 / 2.40	1.80 / 2.32	1.76 / 2.22	1.71 / 2.14	1.67 / 2.08	1.63 / 2.00	1.60 / 1.97	1.57 / 1.90	1.54 / 1.86	1.53 / 1.84
40	4.08 / 7.31	3.23 / 5.18	2.84 / 4.31	2.61 / 3.83	2.45 / 3.51	2.34 / 3.29	2.25 / 3.12	2.18 / 2.99	2.12 / 2.88	2.07 / 2.80	2.04 / 2.73	2.00 / 2.66	1.95 / 2.56	1.90 / 2.49	1.84 / 2.37	1.79 / 2.29	1.74 / 2.20	1.69 / 2.11	1.66 / 2.05	1.61 / 1.97	1.59 / 1.94	1.55 / 1.88	1.53 / 1.84	1.51 / 1.81
42	4.07 / 7.27	3.22 / 5.15	2.83 / 4.29	2.59 / 3.80	2.44 / 3.49	2.32 / 3.26	2.24 / 3.10	2.17 / 2.96	2.11 / 2.86	2.06 / 2.77	2.02 / 2.70	1.99 / 2.64	1.94 / 2.54	1.89 / 2.46	1.82 / 2.35	1.78 / 2.26	1.73 / 2.17	1.68 / 2.08	1.64 / 2.02	1.60 / 1.94	1.57 / 1.91	1.54 / 1.85	1.51 / 1.80	1.49 / 1.78
44	4.06 / 7.24	3.21 / 5.12	2.82 / 4.26	2.58 / 3.78	2.43 / 3.46	2.31 / 3.24	2.23 / 3.07	2.16 / 2.94	2.10 / 2.84	2.05 / 2.75	2.01 / 2.68	1.98 / 2.62	1.92 / 2.52	1.88 / 2.44	1.81 / 2.32	1.76 / 2.24	1.72 / 2.15	1.66 / 2.06	1.63 / 2.00	1.58 / 1.92	1.56 / 1.88	1.52 / 1.82	1.50 / 1.78	1.48 / 1.75
46	4.05 / 7.21	3.20 / 5.10	2.81 / 4.24	2.57 / 3.76	2.42 / 3.44	2.30 / 3.22	2.22 / 3.05	2.14 / 2.92	2.09 / 2.82	2.04 / 2.73	2.00 / 2.66	1.97 / 2.60	1.91 / 2.50	1.87 / 2.42	1.80 / 2.30	1.75 / 2.22	1.71 / 2.13	1.65 / 2.04	1.62 / 1.98	1.57 / 1.90	1.54 / 1.86	1.51 / 1.80	1.48 / 1.76	1.46 / 1.72
48	4.04 / 7.19	3.19 / 5.08	2.80 / 4.22	2.56 / 3.74	2.41 / 3.42	2.30 / 3.20	2.21 / 3.04	2.14 / 2.90	2.08 / 2.80	2.03 / 2.71	1.99 / 2.64	1.96 / 2.58	1.90 / 2.48	1.86 / 2.40	1.79 / 2.28	1.74 / 2.20	1.70 / 2.11	1.64 / 2.02	1.61 / 1.96	1.56 / 1.88	1.53 / 1.84	1.50 / 1.78	1.47 / 1.73	1.45 / 1.70

F-distribution critical values. Each cell gives the 5% point (roman) over the 1% point (bold).

ν_2	1	2	3	4	5	6	7	8	9	10	11	12	14	16	20	24	30	40	50	75	100	200	500	∞
50	4.03 / **7.17**	3.18 / **5.06**	2.79 / **4.20**	2.56 / **3.72**	2.40 / **3.41**	2.29 / **3.18**	2.20 / **3.02**	2.13 / **2.88**	2.07 / **2.78**	2.02 / **2.70**	1.98 / **2.62**	1.95 / **2.56**	1.90 / **2.46**	1.85 / **2.39**	1.78 / **2.26**	1.74 / **2.18**	1.69 / **2.10**	1.63 / **2.00**	1.60 / **1.94**	1.55 / **1.86**	1.52 / **1.82**	1.48 / **1.76**	1.46 / **1.71**	1.44 / **1.68**
55	4.02 / **7.12**	3.17 / **5.01**	2.78 / **4.16**	2.54 / **3.68**	2.38 / **3.37**	2.27 / **3.15**	2.18 / **2.98**	2.11 / **2.85**	2.05 / **2.75**	2.00 / **2.66**	1.97 / **2.59**	1.93 / **2.53**	1.88 / **2.43**	1.83 / **2.35**	1.76 / **2.23**	1.72 / **2.15**	1.67 / **2.06**	1.61 / **1.96**	1.58 / **1.90**	1.52 / **1.82**	1.50 / **1.78**	1.46 / **1.71**	1.43 / **1.66**	1.41 / **1.64**
60	4.00 / **7.08**	3.15 / **4.98**	2.76 / **4.13**	2.52 / **3.65**	2.37 / **3.34**	2.25 / **3.12**	2.17 / **2.95**	2.10 / **2.82**	2.04 / **2.72**	1.99 / **2.63**	1.95 / **2.56**	1.92 / **2.50**	1.86 / **2.40**	1.81 / **2.32**	1.75 / **2.20**	1.70 / **2.12**	1.65 / **2.03**	1.59 / **1.93**	1.56 / **1.87**	1.50 / **1.79**	1.48 / **1.74**	1.44 / **1.68**	1.41 / **1.63**	1.39 / **1.60**
65	3.99 / **7.04**	3.14 / **4.95**	2.75 / **4.10**	2.51 / **3.62**	2.36 / **3.31**	2.24 / **3.09**	2.15 / **2.93**	2.08 / **2.79**	2.02 / **2.70**	1.98 / **2.61**	1.94 / **2.54**	1.90 / **2.47**	1.85 / **2.37**	1.80 / **2.30**	1.73 / **2.18**	1.68 / **2.09**	1.63 / **2.00**	1.57 / **1.90**	1.54 / **1.84**	1.49 / **1.76**	1.46 / **1.71**	1.42 / **1.64**	1.39 / **1.60**	1.37 / **1.56**
70	3.98 / **7.01**	3.13 / **4.92**	2.74 / **4.08**	2.50 / **3.60**	2.35 / **3.29**	2.23 / **3.07**	2.14 / **2.91**	2.07 / **2.77**	2.01 / **2.67**	1.97 / **2.59**	1.93 / **2.51**	1.89 / **2.45**	1.84 / **2.35**	1.79 / **2.28**	1.72 / **2.15**	1.67 / **2.07**	1.62 / **1.98**	1.56 / **1.88**	1.53 / **1.82**	1.47 / **1.74**	1.45 / **1.69**	1.40 / **1.62**	1.37 / **1.56**	1.35 / **1.53**
80	3.96 / **6.96**	3.11 / **4.88**	2.72 / **4.04**	2.48 / **3.56**	2.33 / **3.25**	2.21 / **3.04**	2.12 / **2.87**	2.05 / **2.74**	1.99 / **2.64**	1.95 / **2.55**	1.91 / **2.48**	1.88 / **2.41**	1.82 / **2.32**	1.77 / **2.24**	1.70 / **2.11**	1.65 / **2.03**	1.60 / **1.94**	1.54 / **1.84**	1.51 / **1.78**	1.45 / **1.70**	1.42 / **1.65**	1.38 / **1.57**	1.35 / **1.52**	1.32 / **1.49**
100	3.94 / **6.90**	3.09 / **4.82**	2.70 / **3.98**	2.46 / **3.51**	2.30 / **3.20**	2.19 / **2.99**	2.10 / **2.82**	2.03 / **2.69**	1.97 / **2.59**	1.92 / **2.51**	1.88 / **2.43**	1.85 / **2.36**	1.79 / **2.26**	1.75 / **2.19**	1.68 / **2.06**	1.63 / **1.98**	1.57 / **1.89**	1.51 / **1.79**	1.48 / **1.73**	1.42 / **1.64**	1.39 / **1.59**	1.34 / **1.51**	1.30 / **1.46**	1.28 / **1.43**
125	3.92 / **6.84**	3.07 / **4.78**	2.68 / **3.94**	2.44 / **3.47**	2.29 / **3.17**	2.17 / **2.95**	2.08 / **2.79**	2.01 / **2.65**	1.95 / **2.56**	1.90 / **2.47**	1.86 / **2.40**	1.83 / **2.33**	1.77 / **2.23**	1.72 / **2.15**	1.65 / **2.03**	1.60 / **1.94**	1.55 / **1.85**	1.49 / **1.75**	1.45 / **1.68**	1.39 / **1.59**	1.36 / **1.54**	1.31 / **1.46**	1.27 / **1.40**	1.25 / **1.37**
150	3.91 / **6.81**	3.06 / **4.75**	2.67 / **3.91**	2.43 / **3.44**	2.27 / **3.14**	2.16 / **2.92**	2.07 / **2.76**	2.00 / **2.62**	1.94 / **2.53**	1.89 / **2.44**	1.85 / **2.37**	1.82 / **2.30**	1.76 / **2.20**	1.71 / **2.12**	1.64 / **2.00**	1.59 / **1.91**	1.54 / **1.83**	1.47 / **1.72**	1.44 / **1.66**	1.37 / **1.56**	1.34 / **1.51**	1.29 / **1.43**	1.25 / **1.37**	1.22 / **1.33**
200	3.89 / **6.76**	3.04 / **4.71**	2.65 / **3.88**	2.41 / **3.41**	2.26 / **3.11**	2.14 / **2.90**	2.05 / **2.73**	1.98 / **2.60**	1.92 / **2.50**	1.87 / **2.41**	1.83 / **2.34**	1.80 / **2.28**	1.74 / **2.17**	1.69 / **2.09**	1.62 / **1.97**	1.57 / **1.88**	1.52 / **1.79**	1.45 / **1.69**	1.42 / **1.62**	1.35 / **1.53**	1.32 / **1.48**	1.26 / **1.39**	1.22 / **1.33**	1.19 / **1.28**
400	3.86 / **6.70**	3.02 / **4.66**	2.62 / **3.83**	2.39 / **3.36**	2.23 / **3.06**	2.12 / **2.85**	2.03 / **2.69**	1.96 / **2.55**	1.90 / **2.46**	1.85 / **2.37**	1.81 / **2.29**	1.78 / **2.23**	1.72 / **2.12**	1.67 / **2.04**	1.60 / **1.92**	1.54 / **1.84**	1.49 / **1.74**	1.42 / **1.64**	1.38 / **1.57**	1.32 / **1.47**	1.28 / **1.42**	1.22 / **1.32**	1.16 / **1.24**	1.13 / **1.19**
1000	3.85 / **6.66**	3.00 / **4.62**	2.61 / **3.80**	2.38 / **3.34**	2.22 / **3.04**	2.10 / **2.82**	2.02 / **2.66**	1.95 / **2.53**	1.89 / **2.43**	1.84 / **2.34**	1.80 / **2.26**	1.76 / **2.20**	1.70 / **2.09**	1.65 / **2.01**	1.58 / **1.89**	1.53 / **1.81**	1.47 / **1.71**	1.41 / **1.61**	1.36 / **1.54**	1.30 / **1.44**	1.26 / **1.38**	1.19 / **1.28**	1.13 / **1.19**	1.08 / **1.11**
∞	3.84 / **6.63**	2.99 / **4.60**	2.60 / **3.78**	2.37 / **3.32**	2.21 / **3.02**	2.09 / **2.80**	2.01 / **2.64**	1.94 / **2.51**	1.88 / **2.41**	1.83 / **2.32**	1.79 / **2.24**	1.75 / **2.18**	1.69 / **2.07**	1.64 / **1.99**	1.57 / **1.87**	1.52 / **1.79**	1.46 / **1.69**	1.40 / **1.59**	1.35 / **1.52**	1.28 / **1.41**	1.24 / **1.36**	1.17 / **1.25**	1.11 / **1.15**	1.00 / **1.00**

From George W. Snedecor and William G. Cochran, *Statistical Methods*, seventh ed., © 1980. Reprinted with permission from Iowa State University Press, Ames, IA.

Student's *t* Distribution

Example For 15 degrees of freedom, the *t* value that corresponds to an area of 0.05 in both tails combined is 2.131.

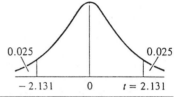

0.025   0.025

−2.131   0   *t* = 2.131

Degrees of Freedom	Area in Both Tails Combined			
	0.10	0.05	0.02	0.01
1	6.314	12.706	31.821	63.657
2	2.920	4.303	6.965	9.925
3	2.353	3.182	4.541	5.841
4	2.132	2.776	3.747	4.604
5	2.015	2.571	3.365	4.032
6	1.943	2.447	3.143	3.707
7	1.895	2.365	2.998	3.499
8	1.860	2.306	2.896	3.355
9	1.833	2.262	2.821	3.250
10	1.812	2.228	2.764	3.169
11	1.796	2.201	2.718	3.106
12	1.782	2.179	2.681	3.055
13	1.771	2.160	2.650	3.012
14	1.761	2.145	2.624	2.977
15	1.753	2.131	2.602	2.947
16	1.746	2.120	2.583	2.921
17	1.740	2.110	2.567	2.898
18	1.734	2.101	2.552	2.878
19	1.729	2.093	2.539	2.861
20	1.725	2.086	2.528	2.845
21	1.721	2.080	2.518	2.831
22	1.717	2.074	2.508	2.819
23	1.714	2.069	2.500	2.807
24	1.711	2.064	2.492	2.797
25	1.708	2.060	2.485	2.787
26	1.706	2.056	2.479	2.779
27	1.703	2.052	2.473	2.771
28	1.701	2.048	2.467	2.763
29	1.699	2.045	2.462	2.756
30	1.697	2.042	2.457	2.750
40	1.684	2.021	2.423	2.704
60	1.671	2.000	2.390	2.660
120	1.658	1.980	2.358	2.617
Normal Distribution	1.645	1.960	2.326	2.576

From Table III of Fisher and Yates: *Statistical Tables for Biological, Agricultural and Medical Research*, published by Longman Group UK Ltd., London (1974), 6th edition (previously published by Oliver and Boyd, Ltd., Edinburgh).

Chi-Square (χ^2) Distribution

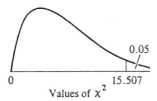

0.05

0

15.507

Values of χ^2

Example   In a chi-square distribution with $v = 8$ degrees of freedom, the area to the right of a chi-square value of 15.507 is 0.05.

Degrees of Freedom v	Area in Right Tail				
	0.20	0.10	0.05	0.02	0.01
1	1.642	2.706	3.841	5.412	6.635
2	3.219	4.605	5.991	7.824	9.210
3	4.642	6.251	7.815	9.837	11.345
4	5.989	7.779	9.488	11.668	13.277
5	7.289	9.236	11.070	13.388	15.086
6	8.558	10.645	12.592	15.033	16.812
7	9.803	12.017	14.067	16.622	18.475
8	11.030	13.362	15.507	18.168	20.090
9	12.242	14.684	16.919	19.679	21.666
10	13.442	15.987	18.307	21.161	23.209
11	14.631	17.275	19.675	22.618	24.725
12	15.812	18.549	21.026	24.054	26.217
13	16.985	19.812	22.362	25.472	27.688
14	18.151	21.064	23.685	26.873	29.141
15	19.311	22.307	24.996	28.259	30.578
16	20.465	23.542	26.296	29.633	32.000
17	21.615	24.769	27.587	30.995	33.409
18	22.760	25.989	28.869	32.346	34.805
19	23.900	27.204	30.144	33.687	36.191
20	25.038	28.412	31.410	35.020	37.566
21	26.171	29.615	32.671	36.343	38.932
22	27.301	30.813	33.924	37.659	40.289
23	28.429	32.007	35.172	38.968	41.638
24	29.553	33.196	36.415	40.270	42.980
25	30.675	34.382	37.652	41.566	44.314
26	31.795	35.563	38.885	42.856	45.642
27	32.912	36.741	40.113	44.140	46.963
28	34.027	37.916	41.337	45.419	48.278
29	35.139	39.087	42.557	46.693	49.588
30	36.250	40.256	43.773	47.962	50.892

From Table IV of Fisher and Yates: *Statistical Tables for Biological, Agricultural and Medical Research*, published by Longman Group UK Ltd., London (1974), 6th edition (previously published by Oliver and Boyd, Ltd., Edinburgh).

Areas Under the Normal Probability Distribution Between the Mean and Successive Values of z

Areas under the standard normal probability distribution between the mean and successive values of z

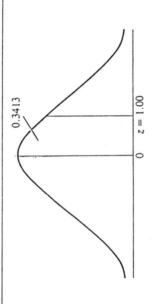

0.3413

0   z = 1.00

Example If z = 1.00, then the area between the mean and this value of z is 0.3413.

z	0.00	0.01	0.02	0.03	0.04	0.05	0.06	0.07	0.08	0.09
0.0	0.0000	0.0040	0.0080	0.0120	0.0160	0.0199	0.0239	0.0279	0.0319	0.0359
0.1	0.0398	0.0438	0.0478	0.0517	0.0557	0.0596	0.0636	0.0675	0.0714	0.0753
0.2	0.0793	0.0832	0.0871	0.0910	0.0948	0.0987	0.1026	0.1064	0.1103	0.1141
0.3	0.1179	0.1217	0.1255	0.1293	0.1331	0.1368	0.1406	0.1443	0.1480	0.1517
0.4	0.1554	0.1591	0.1628	0.1664	0.1700	0.1736	0.1772	0.1808	0.1844	0.1879
0.5	0.1915	0.1950	0.1985	0.2019	0.2054	0.2088	0.2123	0.2157	0.2190	0.2224
0.6	0.2257	0.2291	0.2324	0.2357	0.2389	0.2422	0.2454	0.2486	0.2518	0.2549
0.7	0.2580	0.2612	0.2642	0.2673	0.2704	0.2734	0.2764	0.2794	0.2823	0.2852
0.8	0.2881	0.2910	0.2939	0.2967	0.2995	0.3023	0.3051	0.3078	0.3106	0.3133
0.9	0.3159	0.3186	0.3212	0.3238	0.3264	0.3289	0.3315	0.3340	0.3365	0.3389

z	.00	.01	.02	.03	.04	.05	.06	.07	.08	.09
1.0	0.3413	0.3438	0.3461	0.3485	0.3508	0.3531	0.3554	0.3577	0.3599	0.3621
1.1	0.3643	0.3665	0.3686	0.3708	0.3729	0.3749	0.3770	0.3790	0.3810	0.3830
1.2	0.3849	0.3869	0.3888	0.3907	0.3925	0.3944	0.3962	0.3980	0.3997	0.4015
1.3	0.4032	0.4049	0.4066	0.4082	0.4099	0.4115	0.4131	0.4147	0.4162	0.4177
1.4	0.4192	0.4207	0.4222	0.4236	0.4251	0.4265	0.4279	0.4292	0.4306	0.4319
1.5	0.4332	0.4345	0.4357	0.4370	0.4382	0.4394	0.4406	0.4418	0.4429	0.4441
1.6	0.4452	0.4463	0.4474	0.4484	0.4495	0.4505	0.4515	0.4525	0.4535	0.4545
1.7	0.4554	0.4564	0.4573	0.4582	0.4591	0.4599	0.4608	0.4616	0.4625	0.4633
1.8	0.4641	0.4649	0.4656	0.4664	0.4671	0.4678	0.4686	0.4693	0.4699	0.4706
1.9	0.4713	0.4719	0.4726	0.4732	0.4738	0.4744	0.4750	0.4756	0.4761	0.4767
2.0	0.4772	0.4778	0.4783	0.4788	0.4793	0.4798	0.4803	0.4808	0.4812	0.4817
2.1	0.4821	0.4826	0.4830	0.4834	0.4838	0.4842	0.4846	0.4850	0.4854	0.4857
2.2	0.4861	0.4864	0.4868	0.4871	0.4875	0.4878	0.4881	0.4884	0.4887	0.4890
2.3	0.4893	0.4896	0.4898	0.4901	0.4904	0.4906	0.4909	0.4911	0.4913	0.4916
2.4	0.4918	0.4920	0.4922	0.4925	0.4927	0.4929	0.4931	0.4932	0.4934	0.4936
2.5	0.4938	0.4940	0.4941	0.4943	0.4945	0.4946	0.4948	0.4949	0.4951	0.4952
2.6	0.4953	0.4955	0.4956	0.4957	0.4959	0.4960	0.4961	0.4962	0.4963	0.4964
2.7	0.4965	0.4966	0.4967	0.4968	0.4969	0.4970	0.4971	0.4972	0.4973	0.4974
2.8	0.4974	0.4975	0.4976	0.4977	0.4977	0.4978	0.4979	0.4979	0.4980	0.4981
2.9	0.4981	0.4982	0.4982	0.4983	0.4984	0.4984	0.4985	0.4985	0.4986	0.4986
3.0	0.49865	0.4987	0.4987	0.4988	0.4988	0.4989	0.4989	0.4989	0.4990	0.4990
4.0	0.49997									

Table from *Statistical Analysis for Decision Making*, Fifth Edition by Morris Hamburg, copyright © 1991 by Harcourt Brace Jovanovich, Inc., reproduced by permission of the publisher.

Spearman's Rank Correlation Table

n	$p = .900$	.950	.975	.990	.995	.999
4	.8000	.8000				
5	.7000	.8000	.9000	.9000		
6	.6000	.7714	.8286	.8857	.9429	
7	.5357	.6786	.7450	.8571	.8929	.9643
8	.5000	.6190	.7143	.8095	.8571	.9286
9	.4667	.5833	.6333	.7667	.8167	.9000
10	.4424	.5515	.6364	.7333	.7818	.8667
11	.4182	.5273	.6091	.7000	.7455	.8364
12	.3986	.4965	.5804	.6713	.7273	.8182
13	.3791	.4780	.5549	.6429	.6978	.7912
14	.3626	.4593	.5341	.6220	.6747	.7670
15	.3500	.4429	.5179	.6000	.6536	.7464
16	.3382	.4265	.5000	.5824	.6324	.7265
17	.3260	.4118	.4853	.5637	.6152	.7083
18	.3148	.3994	.4716	.5480	.5975	.6904
19	.3070	.3895	.4579	.5333	.5825	.6737
20	.2977	.3789	.4451	.5203	.5684	.6586
21	.2909	.3688	.4351	.5078	.5545	.6455
22	.2829	.3597	.4241	.4963	.5426	.6318
23	.2767	.3518	.4150	.4852	.5306	.6186
24	.2704	.3435	.4061	.4748	.5200	.6070
25	.2646	.3362	.3977	.4654	.5100	.5962
26	.2588	.3299	.3894	.4564	.5002	.5856
27	.2540	.3236	.3822	.4481	.4915	.5757
28	.2490	.3175	.3749	.4401	.4828	.5660
29	.2443	.3113	.3685	.4320	.4744	.5567
30	.2400	.3059	.3620	.4251	.4665	.5479

From *Practical Nonparametric Statistics* by W. J. Conover, copyright © 1971, reprinted by permission of John Wiley & Sons, Inc.

Uniform Random Numbers between 0 and 1

0.339	0.027	0.911	0.851	0.204	0.712	0.818	0.794	0.968	0.965
0.908	0.740	0.082	0.534	0.081	0.189	0.746	0.424	0.425	0.539
0.500	0.887	0.448	0.822	0.941	0.182	0.104	0.861	0.562	0.303
0.710	0.809	0.697	0.985	0.192	0.742	0.847	0.698	0.090	0.731
0.903	0.203	0.153	0.779	0.922	0.218	0.155	0.290	0.422	0.662
0.028	0.035	0.328	0.872	0.276	0.594	0.034	0.305	0.776	0.919
0.166	0.257	0.629	0.002	0.467	0.602	0.087	0.110	0.046	0.160
0.215	0.952	0.981	0.595	0.842	0.179	0.437	0.002	0.525	0.360
0.556	0.210	0.691	0.391	0.859	0.862	0.340	0.453	0.512	0.520
0.288	0.024	0.564	0.313	0.330	0.229	0.646	0.375	0.187	0.599
0.719	0.834	0.444	0.128	0.068	0.625	0.643	0.185	0.440	0.091
0.852	0.638	0.686	0.002	0.057	0.200	0.738	0.453	0.717	0.608
0.008	0.706	0.538	0.801	0.957	0.146	0.240	0.842	0.929	0.284
0.106	0.102	0.907	0.610	0.082	0.071	0.703	0.147	0.556	0.311
0.317	0.717	0.805	0.596	0.191	0.708	0.092	0.726	0.375	0.604
0.717	0.282	0.043	0.226	0.203	0.959	0.816	0.628	0.141	0.421
0.129	0.661	0.126	0.715	0.362	0.611	0.784	0.013	0.862	0.618
0.469	0.178	0.374	0.062	0.430	0.740	0.853	0.556	0.468	0.383
0.132	0.034	0.399	0.767	0.706	0.958	0.957	0.378	0.244	0.122
0.837	0.060	0.056	0.755	0.785	0.093	0.372	0.305	0.760	0.923
0.205	0.230	0.533	0.132	0.996	0.784	0.742	0.398	0.710	0.678
0.682	0.991	0.806	0.915	0.237	0.186	0.980	0.204	0.408	0.610
0.991	0.451	0.789	0.674	0.942	0.588	0.051	0.014	0.623	0.612
0.059	0.847	0.555	0.706	0.240	0.084	0.348	0.330	0.846	0.104
0.013	0.138	0.714	0.043	0.834	0.611	0.165	0.488	0.446	0.278
0.657	0.440	0.725	0.391	0.824	0.424	0.127	0.944	0.522	0.632
0.097	0.897	0.503	0.950	0.173	0.487	0.359	0.773	0.410	0.504
0.331	0.455	0.749	0.398	0.645	0.295	0.958	0.098	0.966	0.910
0.768	0.421	0.614	0.892	0.827	0.935	0.169	0.604	0.099	0.162
0.077	0.007	0.343	0.995	0.890	0.379	0.268	0.195	0.762	0.814
0.029	0.850	0.836	0.364	0.658	0.675	0.130	0.705	0.060	0.016
0.558	0.207	0.217	0.445	0.712	0.270	0.207	0.815	0.024	0.813
0.661	0.647	0.935	0.786	0.301	0.735	0.699	0.577	0.171	0.831
0.446	0.199	0.180	0.291	0.122	0.118	0.603	0.563	0.945	0.609
0.143	0.379	0.986	0.511	0.189	0.536	0.513	0.253	0.903	0.140
0.714	0.028	0.738	0.180	0.435	0.992	0.041	0.318	0.538	0.364
0.341	0.768	0.534	0.294	0.961	0.121	0.078	0.380	0.575	0.029
0.996	0.717	0.338	0.576	0.419	0.330	0.204	0.256	0.699	0.895
0.074	0.393	0.689	0.598	0.383	0.915	0.043	0.023	0.755	0.322
0.139	0.935	0.362	0.754	0.272	0.840	0.595	0.012	0.717	0.190

INDEX

About the Authors

CHRISTIAN N. MADU is professor and program chair, Management Science, at Lubin School of Business, Pace University, New York. He has published over forty papers in refereed journals such as *IIE Transactions, Journal of Operational Research Society, European Journal of Operational Research, Computers and Operations Research,* and *International Journal of Production Research.* He holds a BSIE from the State University of New York at Buffalo, an MBA in Operations Research, an MSIE from the University of New Haven, an MBA from Baruch College–City University of New York (CUNY), and an MPhil. and a Ph.D. in Management Science from the City University of New York. His research interests are in statistical simulation modeling and reliability, quality, and maintenance modeling. He is the author of *Strategic Planning in Technology Transfer to Less Developed Countries* (Quorum Books, 1992) and author/editor of *Management of New Technologies for Global Competitiveness* (Quorum Books, 1993).

CHU-HUA KUEI is an assistant professor of Total Quality Management, Management Information Systems, and Production/Operation Management at Monmouth College, New Jersey. He received his MBA from the University of New Haven and his Ph.D. in Management Planning Systems from the City University of New York. He has contributed articles to *IIE Transactions, Long Range Planning, Computers and Operations Research, European Journal of Operational Research, International Journal of Production Research,* and others. His current research interests include strategic total quality management, strategic marketing planning, total productivity maintenance, simulation modeling, statistical designs, strategic information systems, management of organization design, and total quality management in higher education.